A GUIDE TO DE\

## SPCK International Study Guides

This SPCK series was originally sponsored and subsidized by the Theological Education Fund of the World Council of Churches in response to requests from many different countries. The books are inter-cultural, ecumenical and contextual in approach. They are prepared by and in consultation with theological tutors from all over the world, but have from the outset been as widely used by students and parish groups in the West as by those for whom English may be a second language. The text and pictures are regularly amended to ensure that both scholarship and relevance to contemporary issues are kept up to date. Fully revised editions are marked (R). Titles at a slightly more advanced level are marked (A).

*General Editors:* Daphne Terry and Nicholas Beddow

IN PREPARATION

SPCK International Study Guide 32

# A GUIDE TO DEUTERONOMY

E. John Hamlin

First published in Great Britain 1995
Society for Promoting Christian Knowledge
Holy Trinity Church
Marylebone Road
London NW1 4DU

Unless otherwise stated the Scripture quotations
in this book are from the Revised Standard Version
of the Bible (Ecumenical Edition), copyrighted
1973 by the Division of Christian Education of the
National Council of the Churches of Christ
in the USA.

The photographs are reproduced by courtesy
of the Church Missionary Society (pp. 6 and 146 *below*),
Britain Israel Public Affairs Centre (p. 190)
Lee/Dennis Methodist Information (p. 181 *below*),
The Observer (p. 201 *top*), The Oriental Institute (p. 48 *top*),
SPCK (p. 181 *top*), E. D. Terry (p. 130), Yaul Braun Jerusalem (p. 36),
and Camera Press Ltd.

British Library Cataloguing-in-Publication Data
A catalogue record for this book is available from the
British Library

ISBN 0 281 04863 0
ISBN 0 281 04864 9 (special edition for Africa,
Asia, S. Pacific and Caribbean)

Typeset by Wilmaset Ltd, Wirral
Printed in Great Britain by
The University Press, Cambridge

# Contents

# Editor's Note: Using this Guide

The plan of this Guide follows much the same pattern as other biblical volumes in the series.

In his General Introduction the author notes the meaning of the title 'Deuteronomy', its place in the Canon of Scripture, and its probable authorship in relation to the history of Israel. He also points to the interest and importance of the book for present-day readers, living as so many people are in conditions of political, social and economic instability, facing radical change—and even danger—in their individual lives.

Study of the book is divided into four main parts, covering in turn the general characteristics of Covenant Teaching experienced under Moses's leadership in the wilderness; interpretation of the Primary Covenant made at Mount Sinai/Horeb as a charter for life; extended interpretation and instruction following renewal of the Covenant in Moab; and finally, an outline of the problems ahead as the Israelites prepared to enter the Promised Land 'after Moses'.

Within each Part the text itself is divided into longer or shorter sections according to the continuity or otherwise of the subject matter, some sections being related to particular themes appearing in a group of chapters rather than working through in the order of the Bible text. The treatment in each section normally consists of:
1. An *Outline* of the passage, listing its main theme or themes;
2. An *Interpretation* of the message contained in the passage as it applied to the people to whom it was addressed, and as we should understand and apply its teaching in our lives today;
3. *Notes* on particular words and allusions of possible difficulty, especially as relating to the history of the time, and to comparable passages and references in other parts of the Bible.

## STUDY SUGGESTIONS AND QUESTIONS

Suggestions for further study and review appear at the end of each section. Besides enabling students working alone to check their own progress, they provide topics for discussion, some of which may involve individual or group research. In most cases they are divided into three main sorts:
1. *Review of Content*: To enable readers to ensure that they have fully grasped the ideas and points of teaching studied.
2. *Bible Study*: To show how the ideas and teaching in each passage relate to those in other parts of the Bible.
3. *Contextual Application*: Chiefly to help readers clarify their own ideas and beliefs, and relate the message and teaching of Deuteronomy to their own lives as Christians and to the work of

vii

the Church today. The best way to use these Study Suggestions is: first re-read the Bible passage; second, re-read the appropriate section of the Guide once or twice, carefully following up the cross-references given; and then do the work suggested, either in writing or in group discussion, without looking at the Guide again except where instructed to do so.

The *Key to Study Suggestions* (p. 205) will enable students to check their work on questions which can be checked in this way. In most cases the Key does not give the answer to a question: it shows where an answer is to be found.

Please note, however, that all these suggestions are only *suggestions*. Some readers may not wish to use them. Some tutors may wish to select only those which are most relevant to the needs of their particular students, or to substitute questions of their own.

SPECIAL NOTES

Separate Special Notes deal in greater detail with certain themes which recur in different parts of Deuteronomy, and with the shape of the book as a whole.

MAP

We cannot be sure of the exact route taken by the Israelites on their journey through the wilderness. Different scholars favour different routes. But the map on p. x shows the geography of northern Egypt, the Sinai peninsular, and Canaan and neighbouring 'nations' at that time, with the route traditionally accepted as being most likely.

INDEX

The Index includes the more important names of people and places which appear in Deuteronomy or are discussed in the Guide.

FURTHER READING

The list below suggests some books which readers wishing to carry their study of Deuteronomy further may find useful.

BIBLE VERSION

The Bible versions chiefly used in the Guide are the *Revised Standard Version Common Bible (Ecumenical Edition)* (RSV) and the *New Revised Standard Version* (NRSV). Reference is also made to the Authorized Version (AV), the Good News Bible/ Today's English Version (GNB/TEV), the Jerusalem Bible (JB), the Jewish Publication Society and New Jewish Publication Society versions (JPS and NJPS), and the New English Bible (NEB), where these help to show the meaning more clearly.

# FURTHER READING

Readers who wish to carry their studies of Deuteronomy further may find the following books useful:

Ian Cairns, *Word and Presence: A Commentary on the Book of Deuteronomy* (International Theological Commentary). Grand Rapids MI USA, Eerdmans and Handsel Press.

Richard Clifford SJ, *Deuteronomy* (Old Testament Message, Vol. 4). Michael Glazier.

Peter C. Craigie, *The Book of Deuteronomy* (The New International Commentary on the Old Testament). Grand Rapids MI USA, Eerdmans.

Leslie J. Hoppe OFM, *Deuteronomy* (Collegeville Bible Commentaries). Collegeville MN USA, Liturgical Press.

Patrick D. Miller, *Deuteronomy: Interpretation, A Bible Commentary for Teaching and Preaching*. Louisville KY USA, Westminster/John Knox Press.

Anthony Phillips, *Deuteronomy* (Cambridge Bible Commentary). Cambridge UK, The Cambridge University press.

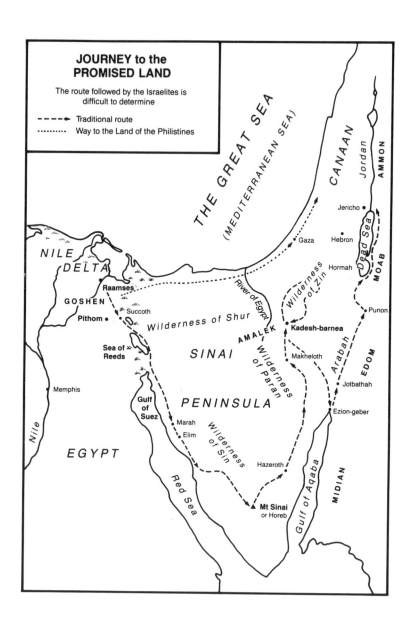

## JOURNEY to the PROMISED LAND

The route followed by the Israelites is difficult to determine

-------► Traditional route

·············· Way to the Land of the Philistines

THE GREAT SEA
(MEDITERRANEAN SEA)

CANAAN

Jordan

AMMON

Jericho

Gaza • Hebron

NILE DELTA

Dead Sea

MOAB

Raamses

GOSHEN

River of Egypt

Wilderness of Zin

Hormah

Punon

Succoth

Wilderness of Shur

AMALEK

Kadesh-barnea

Pithom •

SINAI

Wilderness of Paran

Makheloth

Arabah

EDOM

Sea of Reeds

Jotbathah

Memphis

PENINSULA

Ezion-geber

Gulf of Suez

Marah

Elim

Wilderness of Sin

Hazeroth

Gulf of Aqaba

MIDIAN

EGYPT

Red Sea

Mt Sinai or Horeb

# General Introduction
# Deuteronomy: Book of Life

## THE NAME DEUTERONOMY

'Deuteronomy' comes from the Greek words *deutero* + *nomos* meaning 'second law' or second reading of the law, after the first reading at Sinai/Horeb . This title does in fact describe much of the content of the book as a collection of laws, including the Ten Commandments and especially chapters 12—26.

The Hebrew title of this book is *elleh haddebarim*, which means 'These are The Words'. According to this title, Deuteronomy consists of the words spoken by Moses to 'all Israel' (Deut. 1.1). This is also an accurate description of the contents of Deuteronomy, for we find Moses's words of narrative, command, instruction, and exhortation, which were finally written down in a book (31.9,24).

## PART OF THE CANON OF SCRIPTURE

In the order of the Old Testament books, Deuteronomy is the last book of the Pentateuch. As such it looks back to Genesis, Exodus Leviticus and Numbers. Creation, the call of Abraham, the Exodus, the Covenant at Sinai/Horeb, and the wilderness wanderings all lie behind Deuteronomy. At the same time Deuteronomy is a prelude to the history of Israel found in the books of 1 and 2 Samuel and 1 and 2 Kings. Echoes of the Monarchy and Exile resound in its pages. Deuteronomy builds on the past and prepares for the future.

Deuteronomy was an important part of the Scriptures for Jesus and the New Testament writers. It is one of the four books most often quoted in the New Testament (the others: Genesis, Psalms, Isaiah). Some people claim to have found over 200 direct or indirect references to Deuteronomy in the New Testament.

Jesus quoted from Deuteronomy in His defence against Satan's temptations (Matt. 4.4,7,10; see Deut. 8.3; 6.16; 6.13), and in His conversation with a scribe (Mark 12.28–34; see Deut. 6.4–5). He quoted five of the Ten Commandments to the rich young ruler (Matt. 19.16–20). Paul quoted verses from Deuteronomy several times in Romans (7.7; 10.6–8,19; 12.19; 13.9; 15.10). One scholar has compared Deuteronomy in the Old Testament to Romans in the New Testament: 'These two books lie at the confessional, theological centre of the Bible'.

1

# WHO WROTE DEUTERONOMY?

Deuteronomy is the record of the last words of Moses to his people on the east bank of the River Jordan, just before they were to cross from the wilderness into the Promised Land. The tradition that Moses actually wrote the Book of Deuteronomy is open to question, both because of the style and content of the book and because the book describes Moses's death. Most scholars think that while Moses is the original inspiration for the material, the book was written many centuries later by an unnamed author sometimes referred to as the Deuteronomist, or by the letter 'D'. In this Study Guide we call him the Narrator.

## THE NARRATOR

The Narrator set Moses's words into context, and moulded and formed them into the structure of the book as it appears in our Bibles today (see Special Note E). He gave evidence of his authorship of Deuteronomy by describing the place and time of Moses's words (e.g. 1.1–5; 4.44–49), adding explanatory notes (e.g. 2.10–12, 20–23), describing actions of Moses (e.g. 4.41–49), and telling of the circumstances around Moses's death (32.1–12).

The Narrator probably belonged to a group of reformers who, in the reign of King Hezekiah of Judah (715–687 BC), began gathering old Mosaic teachings, some of which had been preserved in the former Northern Kingdom of Israel. They lived in a time of national and religious crisis, and wanted to lay the foundations for reforming the nation's life and customs according to the Covenant which God had made with the people through Moses at Sinai/Horeb.

At that time the Northern Kingdom 'Israel' had been defeated, and most of its people had been deported to Assyria (2 Kings 15.29; 17.6). The reforming group in Judah supported Hezekiah's reform movement (2 Kings 18.1,5–6). However, during the reign of Hezekiah's son, the corrupt King Manasseh of Judah (687–642 BC; 2 Kings 21.1–17), the reforming group continued to work in secret.

The Narrator probably lived about 100 years later, during the reign of King Josiah (640–609 BC), a great grandson of Hezekiah. Josiah carried out a great movement of reform and national renewal beginning in 622 BC (2 Kings 23.1–25). Many scholars believe that the 'Book of the Law' (2 Kings 22.8–13) found in the Temple at that time was a large part of the present book of Deuteronomy. It may have lain in the Temple archives unnoticed for many years, or perhaps it was placed there to inspire the hoped-for national reform when King Josiah came to the throne as a boy

(2 Kings 22.1). If the Narrator lived at that time, one of his contemporaries would have been the prophet Jeremiah.

When Jerusalem was destroyed in 587 BC, many leading citizens of Judah were carried into exile in Babylonia (2 Kings 24.10–16). The people of Judah turned to Deuteronomy to understand why this great disaster had come to them. They also asked whether there was hope for the future. The Narrator may have written some parts of Deuteronomy or expanded others after the destruction of Jerusalem.

The Narrator gathered, arranged and edited his material for the benefit of people in his own time and for future generations of readers. He bridged the gap between Moses and his own time, presenting Deuteronomy as the prophetic voice and authority of Moses speaking across the generations, calling God's people to lay foundations for new beginnings at each turning-point in their history.

## WHY READ DEUTERONOMY?

First, Deuteronomy as a document of *national reconstruction* is of great interest to people who are trying to find foundations for reform and renewal in times of political instability, economic difficulties, social collapse, and deep discouragement. Such foundations are found in the Ten Commandments (5.6–21) and the Great Commandment (6.4–5).

Second, Deuteronomy teaches us about the importance of *covenantal worship* as a means of maintaining the holiness of God's people and the health of society.

Third, in a time when the rich are tempted to think only of themselves, Deuteronomy calls on us all to conduct our lives with *righteousness and justice*, and to care for the poor and powerless.

Fourth, Deuteronomy will give *hope and courage* to people who live on the borderline between the old and the new, who face radical change in their individual lives, and in the life of their society as a whole.

3

# PART 1: 1.1—4.43

## DISCIPLINE FOR LIFE:
## THE WILDERNESS PERIOD

---

### 1.1–5
## Moses, Interpreter of the Covenant Teaching

### INTERPRETATION

#### BETWEEN THE WILDERNESS AND THE PROMISED LAND

Deuteronomy is set at a crucial turning point in the history of the Israelites. The Narrator pictures Moses standing before his people on the border between the 'great and terrible wilderness'(1.19) and the 'land flowing with milk and honey' (6.3). It was the eleventh month (January-February) of the fortieth year after the Exodus from Egypt (1.3). Six months earlier in that same year Moses's brother Aaron had died (Num. 33.38; Deut. 10.6). Two months later Moses himself would die on Mount Nebo. At the beginning of the following year (March-April) Joshua would lead the people across the Jordan, and they would celebrate their first Passover in the land which God had promised to give them (Josh. 4.19; 5.10).

#### MOSES'S LEGACY

The Narrator shows Moses explaining the meaning of the Covenant Teaching or *Torah* (1.5; see Special Note B) which would be the foundation of life in the new land with its temptations, dangers, and opportunities. The Covenant Teaching was Moses's legacy to his people, later put in writing and entrusted to the Levitical priests (Deut.31.24–25).

#### A NEW GENERATION

'All Israel' (1.1) who heard Moses's words were a new generation. The people who had experienced liberation from slavery in Egypt and entered the Covenant at Sinai/Horeb had become the 'evil generation' (1.35), and had perished in the wilderness (2.14). Those who had been unfaithful at Baal-peor had died (4.3). Moses was speaking to the people who had been born during the years of wandering in the wilderness, had 'held fast to the Lord your God', and were 'all alive this day' (4.4). This new, disciplined generation would enter the new land.

Later readers or listeners, in a similar time of transition, could think of themselves as the spiritual descendants of that wilderness generation ('children and children's children'; 4.25). For example, there was *the generation of those who heard* 'all the words of the law' *read by Joshua at Mount Ebal* (Josh. 8.30–35). Many years later, there was *the generation of those who lived at the time of King Hezekiah*, who 'held fast to the LORD . . . did not depart from following him, but kept the commandments which the LORD commanded Moses' (2 Kings 18.6). Again, there were *the people who joined in the reformation movement of King Josiah*, 'who turned to the LORD with all his heart and with all his soul and with all his might, according to all the law of Moses' (2 Kings 23.25).

Today there are other 'wilderness generations', such as *oppressed people* who are now ready to claim their rights, *ethnic minorities* deprived of opportunities to participate fully in society or to develop their own culture, *young people* who have been alienated from the mainstream of society. People like this listening to Moses's words in Deuteronomy, will be able to learn from their experience in the 'wilderness' of the past, and look forward with hope to the future. They will use their energies to rebuild their society, and bring new life into their congregation.

## NOTES

**1.1. In the wilderness:** The wilderness is a major theme which appears frequently in Deuteronomy. The Israelites remembered the long and dangerous journey through 'the great and terrible wilderness' (1.19; 8.15), when God led them (8.2; 29.5), watched over them (2.7), fed them (8.16), cared for and protected them like a mother eagle (32.10–11), and even carried them like a father or mother (1.31). Although they saw His works (1.31), they repeatedly rebelled against Him in the wilderness (9.7). Moses reminded them that God's purpose in disciplining His people in the wilderness was to do them good (8.2–5; see pp. 72–73). When they crossed over the Jordan River into the Land of Canaan, it was like entering into a restored Garden of Eden (see pp. 158, 160–62).

**1.2. Horeb:** In Exodus (and in Numbers) this mountain is often called Mount Sinai (Exod. 19.11; Num. 3.1). In this Guide we call it Sinai/Horeb to show that both names mean the same mountain.

**1.5. Explain:** The Hebrew word comes from a root word meaning a well of water. The interpretation of God's teaching is like digging a well, making living water accessible to people who would not be able to find it by themselves. Jesus did this for the Samaritan woman (John 4.13–15).

5

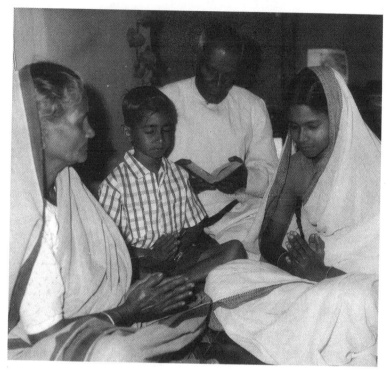

The Narrator presented Deuteronomy as the prophetic voice of Moses speaking across the generations. Every generation of people who love God and try to keep His commandments—like the four generations of this Indian pastor's family—may identify themselves with the generation who experienced the making of the Primary Covenant (see pp. 4, 7, 32).

# SPECIAL NOTE A: 'GENERATIONS' IN DEUTERONOMY

Past, present, and future generations seem to be blended in Deuteronomy. *The Sinai/Horeb generation* had experienced the making of the Primary Covenant, but died in the wilderness. *The wilderness generation* who had been born in the wilderness stood in Moab as Moses reviewed the Primary Covenant (Deut. 1–11), and interpreted it in the renewal of the Covenant in Moab (chs. 12–30). Yet the Narrator portrays Moses as speaking to the wilderness generation in the land of Moab (1.5) in ways which identify them with both the Sinai/Horeb generation and future generations.

The wilderness generation at Moab were witnesses of the events at Sinai/Horeb (4.9–13). Yahweh made the Covenant at Mount Sinai/Horeb not only with the former generation who had died, but 'with us, who are all of us here alive this day' (5.3). Instead of using the pronoun 'they' in his description of events at Kadesh-barnea, Moses, as presented by the Narrator, uses 'you'. He speaks to those at Moab as though they themselves had been that 'evil generation' (1.35). The Covenant at Moab was made not just with those present at that time but 'with him who is not here with us this day' (29.15), meaning future generations, 'children and your children's children' (4.9).

In fact, every generation anywhere, at any time in the world's history, who are faithful to God's Covenant will be one link in the chain of the 'thousand generations' of those who love Him and keep His commandments (7.9). Or they may become 'a perverse and crooked generation' (32.5,20), or the 'third and fourth generation of those who hate' God (5.9; and see 31.16,20). Each generation of those who read Deuteronomy may identify themselves with the Sinai/Horeb generation, the wilderness generation on the border of the Promised Land, and the generations of later years. Deuteronomy is a summons to each new generation to do God's will.

## STUDY SUGGESTIONS

REVIEW OF CONTENT

1. (a) Who was the 'Narrator'?
   (b) When did he live?
   (c) For what reason did he compose Deuteronomy?
2. What two events happened before and after Moses's farewell words? Why are these events important for our understanding of Deuteronomy?
3. Who were the 'wilderness generation' to whom Moses spoke at Moab?

# 1.6–46
# Lessons From the Wilderness Period (1)

Each of the four stages of the wilderness journey from Sinai/Horeb to Moab had important lessons for the people who were preparing to enter the new land. Moses reminds them of these lessons here and will return to the subject later (8.2–5).

## OUTLINE

1.6–18: Lessons at Sinai/Horeb.
1.19–46: Lessons at Kadesh-barnea.

## INTERPRETATION

### LESSONS AT SINAI/HOREB

#### GOD'S CALL TO MOVE ON (1.6–7)

God's plan for the Israelites could not be fulfilled 'at this mountain'. The people had remained long enough at the place where God had made His Covenant with them. God's command to leave the mountain, to 'turn, take your journey, . . . go' was a call for a change in the direction in their lives, and for a decision to 'pack up their tents' and move toward the goal. This call is valid for all generations in every age.

#### THE GOAL: A LAND OF YOUR OWN (1.8)

God's goal for the Sinai/Horeb generation was a land: a place for security with justice, a space for freedom and opportunity for self-development as servants of the living God. Taking possession of the land meant a change of mind from passive to active. It meant taking charge of their own lives, as stewards of the land. In 'setting the land before' them, God was not giving them an absolute right to own the land, but allowing them to 'take possession' of it as a grant, showing His trust in His people to administer it in keeping with His teaching.

From this we can see that in Deuteronomy the word 'land' refers to a specific area. In this case it is the land of Canaan. Today the 'land' which God gives to anyone might mean their native country or nation, land belonging to a family or clan, an apartment in a high-rise housing estate, or a living place of security and freedom not necessarily tied to any particular area. Each of these could be included in God's promise of 'land' to His people and related to His long-range plan for humankind.

## THE WIDER PERSPECTIVE

God's oath or promise to the patriarchs (see note on 1.8) goes back to the call of Abraham when the promise was first made (Gen. 12.1). That first promise came after the collapse of world order described in Genesis 11.1–9. In this wider perspective, God's promise of land for Abraham's descendants was part of His plan for the whole world. With the promise of land came a promise of blessing for Abraham and through Abraham to others (Gen. 12.2–3), including 'all the families of the earth'.

## THE IMPORTANCE OF GOOD LEADERS, 1.9–18

Good leaders were essential not only 'at that time' (1.9), that is, at Mount Sinai/Horeb, but also and especially after Moses's death, when the people would be living in the new land (see 16.18–20, and pp. 106–108).

## THE NEED FOR LEADERS

The leaders were necessary because of three problems that had arisen (1.12):

1. God's own people who should have been a joy to lead, had become a *weight* that Moses could not carry by himself. The Hebrew word translated 'weight' is used only once again in the Old Testament, in Isaiah 1.14, where it is translated 'burden'. There it refers to religious practices that caused Yahweh great sorrow. When we look at the text in Deuteronomy 1.12 alongside this verse from Isaiah, we can draw the surprising conclusion that the nature and number of religious practices actually kept the people from seeing and doing God's will. Instead of opening the people up to God, religion had become an obstacle to faith.

2. The people were a *burden* (using another Hebrew word). Instead of being a joyful witness to God's saving power, they had problems of selfishness, divided loyalties, prejudice, laziness, and thinking of their own group before the common good.

3. There was *strife* among this people who should have been an example of harmonious living. In other parts of Deuteronomy strife takes the form of homicide, disputes over legal rights, or assault (17.8), legal rights of children to inheritance (21.15–17), conflict between parents and children (21.18–21), adultery (22.23–27), kidnapping (24.7), violent quarrels (25.11–12), use of dishonest weights (25.13–16).

## THREE SORTS OF LEADERS

Moses refers to three sorts of leaders:
(a) *Officers* or foremen (as in Exod. 5.6) to oversee common work projects for sanitation, irrigation, road building; to help organize the people for important projects (as in Josh. 1.10; 3.2), and to assist in religious ceremonies (as in Josh. 8.33);
(b) *Judges* to settle disputes; and
(c) *Commanders* in time of war.

## QUALITIES OF GOOD LEADERS

These leaders were required to show three qualities:
1. They should be *wise*: skilled in resolving conflicts, in finding real solutions to difficult problems, in overcoming the forces that threaten to tear the people apart, and in bringing out the good in their people. Wise leaders should listen to the words of wronged people, and keep themselves from any desire for personal gain.
2. They should be *understanding*: having insight into such things as the moral order of the universe, the natural harmony between the human and the natural world, the inner workings of the human heart, and the suffering of the victims of injustice.
3. They should be *known* (AV). Modern translations suggest that the leaders should be 'experienced', or 'of good repute'. A better interpretation is that they should be 'known' by God in the sense of Ps. 139.1,23. This implies a close relationship with and a reverence for God in a way that would help the leaders to 'understand righteousness and justice and equity, every good path' (Prov. 2.9), and be able to reject 'pride and arrogance . . . and perverted speech' (Prov. 8.13) in their public and private life.

## QUALIFICATIONS OF GOOD LEADERS

Moses proposes three tests for these leaders:
(a) They should give fair decisions ('judge righteously').
(b) They should not have favourites, or 'be partial in judgement'.
(c) They should be fearless even when having to give decisions against powerful people, knowing that in the end 'the judgement is God's' (1.17). These tests seem to relate in particular to care for two groups who were most easily victimized: the foreigners living in Israel, and the poor (the 'small' as contrasted with the rich, 'the great').

### LESSONS AT KADESH-BARNEA, 1.19–46

This well-watered oasis, surrounded by green trees, was eleven days' journey (1.2) from Sinai/Horeb. From there a swift and decisive campaign should have enabled the Israelites to take possession of the Promised Land. Yet it turned out to be the place where the Sinai/Horeb generation, fresh from the Covenant on the mountain, became 'this evil generation' (1.35), with no hope of seeing the Promised Land.

This rebellion was not unique. What we find here is an example of behaviour that has lessons for God's people in every age. Moses later told the people that they had been 'rebellious against the LORD from the day that I knew you' (9.24). In his farewell words he reminds them, 'I know how rebellious and stubborn you are; behold, while I am yet alive with you, today you have been rebellious against the LORD; how much more after my death!' (31.27).

## REBELLIOUS ACTION AND INACTION

At Kadesh-barnea there was rebellious *inaction* followed by rebellious *action*. In response to God's command to 'go up, take possession' (1.21), the people refused to attack (1.26). Later, when God commanded 'do not go up or fight, for I am not in the midst of you' (1.42), they 'were presumptuous and went up' (1.43). The causes of rebellion were (1) lack of faith, (2) fear, (3) forgetfulness, and (4) over-confidence.

First, the people's request for a scouting party appears here as a lack of confidence in God's power to give them victory (1.22). They even complained that God was not their saviour but their destroyer (1.27).

Second, they feared what seemed to them the overwhelming military, economic, and political power of the enemy (1.27), and were even more frightened of the unknown: 'whither are we going up?' (1.28; see note on 2.10–11,21).

Third, they forgot how God had fought for them against the power of Pharaoh (1.30), and how He had cared for them in the wilderness (1.31–33).

Finally, they foolishly under-estimated the strength of their adversary, believing they could win the victory without God's help (1.43–44).

## THE CONSEQUENCES OF REBELLION

The results of the rebellion were a warning to all future generations that disobedience is costly. There was humiliating defeat (1.44), a lost generation (1.35), a thirty-eight year delay (2.14), and disappointment for Moses himself, who could not enter the new land on account of the people's rebellion (1.37; see 3.26 and pp. 14–15).

But the Narrator also shows that there were positive lessons to be learnt from this experience of defeat:

(a) God's words 'Do not fear or be dismayed' (1.21; see 31.6) show that rebellion may be avoided by each generation.

(b) God's anger is constructive. God does not want His people to be defeated by their enemies (1.42).

(c) God is still there with His rebellious people during the long journey through the wilderness. God is present by night and day 'to show you by what way you should go' (1.33).

(d) God's purposes focus on the future. Failures in one generation are not the end of the story. New leaders like Joshua (1.38) and future generations (1.39) are always part of God's plan.

## NOTES

**1.8. The land which the Lord swore to your fathers . . . to give them**: God's promise to the fathers is so important to the Narrator that he makes mention of it many times. See 1.8,35; 6.3,10,18,23; 7.23; 8.1; 9.28; 10.11; 11.9,21; 12.20; 19.8; 26.3,15; 28.11; 30.20; 34.4. Alongside this promise is the danger that a disobedient people will 'perish quickly off the good land that the LORD gives you' (11.17; see 28.63).

**1.13. Choose**: The Narrator here emphasizes the responsibility of the *people* for choosing their own leaders as a preparation for their journey through the wilderness toward the Promised Land. In another account of this incident, God commands *Moses* to choose the leaders (Exod. 18.21) as a preparation for the Covenant at Sinai/Horeb. A later passage states that *God* will choose a future king (Deut. 17.15). The Narrator has selected parts of the tradition not found in the Book of Exodus, which emphasize the democratic nature of leadership in the Promised Land. In the time of Hezekiah or Josiah, Deuteronomy would be understood as reminding the king that his authority required the people's assent.

## STUDY SUGGESTIONS

REVIEW OF CONTENT

1. What does 'possessing the land' mean?
2. What were (a) *three* problems for which leadership was necessary, (b) *three* sorts of leaders, (c) *three* qualities of leaders, and (d) *three* tests of good leadership?
3. Kadesh-barnea was a comfortable place, but what happened to the 'Sinai generation' there?
4. What were (a) *two* ways in which the people rebelled at Kadesh-barnea, (b) *four* causes of the rebellion, (c) *four* negative results, and (d) *three* positive lessons from the rebellion?

BIBLE STUDY

5. What more do we learn from Genesis 12.1–3 about God's command to 'possess the land'?

CONTEXTUAL APPLICATION

6. What is *your* 'promised land'? Is it an actual place? If not, what is it?
7. Apply the lessons about leadership in Deut. 1.9–18 to Church leaders, political leaders, and organizational leaders in your own situation.
8. Give examples of how religious practices might 'keep people from seeing and doing God's will' (see p. 9). What sorts of religious practices *do* help people to know what God's will is?

# 2.1—3.29
# Lessons from the Wilderness Period (2)

## OUTLINE

2.1—3.22: Lessons in Transjordan: Reflections on Victory.
3.23–29: Lessons from Unanswered Prayer

## LESSONS IN TRANSJORDAN: REFLECTIONS ON VICTORY

### PREPARATION IS NECESSARY

The defeat at Hormah (1.44) showed that the people were not yet ready for victory. The period of 'forty years' in the wilderness was not a punishment, but a time of training in endurance, humility, and obedience (as in 8.3–5). They gained experience in management, so that they were able to purchase food and water from people along the way. The command to 'turn northward' (2.3) marked the completion of the training period and the resumption of the journey toward the new land.

### NATIONAL AMBITION MUST BE LIMITED

The first lesson the people had to learn was that their national ambition had to be limited *not by their military strength, but by God's will*. The three countries which lay along their northward route were part of God's plan. He had helped Edom, Moab and Ammon to defeat previous occupants of the land (2.10,20–21; see note on 2.10–11,21), and had given each a land of their own

13

(2.5,9,19). God gave specific instructions to the Israelites not to fight with any of them.

## VICTORIES ARE NOT ENDS BUT BEGINNINGS

Moses used the word 'begin' four times to show that these victories were only the beginning of God's work in Israel. The victories would make the peoples of the earth *begin* to respect the Israelites (2.25), and no longer think of them as escaped slaves. God had *begun* a series of actions which would result in victory over the Amorite kings( 2.31). This victory would in turn be the *beginning* of the process of taking possession of the land (2.31). Yet all this, including the victory and the possession of a new land was only a *beginning* of God's work with the Israelites (3.24). It was a time of great possibilities.

## FURTHER REFLECTIONS ON VICTORY

The victories over the two Amorite kings were remembered in song (Pss. 135.10–11; 136.19), in story (Josh. 2.10), in an official document (1 Kings 4.19), and in a Covenant formula (Deut. 29.7) as models of all future victories. Three additional reflections stand out.

1. The *victory was God's*, not Israel's (2.33,36; 3.3). The 'cities fortified with high walls, gates and bars' (3.5), which had so frightened the people at Kadesh-barnea (1.28), were easily overcome with God's help. Victories given by God should be interpreted in the light of God's will: the establishment of a new society under God for the blessing of all nations.

2. The Israelites made a complete *new start* on the land, a new experiment in land administration, free of the corruptions of the previous occupants. This is the inner meaning of the cruel practice of dedicating cities and people to God by a *herem* destruction (2.34; 3.6; see Special Note D).

3. These two victories were only a *first step* in the process of 'taking possession' of the land. Moses's words (3.18–20), addressed to 'all Israel' (1.1), were a warning that victory for one group only would be incomplete 'until the LORD gives rest to your brethren' (3.20). In later years, when King Josiah began his reform, the northern tribes were all in captivity. For them Moses's words would be understood as prophesying that a new beginning in the Southern Kingdom of Judah would not be complete until the people of the northern tribes could be included.

## LESSONS FROM UNANSWERED PRAYER, 3.23–29

### AN UNDERSTANDABLE REQUEST

Moses is shown as presenting his urgent request that God would let him 'go over . . . and see the good land' (3.25), as a fitting reward for his labours. In prayer he pleads that such a great God could certainly do this small favour, which would serve as a witness to His greatness (3.24).

## MOSES'S EXPLANATION

Moses explains to the people that God 'was angry with me on your account' (3. 26). This raises questions in our minds. Was Moses blaming the 'evil generation' who rebelled at Kadesh-barnea? Or was he accepting part of the responsibility because he was not able to convince them of the need for obedience?

## GOD'S ANSWER

Three commands summarize God's answer to this prayer: (1) 'Speak no more to me of this matter' (3.26). In this command God was telling Moses to stop feeling sorry for himself. There was much work to do in preparing the people for their move into the new land. (2) 'Go up to Mount Pisgah and lift up your eyes westward and northward and southward and eastward' (3.27). Moses should not worry about his own future, but see the people's future home. (3) 'Charge Joshua, encourage, and strengthen him' (3.28). Moses should not think of himself as indispensable. Joshua would take up the leadership where Moses left off (see 1.38 and pp. 180–182).

## NOTES

**2.10,11,21. Emim . . . Anakim . . . Rephaim . . . Zamzummim:** These were legendary early inhabitants of the land who were displaced by the Moabites and Ammonites. They were feared because of their unusual size ('great . . .and tall'. 2.10) and warlike reputation (1.28; 9.2).

**3.26. Angry with me on your account:** In Num. 27.14 and Deut. 32.51 Moses's own rebellion is the reason for God's refusal to allow him to enter the Promised Land. See also Deut. 1.37; 4.21–22. Each of these passages gives an answer to the question that troubled many of the people: why was Moses not allowed to complete his career by entering the land?

## STUDY SUGGESTIONS

### REVIEW OF CONTENT

1. For what reason were the Israelites forbidden to take lands belonging to Edom, Moab, and Ammon?
2. List *five* things we can learn from Moses's account of the victory over the two Amorite kings.

3. Give two possible explanations for Moses's words that God was angry with him 'on your account'.
4. What were God's three answers to Moses's request that he should be allowed to enter the Promised Land?

### BIBLE STUDY

5. Compare Deut. 3.18–20 with Hebrews 11.39–40. What similarities and differences can you see?
6. Compare the references to new beginnings in Deuteronomy 2.25,31;3.24 with Mark 1.1; Acts 1.1, and Philippians 1.6. What are the differences, and similarities?

### CONTEXTUAL APPLICATION

7. 'God was not giving them an absolute right to own the land' (p. 8). Do you think that God ever does give tribes or nations an 'absolute right' to the land they live on? What is likely to happen if they believe He has done so? Give examples and reasons for your answers.
8. David conquered the Moabites, Edomites, and Ammonites (2 Sam. 8.11–12). According to 2 Sam. 8.14, God gave him victory.
(a) Did David's victory mean that God's gift of land to these three peoples (Deut. 2.5,9,19) was no longer valid (see Jer. 48.47; 49.6)? If not, what did it mean?
(b) What was the effect of David's victories on Solomon (1 Kings 11.5–8)?

# 4.1–14
# Encounter with the God of Life (1)

The most important part of the 'discipline for life' during the wilderness period was the Israelites' encounter with the God of Life at Mount Sinai/Horeb. It was this profound experience, described in ch. 4, which formed them as a people and gave them their identity among the other peoples of the world.

The expression 'and now' (4.1) shows a change in emphasis, from the events just reviewed in chs. 1—3, to the events at Sinai/Horeb and their significance for the Moab generation as they prepare to enter the Promised Land. In this 'now' Moses is shown as preparing his people spiritually for the new era, by recalling the formative experience of the previous generation at Sinai/Horeb in order to give them their identity, goals, and direction.

## OUTLINE

4.1–8: Who are We?

4.9–14: The Most Important Day of Our Lives.

## INTERPRETATION

### WHO ARE WE?

A SENSE OF IDENTITY

A sense of identity, of who we are, is important for individuals as well as for groups of people who are living in a time of transition between the old and the new. It was especially urgent for the people of Israel as they prepared to enter the new land with its risks and temptations. Christians also need a sure sense of their identity in order to be true to their faith in Jesus and maintain their loyalty to Him, because they live both in the new age of the Kingdom of God and in a society with many values and ways of life which conflict with the Christian way. What made the people of Israel distinctive was that through Moses they had entered into a special relationship with God. Their unique blessings given by God's grace, and their faithfulness to God's Covenant, would set them apart from their surrounding cultural environment.

Archbishop Desmond Tutu in South Africa has referred to the problem of confused identity as 'faith schizophrenia' or split personality. He was thinking of Africans whose lives are split by having to live in two seemingly opposed worlds, the traditional and the Christian. Some ways of dealing with this problem are: (a) to make a complete break with the traditional ways; (b) to keep the traditional ways, but put on the Christian ways as a sort of coat; (c) to reject both the traditional and the Christian ways and become a 'modern' secular person; and (d) to allow the power of God to cleanse, reform, and renew the traditional ways.

TWO PRICELESS TREASURES (4.7–8)

Two gifts from God set the Israelites apart from other peoples. The first was the presence of God himself 'so near . . . as the LORD our God is to us, whenever we call upon him'. This is a joyful message that echoes throughout the Bible: 'The Lord is near to all who call upon Him, to all who call upon Him in truth' (Ps. 145.18). The second was 'statutes and ordinances so righteous as all this law which I set before you this day'. God who is near to His people also makes demands on them by giving them guidelines which lead along the path of life.

The people should respond by making the 'statutes and ordinances' their own in four ways: (a) by attentive *listening* to Moses's words (Deut. 4.1); (b) by *keeping* the guidelines in their memory, making them part of their consciousness and way of life (4.2,6); (c) by *doing* them, living by them in their daily lives (4.1,5,6); and (d) through it all, by *holding fast* to their Lord instead of accepting other values and gods (4.3–4).

## UNIQUE BLESSINGS FROM GOD'S GRACE

When the people respond to God's gifts in this way, four results will follow.

1. They will be able to 'live', that is, to find *true life* (4.1).
2. They will be able to 'possess', that is take *control of the land* (4.1; see p. 8).
3. They will attain *wisdom and understanding* (4.6; see p. 10) to create a peaceful, just, and sustainable national life on the land.
4. From God's wider perspective (4.6; see p.8), they will be an *inspiration for the peoples* among whom they live (see note on 4.6).

## THE MOST IMPORTANT DAY OF OUR LIVES, 4.9–14

### LEST YOU FORGET (4.9)

God's people live by making past experiences ('the things which your eyes have seen') become real again. Memory guides them in the present and prepares them to face the future.

The entire people including each family and individual must make a conscious effort ('take heed and keep your soul diligently') to guard against loss of memory ('lest they depart from your heart'). Each generation that followed must live through the same experience and pass it on to the next generation. Without the ever-renewed memory of the events of that day, the Israelites would lose their identity in the new land. They would be in danger of forgetting the Covenant (4.23), and even forgetting God (6.12; 8.11,14,19).

Israel's way of remembering was to tell and retell the story, perhaps in the form of drama, often in the context of a festival when all the people gathered together. Retelling the story would make 'the day of the assembly' (10.4) become 'now' (4.1), 'this day' (4.39,40) for the listeners. They could say, 'that was the day when *we* heard the voice of God'.

### A FRAMEWORK OF WORSHIP (4.10)

The remembrance of the experience of the people gathered at the mountain would give them a framework of worship for their life together in the new land. It would remind them that: (a) worship was a corporate activity of the whole people; (b) the heart of their worship was hearing God's words; and (c) worship was also to be a

The most important part of the 'discipline for life' in the wilderness was the Israelites' encounter with the God of Life at Mount Sinai/Horeb (p. 20 and see 4.11–13). Today, above the Monastery of St Catherine on the lower slopes of Mount Sinai, a priest of the Greek Orthodox Church waits to act as guide for tourists climbing the 'Mountain of Moses'.

way of teaching succeeding generations of children to reverence God.

## REMEMBERING THE FIRE (4.11)

The first thing the people saw on that day was the towering fire rising from the mountain to 'the heart of heaven'. The miracle was that God who ruled heaven and earth (4.39; see also 10.14) came down 'in fire' (Exod. 19.18) to meet with His people.

Fire has two meanings when it refers to God's presence. First it is the shining *light* of God's glory (Exod. 24.16–17), which is present in the Temple (Exod. 40.34–35), and which will fill the whole earth (Num. 14.21). Secondly, it *burns* as a 'devouring fire' (Deut. 4.24), symbolizing God's judgement. The people's anxiety in the presence of this fire (5.5,25) is understandable. God's anger at injustice and evil-doing could kindle a fire that would destroy nations and peoples all over the earth (32.22), including the Israelites themselves (5.25).

## REMEMBERING THE MYSTERY (4.11)

The 'darkness, cloud, and gloom', which surrounded the fire on the mountain shows that God is beyond human powers of observation, analysis or control. There was no visible form for a craftsman to take as a model for an image of God which could be controlled. According to Isaiah 45.15, God hides himself from human sight and control. Humans cannot 'manage' God.

## REMEMBERING THE VOICE (4.12–13)

The most important event of that day, however, was not fire and darkness but 'the sound of words' with two messages: (a) a life-giving *Covenant*, or relationship with the Lord of heaven and earth (see Special Note D), and (b) ten *rules of life* (the Ten Commandments, as we call them, or 'Ten Words', RSV margin) inscribed on stone by God, to guide His people in the new land.

The Israelites never ceased to marvel that they had survived this tremendous experience which made them different from all other peoples (5.26).

Today we may ask what was meant by the statement that God personally 'declared', or enabled the Israelites to understand, the meaning of the Covenant and the Ten Commandments (4.13). Some possible explanations are: (a) that God spoke so plainly that all the people could hear (see 5.4), and they could have recorded the words on a tape recorder if one had been available; (b) that God's words were not clear to the people (see John 12.29), so Moses had to relay them to the people (see 5.5); (c) that the people were so frightened by the sound of God's voice that they did not remember them, so they asked Moses to make God's message clear to them (see 5.27); (d) that God only communicated the *Covenant relationship* to the people of that time (4.13), but the people of Israel came to know these Ten Commandments later on as a summary of what God had taught them over the years. Perhaps we may conclude that *how* this was communicated to the people is not as important as the fact *that* it came from God to them and to us.

## NOTES

**4.2. You shall not add . . . nor take from it:** Some scholars have interpreted this to mean a rigid adherence to the letter of the word which Moses taught, leaving no room for interpretation. Another view is that nothing should be added that would contradict the original Covenant Teaching. New interpretations are always necessary to deal with new situations, but these interpretations should remain faithful to the Covenant Teaching. The advice of a later Israelite teacher of wisdom was not to 'add to God's words, lest he rebuke you and you be found a liar' (Prov. 30.6). On the other hand, we know from the prophets that God's word cannot be limited to the words of Moses (Jer. 26.2). We find a similar command regarding 'the words of the prophecy' in Rev. 22.18–19.

**4.3. What the LORD did at Baal-peor:** This is a reference to Num. 25.1–9. Some scholars have found evidence of an outbreak of the disease bubonic plague. They believe that the Israelites tried to stop it by joining the Midianites in a ritual of sexual coupling, to appease angry spirits of the dead who were believed to have caused the disease. This close contact with the Midianites only spread the disease. We find other references to this famous example of turning away from God in Josh. 22.17; Ps. 106.28–31; 1 Cor. 10.8 (see Deut. 4.46 and p. 32).

**4.6. When they hear all these statutes:** This points forward to a future time when other nations' 'dread and fear' of Israel (Deut. 2.25) would change to admiration. Reference to the peoples' 'hearing' the statutes may mean that some members of the other peoples of Canaan were listening to the reading of the Covenant Teaching at festival time (see Deut. 31.9–13). In the days of the monarchy members of foreign peoples may have been royal guests. We may think of the reaction of the Queen of Sheba (1 Kings 10.7–9) or of the many foreign kings who came to Solomon's court (1 Kings 4.34; 10.24). Solomon's prayer at the dedication of the Jerusalem Temple also includes a reference to foreigners who come and pray toward the Temple to the God of Israel. Solomon calls on God to answer their prayers, 'in order that all the peoples of the earth may know thy name and fear thee, as do thy people Israel' (1

Kings 8.43; see 8.59–60). We learn from Deut. 4.6 that the well-being of all the nations was God's ultimate goal in calling Israel.

**4.7. Great nation:** This description does not fit the situation of the Israelites on the plains of Moab before their entry into the Promised Land. More probably it refers to the future, most likely the time of David and Solomon. Afterwards, in the days of Hezekiah, Manasseh, or Josiah, people would remember the time of David and Solomon as the golden age of the past when Israel had truly been a 'great nation'.

**4.7. Whenever we call upon him:** We know from the Book of Judges that the Israelites only called on God after they had turned away from Him and been in trouble for many years (Judges 3.9,15, etc.).

**4.9. The things which your eyes have seen:** In Hebrew thought experiences came through the eye. Thus the eye could be called the experiencing person. See 1 John 1.1 for an application of this phrase to the first-hand experience of people who had been with Jesus. Moses spoke to the new generation as though they had been there at the mountain themselves (see Special Note B).

## STUDY SUGGESTIONS

### REVIEW OF CONTENT

1. What are (a) God's *two* gifts, (b) the *four* ways in which the people should respond, and (c) the *four* blessings that make God's people distinct from others?
2. What method did the Israelites use to remind themselves of the most important day in their national life?
3. What *three* things can we learn about our own worship from the Israelites' experience on the mountain?
4. (a) What are the *two* meanings of the fire they saw on the mountain?
   (b) What do the 'darkness, cloud and gloom' have to tell us about God?
5. What were the *two* messages which came from the 'sound of words' out of the fire?

### CONTEXTUAL APPLICATION

6. Give examples of 'faith schizophrenia' or split personality (p. 17) in your own society. Which of the alternative ways of dealing with this problem suggested on p. 17 do you prefer? Give reasons.

# 4.15–43
# Encounter with the God of Life (2)

## OUTLINE

4.15–31: Risk and Promise.
4.32–40: The Creating and Liberating God.
4.41–43: Cities of Life in Transjordan.

## INTERPRETATION

### RISK AND PROMISE, 4.15–31

After the Narrator's description of the memorable experience at the mountain, he pictures Moses explaining to the people that entering into a Covenant with the One who spoke from the fire meant both risk and promise. The risk was that the God of the Covenant is 'jealous'. The promise was that God is also 'merciful' (4.31). Both 'kindness and severity' (Rom. 11.22) are aspects of God's passionate concern for re-establishing the goodness of a corrupted creation.

### THE RISK

The risk is that God's people will arouse His 'jealous' or 'passionate' (NJPS) anger by *corrupting* right relationships between humans and God, among humans themselves, and between humans and nature (4.16,25; see 9.12 and note on 4.24).

Four sorts of corruption could bring disaster:

1. The people would *make and worship images* of what God called 'good' — idols in the form of men or women, animals, birds, creeping things, or fish (4.16–18,23,25; see Gen.1.20–27).

2. They would *worship and serve God's creations*, for example the sun, moon and stars as though they were divine (Deut.4.19; see Gen. 1.14–18).

3. They would *do what is evil* in God's sight (Deut. 4.25).

4. In short, they would '*forget the Covenant* of the LORD your God' (4.23).

In the words of Paul, this means exchanging 'the truth about God for a lie', and worshipping and serving 'the creature rather than the Creator' (Rom. 1.25). St Paul goes on to describe the disastrous consequences in a way that reminds us of Deuteronomy (Rom. 1.26–31).

Corruption of God's good creation goes back to the period

before and after Noah (Gen. 6.12; 8.21). However, God's people, as a new creation in the midst of the old, should have the 'wisdom and understanding' to preserve this right relationship as a model for others (Deut. 4.6). Nevertheless, as Moses foresaw (31.29; see 32.5), and Isaiah observed (Isa. 1.4), God's people were always in danger of behaving corruptly like the peoples around them. How then could they help others to turn from evil ways? It would be like a blind person trying to lead another blind person (see Matt. 15.14).

The consequences of corrupt actions are a reversal of the promises made to the patriarchs. (1) The Israelites who receive their own land as a gift according to God's promise (Gen. 12.1) will become *landless* (Deut. 4.26). (2) Those who should become a 'great nation' (Gen. 12.2) will end as a *scattered remnant* (Deut. 4.27). (3) Those who should bear God's blessing to the nations around them (Gen. 12.3) will have to 'serve gods of wood and stone, the work of men's hands' (Deut. 4.28; 28.64), as *part of the corrupt society* of the nations.

THE PROMISE (4.28–31)

The other side of the risk is the promise that God will be merciful. Though God's people may forget, God will not forget the Covenant. Though the fire of God's anger may reverse the blessings promised to the ancestors, the gentle dew of His mercy will bring new life and hope (Deut. 33.28; see Hos. 14.5; Isa. 26.19). The good news is that there is always the possibility of a new beginning.

*A turning point for the Israelites*: Moses's words look forward to 'the latter days' (see note on Deut. 4.30), when God's people will come to understand His mercy and love after they have endured the loss of land, nation, and freedom. They will see a vision of a new order of justice and peace without the corruptions of the idols in the old society. According to 4.29–30, this landless, weak and poor remnant will gain freedom from their slavery to the idols of their captors by seeking (see note on 4.29) and finding the 'merciful God' who is 'so near' (4.7,31). Then, like the prodigal son in Jesus's parable, they will remember God's mercy, give up their idols and come back to serve God as in the beginning (Deut. 4.30, 31; Luke 15.18).

*A turning point for the nations*: Jeremiah described Israel's return to God in the wider context of the peoples of the world. He said that Israel's resolute return to God would lead the nations to say to themselves 'Our fathers have inherited naught but lies, worthless things in which there is no profit' (Jer. 16.19). He saw an opportunity for them to leave their idols and 'be built up' again in the midst of God's people (Jer. 12.16).

## THE CREATING AND LIBERATING GOD, 4.32–40

The Sinai/Horeb experience taught the Israelites that the God of the Covenant was also the creating and liberating God.

### GOD WHO CREATES (4.32)

The words 'since the day that God created human beings on the earth' puts the whole experience at Sinai/Horeb in a context of creation (4.32 NRSV). God who created the nations (26.19) also cares for the nations. At this moment, when the Israelites were preparing to enter the Promised Land, it comes as a surprise to read that Moses told his people to make a survey of the experience of other peoples by asking two questions (4.32–33). First, has any other people experienced what we have experienced at Sinai/Horeb? Second, has any other god done what our God has done in taking 'a nation for himself from the midst of another nation'?

Perhaps the Narrator was thinking of a time when the Israelites were scattered among the peoples and were seeking God 'with all your heart and all your soul' (4.29). He was telling them that they should invite the nations to learn wisdom and understanding (4.6; see 33.18–19 and note on 4.6). Isaiah 49.1 pictures Israel as doing just this: 'Listen to me, O coastlands, and hearken, you peoples from afar'.

### GOD WHO LIBERATES (4.33–34)

The implied answer to the two questions is that Israel is a unique new creation brought into being by God's *risk-taking* when He attempted 'to go and take a nation for himself', by His *bold action* in Egypt by 'a mighty hand and an outstretched arm', and by His *creative words* out of the fire (4.33–34). In the midst of great crisis by 'trials . . . signs . . . wonders . . . war . . . terrors', God's liberating action and words of power gave the people new form and purpose.

### GOD OF LOVE AND SELECTIVE PURPOSE (4.35–40)

God's personal involvement in this new creation is shown in the words 'loved', 'chose', and 'with his own presence' (4.37). God's purpose for His people is threefold: (1) They should come to understand ('lay it to your heart', 4.39), that the God of the Exodus and Covenant is also the one Creator God, Lord of all powers of nature 'in heaven above', and Lord of all humankind 'on the earth beneath', and that there is in fact 'no other' (4.35,39). (2) They should learn to accept God's *spiritual, social and moral discipline* in their personal and public life as commanded by Moses (4.36,40; see 8.2–5). (3) They should use their *freedom to create a new society* on the land as their 'inheritance' (4.38). As they submit to God's discipline they will prolong their days and generations on the land (4.40).

## CITIES OF LIFE IN TRANSJORDAN

At this point the Narrator has inserted an interlude between parts one and two of Deuteronomy. He tells his readers that Moses designated three cities of refuge in Transjordan. The purpose of these three cities of refuge was to maintain the health of society by preventing the spread of unchecked violence and bloodshed. A person who killed another by accident, and was therefore not guilty of murder, could escape the blood vengeance of the dead person's next of kin by taking refuge in one of these cities. By describing Moses's action in setting these cities apart in Transjordan, the Narrator suggests that the new society was already beginning before the people crossed the Jordan. (The Narrator tells about another three such cities of refuge on the west side of the Jordan River in 19.1–10; see Num.35.1–28 and Josh. 20.1–9).

## NOTES

**4.10. That they may teach their children so:** The duty of parents to teach their children is emphasized in this statement from the Jewish law code, the *Talmud*: 'He who teaches his child the Torah is considered as if he taught Torah not only to his child but to his children's children, and their children to the end of time. A grandchild taught by his grandfather is considered as if he had received the Torah at Sinai'.

**4.19. Things which the LORD your God has allotted to all the peoples under the whole heaven:** The Israelites believed that God created (Deut. 26.19; Ps. 86.9), blessed, and made a Covenant with all the different nations (Gen. 9.1,9). As a part of this blessing, they believed, God allotted lands to the nations (Gen. 10.5,20,31; Deut. 2.5,9,19; 32.8), and assigned to them divine beings who would act as guardians to defend the interests of their people, and maintain justice and freedom according to the Creator's will (Deut. 4.19; cf. Ps. 82:3–4). These beings were believed to control the forces of nature including 'the sun and the moon and the stars', but were *not* to be treated as idols or worshipped, as some of the nations did.

In the Book of Daniel these angelic guardians are called 'princes' of a particular country (Dan. 10.20). In the New Testament they are called 'thrones or dominions or principalities or authorities . . . created through . . . and for' Jesus Christ (Col. 1.16).

Though created and blessed by God, the nations are under God's judgement. One way of explaining this was that the 'divine' beings failed in their assigned task. In the judgement scene described in

When 'covenants' or treaties are agreed between nations, interpreters can help the two sides understand each other. But God's Covenant was not merely a political treaty. It was more like the agreement between Nelson Mandela and President de Klerk in South Africa, offering 'a vision of a new order of justice and peace'. And Moses was not simply 'translating', he was like someone 'opening a well of living water to let the people drink'.

Psalm 82, God condemns these 'divine' overseers because they 'judge unjustly and show partiality to the wicked'. They have no power to 'rescue the weak and the needy' or 'deliver them from the hand of the wicked' (Ps. 82.2,4). According to Deuteronomy God says that 'the peoples that are under the whole heaven' will be in 'dread and fear', and will 'tremble and be in anguish' at the arrival of Israel (Deut. 2.25). God will deprive them of power because of their wickedness (9.5), and give their land to His own people. However, in due time they will learn from the wisdom and understanding of the Israelites (4.6).

**4.24. A jealous God:** See also Deut. 5.9; 6.15; 29.20; 32.16,21. Other translations are 'impassioned' (NJPS) and 'tolerates no rivals' (TEV). God's 'jealousy' has been described as 'the extravagance of His love' (JB note). The Hebrew word which, as an adjective, is translated 'jealous' may also, as a noun, be translated as 'zeal' (Isa. 9.7; see John 2.17).

**4.29. If you search after him:** Such searching is done 'with all your soul', like Daniel 'by prayer and supplications, with fasting and sackcloth and ashes' (Dan 9.3). It must also be done with 'all your heart', that is, with strenuous effort of mind and strong determination.

**4.30. In the latter days:** Some scholars believe that the apparent reference to a return from Exile (Deut.4.29–30) means that these verses were added to Deuteronomy during the Babylonian Exile itself (see General Introduction). Others believe that they may refer to the Exile of the northern tribes at the time of the Assyrian conquest (2 Kings 1.5–7). But we can be sure that each generation would apply words preserved in Deuteronomy to their own situation, and might believe they were living 'in the latter days'.

**4.31. A merciful God:** This is one of the most commonly used descriptions of Israel's God (see Exod. 34.6; Joel 2.13; Jonah 4.2; Pss. 86.15; 111.4; 112.4; 145.8; Neh. 9.17; 2 Chron. 30.9). The Hebrew adjective is related to the noun meaning a mother's womb, and might be translated as 'compassionate' (NJPS), or 'loving like a mother' (see Isa. 49.15).

## SPECIAL NOTE B:
## COVENANT TEACHING, TORAH, OR LAW

The Hebrew word *Torah* appears 21 times in Deuteronomy. In each case the RSV translates it as 'law', except in 17.11, where it is translated 'instructions'. A better translation might be 'Covenant Teaching', as it contains much more than law codes.

When Moses undertook to expound, or interpret this law or Covenant Teaching (see 1.5), he was not a lawyer pointing out details of a legal code, nor merely translating God's words into a different language. He was more like a person opening up a well of living water to let the people drink (see note on 1.5).

'This law' included:

(a) the story of God's grace and Israel's rebellion or obedience during the wilderness period (1.6—3.29), and the encounter with God at Sinai/Horeb (4.1–43);

(b) the Ten Commandments (5.6–21), the Great Commandment (6.4–5), and the other guidelines of the Primary Covenant, along with sermon-like appeals for obedience (chs. 5—11);

(c) constitutional guidelines for Covenant living ('testimonies, statutes and ordinances') of the Covenant in Moab (chs. 12—25);

(d) promises of reward for obedience (e.g. 30.9–10), and warnings of disaster as punishment for disobedience (e.g. 29.21).

The Covenant Teaching was to be written on stone tablets for all to read (4.13; 5.22; 27.3,8). In written form it would serve to guide the king in governing the people (17.18). The priests would have a copy for their careful study (31.9). They would read it before all the people of Israel at least every seven years (31.10–11), and teach it to them (33.10), so that each generation in every place might 'hear and learn to fear the Lord your God' (31.12).

The Covenant Teaching as the treasured 'possession' for the Israelites was a sign of God's love (33.3–4), their way to show love for God, and the basis for their wisdom and understanding in the sight of all nations.

## STUDY SUGGESTIONS

### REVIEW OF CONTENT

1. What are the *two* seemingly opposite descriptions of God in 4.24 and 31?
2. In what *four* ways do God's people corrupt the created goodness of the world? What did St Paul say about this?
3. What *two* questions did Moses tell the Israelites to ask, and among whom should they ask them? What is implied by the questions?
4. What are God's *three* purposes for His people?
5. The *Torah* or Covenant Teaching contains much more than law codes (p. 28). Say briefly what it contains.

### BIBLE STUDY

6. Use a concordance to look up all the references to 'day' or 'days' in Deuteronomy 4. What can you learn from them about the 'days' of your own life and situation?

CONTEXTUAL APPLICATION

7. Hebrews 12.18–24 shows the contrast between the experience of the Israelites at the mountain and the experience of Christians at 'Mount Zion'. What are the differences? Why is it important for Christians to remember the experience described in Deuteronomy?

8. Young people in many countries today feel no hope in the future because they have lost contact with the basic teaching of their faith. How can a study of Deuteronomy 4 help people to find hope for the future?

9. Deuteronomy 4.34 suggests that God took a risk in creating a new nation for Himself (4.33). What was that risk? What sort of risks should we be willing to take in our effort to follow God's will?

10. What sorts of 'graven' images are used for religious purposes by people in your country today? In what ways are they used, and how far do you agree with Deuteronomy 4.25 that any such use is to 'act corruptly' (Deut. 4:16) and against God's will?

11. Read Special Note B on *Torah* or Covenant Teaching or Law in Deuteronomy. Then read John 1.17. Does the 'grace and truth' which came through Jesus Christ mean that the *Torah* which was 'given through Moses' is of no value to Christians? Give reasons for your answer.

12. What are the 'law codes' and 'constitutional guidelines' that provide the 'foundations of life' for the people of your nation today? By what 'authority' are such laws and guidelines established and administered?

# PART 2: 4.44—11.32

# CHARTER FOR LIFE:
# THE PRIMARY COVENANT

## INTRODUCTION

The Ten Commandments which we find in Deuteronomy ch. 5 and Exodus ch.20 are a brief statement of the basic religious and ethical principles holding society together. They have had a great influence in Europe, North and South America, Australia and New Zealand, parts of Africa, and other areas where Judaism and Christianity have spread. The Laws of Manu have had a similar influence as a guide to religious and ethical standards for most peoples on the Indian subcontinent.

In places where Christianity is a minority religion, the Ten Commandments provide fundamental guidelines for righteous living for believers, and a treasure to be shared with others. These commandments have a universal quality which makes them relevant to all societies and situations. Many countries today are experiencing a moral and spiritual crisis. Old traditions have broken down. People need some commonly accepted standards which will enable them to live justly and peaceably together.

In Part 2 of Deuteronomy, the Narrator shows Moses continuing his words in 4.9–14 by reviewing for the Moab generation the Primary Covenant at Sinai/Horeb. The Ten Commandments were the most important part of this Covenant, which was to be valid for them in Moab and for every future generation. As we have seen, the Narrator himself lived at later period of crisis, when similar guidelines were urgently needed. The account of King Manasseh's reign (2 Kings 21) and Jeremiah's temple sermon early in the reign of King Jehoiakim (Jer. 7.1–20) reveal a society that had broken down. In that critical time the Narrator was building on the Moses tradition to plead with the people to follow the Covenant way of life.

# 4.44—5.15
# Ten Rules of Life (1)

## OUTLINE

4.44–49: The Narrator Sets the Stage.
5.1–5: Moses's Introduction.
5.6–15: Four Rules for Life With the God of the Covenant.

## INTERPRETATION

### THE NARRATOR SETS THE STAGE

As at the beginning (1.1–5), the Narrator once again describes the setting for Moses's explanation of the Primary Covenant which follows (chs. 5—11). Three key words show the Narrator's idea of the great importance of this Covenant. The first word is *Egypt* (4.45,46), frequently mentioned in Deuteronomy as 'the house of bondage' (e.g. 5.6; see 26.6). Without the Covenant, those who had been liberated from oppression ('came out of Egypt') might be interested only in protecting their own freedom, and turn to oppress others.

The second key word is *Beth-peor* (4.46), the home of the Baal of Peor (see note on 4.3, p. 21). The Narrator's repetition of this name points to the importance of the Primary Covenant as a protection against the temptations and dangers of the worship of false gods in the Promised Land (see 6.14–15).

Third, the people were 'under the slopes of *Mount Pisgah*' (4.49). Here Moses stood for his last view of the Promised Land (3.27; 34.1) before his death. This mountain would be a reminder that the people would have to begin their new life in the land of opportunity and temptation without Moses! Remembering the ten rules of Life, together with the guidelines to follow, would be the only way of continuing under Moses's guidance.

### MOSES'S INTRODUCTION

#### TO EACH GENERATION

Moses's address to 'all of us here alive this day' (5.3; see p. 7) make his words an urgent summons to each generation of God's people to return to God and join in the Covenant again, to hear the words afresh, and experience anew the wonder and dread of God's presence (5.4). 'All Israel' (5.1) would include 'men, women, and little ones, and the sojourner' (31.12), parents ('our fathers' 5.3), children and grandchildren (4.9) in each period of time.

## AN EDUCATIONAL PROCESS

Referring again to applying the rules of life (see 4.1–6 and p. 18), the Narrator shows Moses describing a continuous life-changing educational process. This will help the people to make the demands of the Covenant a part of their lives: (1) The process begins with *hearing* (see 4.1) the spoken words, perhaps in a religious ceremony, as in Deuteronomy 31.10–13, or Joshua 8.33–35. (2) Education continues as the interpreters undertake to '*declare* [literally to 'make plain'] to you the word of the LORD' (as in Neh. 8.7–8). (3) The people must then *learn* (5.1) the meaning of the rules of life by repetition, reinforcement, and practice, until they become firmly fixed as attitudes and habits, and the people know instinctively that some things are 'not done in Israel' (2 Sam. 13.12). (4) The people are constantly on the alert to *apply* these rules in each new situation (be 'careful to *do* them' Deut. 5.1; see 4.1).

## FACE TO FACE

Finally, Moses reminds the people of the central importance of what is to follow. Both here and in the conclusion (5.22) Moses sets these particular rules apart from all other laws because they were spoken directly by God to the people 'face to face'.

## FOUR RULES FOR LIFE WITH THE GOD OF THE COVENANT

The Ten Commandments fall into two sections. The first four deal with our relationship with God; the last six provide standards for our relationship with our neighbours. In God's own introduction or prologue (5.6), we learn two things about the covenant God: First, He is a God who speaks directly to His people in building a Covenant relationship: 'I am the LORD your God'. This short sentence will define the people's identity and their way of life (see Lev. 23.22; 25.17). God's love leads to the rules for life. Second, in the phrase 'who brought you out of the house of bondage' (Deut. 5.6), God's people know that their liberation and re-creation were the result of a victorious struggle against the forces of death (see pp. 34, 37).

**1. You shall have no other gods before me** (see note on 5.7). The command 'no other gods before me' has two sides to it:

1. Positively, it means centring the whole of life under the Lordship of the one true God and holding fast to the God of life. A

psalmist declared his faith with the words, 'Whom have I in heaven but thee? And there is nothing upon earth that I desire besides thee' (Ps. 73.25). It means accepting both the risk and the promise of discipleship.

2. Negatively, this command means resisting the fascination of 'other gods', who are assumed to be agents of death, but are often disguised as bearers of life (See note on 5.7).

**2. You shall not make for yourself a graven image** (5.8–10; see pp. 37–48). An 'image' is something people 'make' to serve human purposes ('for yourself', see 4.28). Danger comes when people 'bow down' (5.9) in an act of submission, and worship as idols the work of human hands. 'Idols' may be visible, such as an image or an object or a person. Or they may be invisible, such as the special interests of a class, a small power élite, a revolutionary group, a nation, an individual.

People may be 'ensnared' (7.25) or fascinated by the power of the idol. Hosea's words describe the mystery of this sort of deception: 'My people inquire of a thing of wood . . . a spirit of harlotry has led them astray, and they have left their God to play the harlot' (Hos. 4.12; see Isa. 44.18–20).

Once in the power of the idols of death, the people then 'serve them'. Serving the idols may involve personal or community sacrifice, 'abominable practices' (Deut. 20.18), acts of great cruelty and tricks to deceive others. Even the enthusiasm of 'fans', who idolize individual TV personalities or sports champions, may lead to dishonesty, corruption, or violence.

Positively stated, this rule means that we should dedicate the work of our hands to the service of God's purpose, in order to be worthy of God's blessing (14.29; 28.12). If we worship as idols things we ourselves have made, or people we especially admire, we risk 'provoking him to anger' by setting them in the place of God (see 31.29; see note on 5.7).

One person has stated that the greatest danger to Christianity in the 20th century is not heresy (i.e. wrong belief) but idolatry. Modern people try to define all parts of life apart from God, and to set up their own 'idols'.

**3. You shall not take the name of the Lord your God in vain** (5.11). Another translation of this commandment is 'You shall not make wrongful use of the name of the LORD your God' (NRSV). People must not use God's name to claim divine support for their own evil purpose (the real meaning of the Hebrew word translated 'in vain'). This might be done, for example, by using God's name in curses, spells or incantations to harm enemies, or to pretend that our national or personal ambitions have His blessing.

God's people are 'called by the name of the LORD' (28.10), and whatever they do reflects on the name of their God either for praise (as in Jer. 13.11) or for shame (as in Jer. 34.16).

Some right ways to use God's name, as found in Deuteronomy, are: (a) to make promises (to 'swear', 6.13; 10.20) in Yahweh's name instead of in the name of 'other gods' (18.20); (b) to rejoice before 'the LORD your God' in the place which bears His name (12.11–12); (c) to show reverence for God's name and to 'proclaim the name of the LORD' in all words and actions (28.58; 32.3); (d) to be a blessing to the people; (e) to help others to know His name; and (f) to settle disputes in God's name (10.8; 21.5).

**4. Observe the Sabbath day, to keep it holy** (5.12–15). This longest commandment is a fitting climax to the first three rules which warn against 'other gods', 'graven images', and the wrong use of God's name. The fourth commandment is positive. In order to heed the warnings, God's people must reserve one day of each week to rejoice in, and learn to imitate the creating and liberating God.

As God *worked* for six days to complete His good creation (Gen. 1.31; Exod. 20.11), so God's people must learn to think of their work for 'six days' as a *continuation of God's work of creation* (Deut. 5.13; see John 5.17–18). As God *liberated* His people from oppression, so God's people must 'remember' with gratitude, and consider how they may help to *liberate* those in any kind of suffering or oppression (Deut. 5.15). As God *rested* on the seventh day from His labours and *was refreshed* (Gen. 2.2,3; Exod. 31.17), so God's people must *rest and be refreshed* (Deut. 5.14). As God *gave the Sabbath day* to His people so that they could share God's rest (Ezek. 20.12), so God's people must *give a Sabbath rest* to all those dependent on them, including servants, foreigners, and animals (Deut. 5.14). As God *set the seventh day apart* from the other days as holy time (Gen. 2.3), so God's people must *set this day apart* to 'keep it holy' (Deut. 5.12).

Each Sabbath day is like the seventh day of creation and the day of celebration of release from bondage. God's people are restored in body and spirit, and get a new view of themselves as a part of God's new creation. They know that this new perspective is meant for all peoples. 'From sabbath to sabbath, all flesh shall come to worship me' (Isa. 66.23).

## NOTES

There are three traditions for numbering the Ten Commandments as found in Deuteronomy and Exodus:

'Observe the sabbath day, to keep it holy.' As God rested on the seventh day, so God's people must rest from their work and 'be refreshed'. In countries where Christians or Jews are a minority it may not be easy for them to 'observe the sabbath'. But Jewish custom everywhere is to gather for a special meal, lit by 'sabbath candles', on that day.

|    | Jewish | | Catholic/Lutheran | | Greek/Protestant | |
|----|--------|--------|--------|--------|--------|--------|
|    | Deut. | Exod. | Deut. | Exod. | Deut. | Exod. |
| 1  | 5.6 | 20.2 | 5.7–10 | 20.3–6 | 5.7 | 20.3 |
| 2  | 5.7–10 | 20.3–6 | 5.11 | 20.7 | 5.8–10 | 20.4–6 |
| 3  | 5.11 | 20.7 | 5.12–15 | 20.8–11 | 5.8–10 | 20.7 |
| 4  | 5.12–15 | 20.8–11 | 5.16 | 20.12 | 5.12–15 | 20.8–11 |
| 5  | 5.16 | 20.12 | 5.17 | 20.13 | 5.16 | 20.12 |
| 6  | 5.17 | 20.13 | 5.18 | 20.14 | 5.17 | 20.13 |
| 7  | 5.18 | 20.14 | 5.19 | 20.15 | 5.18 | 20.14 |
| 8  | 5.19 | 20.15 | 5.20 | 20.16 | 5.19 | 20.15 |
| 9  | 5.20 | 20.16 | 5.21a | 20.17a | 5.20 | 20.16 |
| 10 | 5.21 | 20.17 | 5.21b | 20.17b | 5.21 | 20.17 |

**5.7. Other gods:** People in ancient Israel knew that other nations treated as gods different parts of the natural environment allotted to them by the Creator of the nations (4.19; 6.14; Ps. 86.9; and see a list in Judges 10.6). Today we could think of these 'gods' as expressions of the personalities, individual talents and energies, policies, customs and social structures of particular nations or peoples. For example, the gilded image 'Lord Siam' in Bangkok, Thailand, is a symbol of the Thai nation.

When these created 'gods' or 'idols' are recognized as gifts of the one good creator God, they are blessings. When they are put in the place of God they become part of the destructive forces of the world. For example, love of our own nation is a good thing, but it will become evil if it is worshipped, as in the case of German nationalism under Hitler. Racial differences are part of God's good creation, but when one group thinks of itself as superior to other races, that group becomes an enemy of God. Wealth is a good thing, but if rich people or nations use economic power to gain unfair advantage over weak people or small nations, this defeats God's good purpose in creation. Those who serve other gods like these will do 'abominable practices' (Deut. 20.18) and become 'a root bearing poisonous and bitter fruit' among the people of God (Deut. 29.18).

**5.13–14. All your work . . . any work:** The Hebrew word translated 'work' is also used of God's 'work' in creation (Gen. 2.2). It is formed from a root word which means to send a messenger, and is very similar to the word often translated 'angel' (Gen. 19.1). 'Work' is an expression of the creative power of God and humans, and whatever is created bears a message from the person who 'works'. For this reason it is necessary for humans to stop their 'work' every seventh day in order to see it in relationship to the creating and liberating God.

Christians at first observed the Sabbath on the seventh day, as well as the Lord's day on the first day when Christ rose from the dead. Eventually they transferred the meaning and the law concerning the Sabbath to the Lord's day.

## STUDY SUGGESTIONS

### REVIEW OF CONTENT

1. What do the words 'Egypt', 'Peor' and 'Pisgah' mean in the Narrator's introduction?
2. What *four* actions listed in 5.1 describe a life-changing educational process?
3. What are the positive and negative meanings of 'have no other gods'?
4. What is meant by 'bowing down to' and 'serving' idols?
5. What are some wrong and right ways to use God's name?
6. In what way is Sabbath observance an 'imitation' of God?

### BIBLE STUDY

7. (a) What sorts of 'work' was Jesus doing when he was accused of breaking the Sabbath according to Matt. 12.1–2,13; Mark 6.2; Luke 4.31–35; 13.10–17; 14.1–4; John 5.9–17; 9.14?
   (b) Read Matt. 5:17 and say whether in each of these cases, you think Jesus was fulfilling or abolishing the fourth commandment. Give reasons for your answers.

### CONTEXTUAL APPLICATION

8. What sorts of activities are described in the following passages as breaking the sabbath?
   (a) Num. 15.32   (b) Neh. 13.15–18   (c) Isa. 58.13   (d) Jer. 17.21–22   (e) Amos 8.5.
   For each passage suggest some modern activities by which Christians in your country might be described as profaning the sabbath.

# 5:16–33
# Ten Rules of Life (2)

## OUTLINE

5.16–21: Six Rules for Living With Covenant Neighbours.
5.22–33: Moses's Conclusion.

## INTERPRETATION

### SIX RULES FOR LIVING WITH COVENANT NEIGHBOURS

**5. Honour your father and your mother (5.16).** This rule is a bridge from God to neighbour. Reverence for God is like honouring parents. The neighbours closest to us are our parents. The model for our other relationships is the family, and a continued good life in the Promised Land depends on a proper relationship between parents and children.

Honour is due to parents because of their role in bringing children into the world, and in teaching them so that they will learn to honour God and obey His Covenant Teaching in every situation (6.7; 11.19; see note on 4.10). Parents are the tellers of the sacred stories of the past (32.7) and the interpreters of the Covenant Teaching (6.20–25) for their children. Parents follow the example of Covenant Teaching by giving their children the same opportunity of Sabbath rest as they themselves enjoy (5.14), and by ensuring that their children enjoy the festivals at which the Covenant Teaching is read (16.11,14; 31.13; and see Ps. 78.5–8). The inclusion of the 'fatherless' in these festivals suggests that there were people who acted in the place of parents for them, just as 'foster parents' do for orphans and needy children today.

Of course parents may exercise an evil influence on their children and grandchildren (4.25). Some may even sacrifice a son or daughter to a false god (18.10) in imitation of the ways of Canaan (12.31). When parents mislead their children by choosing 'new gods' not known by their ancestors (32.17), the children grow up to be a new 'perverse generation, children in whom is no faithfulness' (32.20).

The original meaning of this commandment probably referred to the respect due to aged parents by their adult children. Respect for parents is not innate in human nature. Behind this rule are those who dishonour (Deut. 27.16), curse (Prov. 20.20; 30.11), or rob their parents (Prov. 28.24). In the background we can see a son or daughter committing violence against an aged parent, or driving an infirm mother away from their family home (Prov. 19.26). Respect for the dignity and worth of parents in their later years is basic to Covenant teaching.

**6. You shall not kill (5.17).** Positively considered, this rule means to respect and protect the life of covenant neighbours, who are made in God's image (Gen. 9.6). The word 'kill' refers to intentional and evil violence as in the case of someone 'attacking and murdering his neighbour' (Deut.22.26), or who 'slays his neighbour in secret' (27.24), 'wilfully attacks another to kill him treacherously' (Exod. 21.14), or people who 'lie in wait for blood' of the innocent (Prov. 1.11). In the context of this passage, this commandment does not refer to the killing which takes place in wartime (Deut. 20.12–13), nor to a judicial act of punishment (22.22), nor to accidental or unintentional manslaughter (4.42).

Respect for the life of our neighbours is a basic condition for living together in a Covenant society.

**7. Neither shall you commit adultery (5.18).** Respect for and protection of the marriage covenant of our neighbours, and the institution of the family are the subject of this rule. Marriage and family are not seen as a private affair between two separate individuals, but rather as a part of the structure of life in a covenant society. The power of love which is related to the good sex drive given to us by God's good creation can be a 'raging flame' (Song of Sol. 8.6 NRSV). If it is to be creative and not destructive, it must be guided along covenantal lines.

The term 'adultery' in ancient Israel meant having sexual relations with a person who was part of another family. In a patriarchal society that meant primarily a man having relations with a married or a betrothed woman (Lev. 18.20). It did not refer to sexual relations with an unbetrothed virgin (Exod. 22.16) or with a prostitute (Prov. 6.26).

The effects of adultery are four-fold: (1) the break-up of the neighbour's marriage covenant; (2) the self-destruction of an individual's own life (Prov. 6.32), and (3) in many cases the misery and break-up of his family; (4) the weakening of Covenant society as a whole (Hos. 4.2; Jer. 7.9; Mal. 3.5; Matt. 15.19). For this reason the Covenant society took a very serious view of violations, imposing the death penalty on both the man and the woman (Lev. 20.10).

**8. Neither shall you steal (5.19).** Taking what belongs to someone else, whether an individual, a family, a clan or a larger group, is a violation of personal or group dignity, security, and identity. In a positive sense, members of a Covenant society should show respect for and protection of their neighbours' right to personal possessions.

This command is directly relevant to the realities of Israelite society, which are not unlike those of the present day. *False weights and measures* (Deut. 25.13–16; see Amos 8.5–6) which cheat the poor are like false advertising, shoddy workmanship or price-fixing. *Holding back the wages of a worker* (Deut. 24.14–15) is like paying starvation wages to children or women, or to the very poor. Getting *dishonest profit from exploitation of the foreigners, widows or orphans* (Exod. 22.21–22) is like depriving guest workers, refugees, unemployed, disadvantaged or homeless people of the justice due to them. *Luxurious living at the expense of the poor* (Amos 4.1) is often practised by wealthy nations and corrupt rulers, as well as by individuals today. The *use of wealth and power to 'join house to house . . . add field to field'* (Isa. 5.8) is like the growth of great international business enterprises in Third World countries. They seize peasant holdings once used for local food production, or forest lands which provided livelihood for the forest people and water resources for the nation, and then convert such land into plantations for production of export crops. The result is that forest dwellers and previously independent peasants become labourers on what was once their own land. *Fouling water and land* by powerful or careless people (Ezek. 34.17–18) is like pollution of rivers, lakes, and land by industrial waste in our time. The *kings who had 'eyes and heart only for . . . dishonest gain'* (Jer. 22.17) were like company bosses and factory owners today who think only of profit, without regard for the social consequences of their acts. The *power of bribes* (Isa. 1.23) to corrupt the law courts (Isa. 5.23), government, and religion (Mic. 3.11) is widespread today as well.

**9. Neither shall you bear false witness against your neighbour (5.20).** Bearing false witness against a friend or neighbour is more easily hidden than the overt acts of killing, adultery, or theft. The falsehood can remain hidden for some time. Often the judge, the court, and the public do not know of the secret bribe, the selfish interest, or the personal grudge that has influenced the untruthful words. Only the victims know of the ruin caused to their reputation, honour, security, and even life itself.

The opposite of falsehood is truth. The God of truth (Isa. 65.16) desires truth in people's hearts (Ps. 51.6), and in their speech (Ps. 15.2). 'A faithful [true] witness' (Prov. 14.5) will respect other people's honour and reputation, and protect the innocent from false charges. If a witness tells lies, other people are destroyed and the judicial system breaks down (Exod. 23.1). When people are no longer careful to tell the truth (Jer. 7.28), suspicion, lies and slander tear apart the bonds that should hold society together (Jer. 9.4–5).

**10. Neither shall you covet . . . desire . . . anything that is your**

**neighbour's (5.21)**. The proper way to love, respect and protect our neighbour is by controlling our own desires. No legislation can be effective against greed, or craving for what belongs to a neighbour. The word 'neighbour' appears three times in this commandment, as though to summarize the other five ways of loving our neighbours. According to this commandment the root cause of murder, adultery, theft, and false witness lies in the heart (see Mark 7.21–23).

Covetousness is corruption of the ability which God has given us to enjoy what is good, true and beautiful. The Hebrew words translated 'covet' and 'desire' in this commandment have both positive and negative meanings. The trees in the Garden of Eden were '*pleasant* to the sight and good for food' (Gen. 2.9). Lovers take *delight* in each other (Song of Sol. 2.3; Ps. 45.11), and God's teaching is to be *desired* more than gold (Ps. 19.10).

Corruption comes when the forbidden fruit is '*desired* to make one wise' (Gen. 3.6), when the people in the wilderness get a *craving* for more than they need (Ps. 106.14), when Achan *covets* articles belonging to God (Josh. 7.21), or when rich and powerful people '*covet* fields' belonging to others (Mic. 2.2). The wicked king Jehoiakim had 'eyes and heart only for . . . dishonest gain' and the result was 'shedding innocent blood . . . oppression and violence' (Jer. 22.17).

Jeremiah, who spoke of the commandments being broken in Jerusalem during the reign of Jehoiakim (Jer. 7.9), called on the people of Judah and Jerusalem to cleanse their hearts of evil thoughts (4.14), and to return to God with the 'whole heart' (3.10). Yet he was aware of the 'stubborn and rebellious heart' of Israel (5.23), and the 'deceitful . . . desperately corrupt' heart of humans in general (17.9). This is why Moses says that God will 'circumcise your heart' (Deut. 30.6). Radical action by God is necessary to make obedience to the tenth rule possible.

## MOSES'S CONCLUSION, 5.22–33

In his conclusion, Moses first (5.22) re-emphasizes the central importance of these ten rules of life in the Promised Land.

1. Yahweh 'added no more'. These rules are *uniquely authoritative*, and stand behind all other laws and regulations.

2. Yahweh inscribed the ten rules of life on stone (see 4.13). They are of *permanent value* and are an enduring reminder of Yahweh's requirements from the people who heard them.

3. Yahweh entrusted the inscribed stone tablets to Moses (see 9.10). The rules of life must have *interpreters*—Moses and his successors—to proclaim and explain them to later generations. The leaders of Israel, unable to endure a second experience of fire and

deep gloom, petitioned Moses to act as mediator to stand between the Lord and the people (5.5; see 4.12–13 and pp. 20, 21). At the same time they identify themselves with all humans ('man', Hebrew *adam*; see 4.32) and all people of the world ('all flesh', 5.24,26). In the fire and gloom of the presence of 'the living God', this people who share with all humankind a fear of death (see pp. 18, 20) and a longing for life are given the secret of life. In the wider context we can see that the ten rules of life were not for the Israelites alone, but for 'all flesh'.

At the very moment of the people's high resolve, however, when they promise to 'hear and do' God's will as interpreted by Moses, we meet the melancholy words, 'Oh that they had such a mind as this always . . .'! We can sense God's sadness at Mount Sinai/Horeb, which was shared by Moses on the plains of Moab (1.12; 31.27,29 and see p. 9). Indeed, this very human weakness is what makes the ten rules of life so important as the standard by which to measure both the inward obedience called for by the first and tenth rules, and the conduct of life described in the other eight.

This is stressed in the frequent warnings against proud boasts in 'my power . . . my righteousness' (8.17; 9.4), a 'base thought' (15.9), ignorant turning to other gods (11.16), hearts hardened against poor neighbours (15.7), and stubborn insistence on selfish ways (29.19).

The same awareness of human frailty is shown throughout Israel's history by poets (Ps. 95.7c; Isa. 48.18), by the prophets (Hos. 4.1–4; Jer. 7.8–10), by Jesus himself (Matt. 23.37) and by Paul (2 Cor. 4.7). In choosing the frail human community of the Israelites from 'all flesh' for the sake of 'all the families of the earth' (Gen. 12.3), God accepted the risk and vulnerability (see pp. 23, 24 for the people's risk).

God's words to Moses are all the more urgent: 'but you *stand by me* here'! Moses is not only to bow down in humble worship or access to the divine presence, but to stand by God's side in partnership with the divine in forming a people worthy of their high calling. Again the verbs of action are important. First, God *tells* Moses how He wants the people to apply the ten words. Moses then *declares* (makes plain, Deut 5.5) God's words of life, and *teaches* the people how to 'do them'.

## NOTES

**5.16. Honour:** In the New Testament this command is interpreted to mean that children should obey their parents 'in the LORD, for this is right'. Parents in turn must not 'provoke your children to anger' (Eph. 6.1–4).

**5.20. Neighbour**: This word appears for the first time in this commandment. The Hebrew word means 'trusted friend' (Prov. 17.17; Ps.41.9) or associate in work or business or neighbourhood.
**5.22. The LORD**: In the RSV this word, printed in capital letters, is a substitute for 'Yahweh', the name of God which Moses received at the burning bush (Exod. 3.16,18). The text of the early Hebrew Bible was written without vowels, making the name Yahweh only the four consonants YHWH. Because Jews believe the name is too sacred for humans to speak, they substitute the word *adonai* which means 'Lord'. When vowels were added to the Hebrew text, the vowels for Adonai were added to the consonants of Yahweh to remind the Jewish readers that they should not read Yahweh, but Adonai. The result was the name YaHoWaH, or Jehovah.

## SPECIAL NOTE C: COVENANTS IN DEUTERONOMY

At this point we may usefully summarize the three covenants between God and His people which are described in Deuteronomy.

1. *The Covenant with the ancestors*, Abraham, Isaac and Jacob (4.31). According to this Covenant God promised to bless His chosen people (7.13–15). Blessing on them in the land of Israel would be a confirmation of this Covenant promise (8.18). We may date this covenant to the time of Abraham, about 1800 BC.

2. The *Covenant made at Mount Sinai/Horeb* (4.13; 5.2). This is the Primary Covenant which formed the people of Israel, bound them to Yahweh, and promised them long life in the land (5.33). This Covenant is identified in Deuteronomy 4.13 as the Ten Commandments which appear in 5.7–21 and were inscribed on stone tablets (4.13; 9.9,11,15)) as a constant reminder to the Israelites not to forget (4.23), transgress (17.2), or break (31.16,20) this covenant. The Great Commandment (6.4–5) and chs.7—11 are a further application of the Ten Commandments. We may date this Covenant about 1250 BC.

3. The *Covenant in Moab* (29.1) was a renewal of the Covenant at Mount Sinai/Horeb (5.2–3), in a new situation. This Covenant contained 'statutes and ordinances' giving a further set of guidelines for life in the Promised Land. It was just as binding as the Primary Covenant, again promising the people prosperity 'in all that you do'(29.9; 30.9–10). The review of the Primary Covenant and the guidelines included in the Covenant in Moab were written in a book and given into the care of the Levitical priests and also placed in the Ark of the Covenant. This was known as the Covenant Teaching or *Torah* (see Special Note B), and was read in the hearing of the people every seven years (31.9–11). This covenant should be dated about 1200 BC.

## STUDY SUGGESTIONS

REVIEW OF CONTENT

1. What were some practices among the Israelites that did not 'honour' parents?
2. What was the word 'kill' in the sixth commandment understood to mean in ancient Israel?
3. What are the chief effects of adultery?
4. What sorts of activity as described in other parts of the OT should be included in the meaning of 'steal'?
5. What is the effect when people 'bear false witness' against a neighbour?
6. Name some of the things described in the OT as being coveted or desired.
7. God did not command Moses to bow down before Him. What did God tell Moses to do?
8. (a) What are the three Covenants between God and His people described in Deuteronomy?
   (b) What did God chiefly promise, according to each covenant?
   (c) What is the approximate date of each Covenant?

BIBLE STUDY

9. What is the difference between the taking of human life by each of the following?
   (a) Moses   (Exod.   2.12)   (b) Abimelech   (Judges   9.5)
   (c) David (2 Sam. 12.9)   (d) Ahab (1 Kings 21.19)
   What do these examples tell us about the sixth commandment?
10. What does each of the following passages tell us about the meaning and importance of the seventh commandment?
    (a) Gen. 39.2–20   (b) 2 Sam. 11.1–12.24   (c) 2 Sam. 13.1–19   (d) Prov.   7.6–23   (e) Jer.   29.23   (f) Matt.   5.28
    (g) John 8.1–11
    Give similar examples from present day society. Do you agree with Prov. 6.32? Give your reasons.

CONTEXTUAL APPLICATION

11. How would you relate each of the following to the sixth commandment?
    (a) modern warfare   (b) abortion   (c) the death penalty
    (d) the use of medical techniques to prolong the life of a terminally ill person   (e) careless use of toxic chemicals
12. The most famous case of false witness in the Old Testament is found in 1 Kings 21.1–19, esp. v.13. Who gave the false witness, who prompted them to do so, and for what reason? Who was the victim? Which other commandments were

broken by the people described in this passage? What was the result foretold by Elijah the prophet? Give examples of this sort of false witness among rich or powerful people today.
13. In what ways does the commandment against false witness relate to the following activities in the modern world?
(a) commercial advertising    (b) government service
(c) business ethics

# 6.1–25
# The Great Commandment: To Love God

## OUTLINE

6.1–3: *The* Commandment Above All Others.
6.4: Who is God?
6.5: You shall Love the Lord your God.
6.6–9: Love for God in Daily Life.
6.10–11: God's Good Gifts of Love.
6.12–19: Love for other gods.
6.20–24: Love for God in Every Generation.
6.25: The Gift of Righteousness.

## INTERPRETATION

What is the most important rule for human behaviour? What is the beginning point for Christian ethics? When Jesus called Deuteronomy 6.5 'the great and first commandment' (Matt. 22.37–38) and linked it with Deuteronomy 6.4 (Mark 12.29–30), He gave God's answer to these questions. As a consequence, these two verses which link the Old and New Testaments together are of basic significance for all Christians everywhere. Here we should look at the context of Deuteronomy 6.

### *THE* COMMANDMENT ABOVE ALL OTHERS, 6.1–3

At the beginning of ch. 6, we see Moses beginning to teach the people about 'the commandment', which in the singular form refers to the great commandment to love God (see note on 6.1). After the giving of the Ten Commandments, God told Moses to come near to learn about '*all the commandment*' so that he might teach it to the people (5.31). 'The commandment' is not an addition to the ten (see 5.22, and p. 42), but a deepening of the first commandment

(5.7), and indeed a summary of all the others in positive form (see Rom. 13.10). The phrase 'all this commandment' in 6.25 includes all that is meant by the commandment to love God.

## WHO IS GOD? 6.4

### A CALL TO LISTEN WITH CAREFUL ATTENTION

The words 'Hear O Israel'! are an urgent appeal which emphasizes the most important meaning of the words which follow for the people of God. These words come with fresh urgency to each generation in every age and place. Hearing is an act of will, a choice which humans must make each day. The appeal to 'hear' implies the possibility that God's people may refuse to hear ('hearken to') God speaking through Moses (1.43). Even after Covenant words have been spoken, that 'this day you have become the people of the LORD your God' (Deut. 27.9), the people may lack the will to hear God's appeal (30.17; see Isa. 6.9; 42.18–20; Jer. 6.10). In this they are like the disciples of Jesus (Mark 8.18), and like Christians today. Behind the appeal to 'hear' lies the hope that God will give His people 'ears to hear' when they turn to Him (Deut. 29.4; see Isa. 29.18; 35.5; 50.4–5; Mark 7.37).

### OUR GOD IS YAHWEH!

In Thailand, people often use the phrase 'all things holy' in wishes for good fortune or blessing. For them the phrase covers the many spiritual beings of the unseen world. For Israel, the name Yahweh is much more specific than this popular term. Yahweh is the God of the Exodus who saves and delivers His people (Deut. 5.6). Yahweh is the God who made the Israelites into a people by His Covenant at Mount Sinai/Horeb and does so again and again at each Covenant renewal (5.3).

### YAHWEH IS ONE!

Human beings have always wondered about the 'non-human' world of spirits, gods, ghosts. In ancient Canaan people believed in *baals* which they thought inhabited trees and rivers, and in a high god *Baal*, his consort *Asherah*, *Mot*, the god of the world of the dead, and many other gods. The same was true of the Egyptians, Babylonians and Assyrians. Hindus believe in many gods and goddesses. According to Chinese traditional religion there are many gods, such as the god of wealth, the kitchen god, the gods of the earth and the sky. And the same is true of many traditional religions in Africa, Central and South America, and the South Pacific. Primal religion teaches that the world is inhabited by many

6.1–25

'You shall have no other gods' nor 'make for yourself an idol' (NRSV). In ancient Canaan people believed in 'baals': gods of the forces of nature, or national leaders; and worshipped images like this gold-covered statuette discovered by archaeologists at Megiddo.

Moses warned that ruin follows if people worship images they themselves have made, or 'bow down' to such 'idols' as political power, financial profit or popular 'heroes' like the footballer Diego Maradona.

unseen deities. In contrast to this world-view is the affirmation that 'Yahweh is one'!

The word 'one' here has three meanings:

1. Yahweh is *the only God for Israel* (Deut. 4.35,39; 32.12). Although other peoples worship and serve other gods, the Israelites are loyal only to Yahweh 'our God' (see Micah 4.5). This was not thought to rule out the existence of other gods.

2. Yahweh, Israel's Saviour, is *one and the same as God the Creator of heaven and earth, of all living creatures, and all human beings* (see p. 25). This binds Israel and the nations together under the one Creator and Saviour God, as one humanity (4.6; see pp. 21, 25).

3. Yahweh is unique, *the only true God*, 'there is no other' (Deut. 4.35,39; 32.39). This one true God created the powers which other peoples worship as gods (see note on 4.19). Yahweh is King over all the earth, and one day will reign supreme (see note on 6.4).

The three great monotheistic religions, Judaism, Christianity and Islam teach the unity and uniqueness of God, though each gives this teaching a specific meaning related to its own history and theology. Jews recite the '*Shema*' (Deut. 6.4) each Sabbath. It has given them courage in times of persecution in Europe during the Middle Ages, and more recently at the time of the Nazi slaughter of six million Jews during the Second World War. In ancient times, Rabbi Akiba recited the Shema as he was being tortured before his death as a martyr. When asked why he did so, he replied, 'All my life I have recited this verse and have hoped for the hour when I could fulfil it. I have loved Him with all my heart . . . and all my fortunes. Now I have the opportunity to love Him with all my soul'.

The Nicene Creed of the Christian religion begins with the words 'We believe in one God the Father almighty, maker of heaven and earth, of all that is, seen and unseen'. Muslims say 'There is no God but Allah, and Muhammad is His prophet'.

## YOU SHALL LOVE THE LORD YOUR GOD, 6.5

Human love is the response to God's love. It is a joining of our lives with the will and purpose of God in the world, and excludes relationship with any other power. It is an act of the whole mind and will ('heart'), all feelings and affections ('soul'), and the entire abundance of energy ('might'). Such love should unify the life of a people or nation of individuals around the one God and God's purpose for all creation.

Six expressions which occur together with the verb 'love' in Deuteronomy tell us how God's people should show their love for God:

1. Loving God with all their feelings and affections ('soul'), each person will *cleave to God* alone (NRSV has 'hold fast' in 10.20; 30.20; see also Ps. 63.8) in surrender to the holy will of the one God. This requires the discipline of prayer, and results in a personal emotional bond between the Israelites and God. It is like the marriage bond which creates a new solidarity between two people (Gen. 2.24); or like the bond between a child and a parent, affirming family solidarity (Ruth 1.14). Cleaving to God alone (Deut. 13.4) rules out following Solomon's example of cleaving to other gods (1 Kings 11.2).

2. Loving God with all their feelings and affections, the people will *fear God* (Deut. 6.2,13,24). They will show deep respect and awe for the vast power and holiness of the Creator, who is also Judge of unrighteousness and injustice. This attitude of awe, respect and honour is not natural to humans, but must be learned, for example at festival time (14.23), at solemn ceremonies of Covenant renewal (29.12,13), and by the examples of struggle against wickedness in society (13.11; 17.13).

3. Loving God with all their mind and will ('heart'), the people will *serve God* (6.13;10.12) alone, in work and worship, 'with joyfulness and gladness of heart' (28.47). The Hebrew word *abad*, translated here as 'serve', means service in both worship and work.

4. Loving God with all their mind and will, they will *obey His voice* (13.4; 30.20; see Exod. 19.5). (The Hebrew word *shema* means to hear, listen, and obey.) They will listen *for*, and conform their lives *to* the voice of Yahweh in each new situation, to gain fresh insight into the meaning of the commandments. The voice which spoke from the fire to discipline His people (4.36) may add new words in ever-changing situations. Each generation must listen for the voice of God (Ps. 95.7; Isa, 6.8). Commandments require continuing interpretation.

5. Loving God with the entire abundance of their energy ('might'), they will *keep His commandments* (6.2,25), that is, put them into practice in daily life with untiring zeal (see p. 51).

6. Loving God with the entire abundance of their energy, the people will *walk in God's ways* (10.12; 11.22), according to their Covenant oath (26.17). Walking in God's ways means living in ways which follow the pattern set by God, as revealed in the Bible. God's ways are seen in His loving acts of creation, discipline, forgiveness, justice, righteousness, and peace-making (see pp. 36–38 on following God's way in the fourth commandment).

God's ways are different from human ways (Isa. 55.8–9). They stand in sharp contrast to the 'customs of the nations' (2 Kings 17.8), which are marked by stubborn self-will (Deut. 29.19; Jer. 11.8), or destructive attitudes and actions (Col. 3.5–8). According to the Deuteronomic historian only David (1 Kings 11.33) and Hezekiah (2 Kings 20.3) walked in God's ways. In fact, walking in God's ways is possible only with God's help (Ezek. 11.20; see Deut. 30.6).

God's ways are revealed to Christians most clearly in the life of Jesus. Jesus's acts of love (John 15.12) are a model for His followers (John 14.12; see 1 John 2.6). The Christian faith was originally called 'the Way' (Acts 9.2; 24.22).

## LOVE FOR GOD IN DAILY LIFE, 6.6–9

### AT ALL TIMES AND IN ALL ACTIVITIES

1. Love for God *with the Mind* ('these words shall be upon your heart'). God's people will make their thinking, planning and decisions an expression of their love to God, rather than their own self-will (8.14; 29.18–19; see Jer. 5.23).

2. Love for God *in the Family* ('when you sit in your house'). Families will discuss and practise the meaning of loving God in their homes from day to day, and at times of marriage, birth, joys, sickness and death.

3. Love for God *in Public Life* ('when you walk by the way'). The people will explore the meaning of love for God in their ordinary relationships with neighbours, in the market-place, the law courts, and in places of political and military power (see Prov. 1.20).

4. Love for God *at Night and in the Morning* ('when you lie down, and when you rise'). In Hebrew usage, to 'lie down' can refer to sleep, sexual relations, or death. The verb 'rise' can refer to getting up in the morning, recovery from illness, beginning a piece of work, or rebelling against oppressive power. Love for God will govern all these activities of daily life.

5. Love for God *Controlling All Actions* ('bind them as a sign upon your hand'). In Hebrew thought, the hand represents the whole person in action. Binding the command to love God on the hand means making all actions an expression of love for God, for example, producing goods and services, helping the poor, supporting just causes, protecting the environment.

6. Love for God *Controlling Desires and Ambitions* ('they shall be as frontlets between your eyes'). In Hebrew thought, the eye represents the whole person, showing pride or humility, greed or modest desires, and selfishness or generosity. Without the control of love for God, everyone will do 'whatever is right in His own eyes' (Deut. 12.8), or they will be 'wise in their own eyes' (Prov. 3.7; Isa. 5.21). Bribes will blind their eyes (Deut. 16.19). Greed for dishonest gain will be their ambition (Jer. 22.17; see Eccles. 4.8).

Those who love God will control their desires and ambitions, so that their seeing, watching, desiring, and wanting will be without self-seeking. Their desires will be limited, and their wanting modest.

## AS A DECLARATION TO OTHER PEOPLES

1. A Public Declaration that *Love for God Rules Each Home* ('write them on the doorposts of your house'). By writing Deuteronomy 6.5 at the entrance to their homes, God's people will make public to all who pass the door or who come in to visit, that love for God is the governing principle of life in their homes. Those who live there will set aside a portion for the needy (Deut. 26.12), and welcome the homeless poor (Isa. 58.7). There will be integrity (Ps. 101.2) rather than wickedness (Prov. 3.33) or strife (Prov. 17.1).

2. A Public Declaration that *Love for God Rules the Whole Community* ('Write them . . . on your gates'). By writing Deuteronomy 6.5 on the gates of the town, public officials will declare that love for God will control the corporate life of the people. Laws, government, education, public care for the weak, care for the earth will show the whole community's love toward God.

### GOD'S GOOD GIFTS OF LOVE, 6.10–11

'We love because He first loved us', wrote John (1 John 4.19). God's love for His people is the basis of the great command to love God. God shows His love for His people by giving them a beautiful natural environment (a *'good* land' Deut. 6.18), 'flowing with milk and honey' (6.3), with olive orchards and vineyards and a constant supply of water (cisterns, 6.11). Jeremiah called it 'a plentiful land [with] . . . fruits and its good things . . . a heritage most beauteous of all nations' (Jer. 2.7; 3.19). God also gave them a fine political, social, and economic environment (*'goodly* cities', Deut. 6.10), where, 'people [would] blossom in the cities like the grass of the field' (Ps. 72.16, NRSV). The third gift of God's love was a pleasing family environment ('houses full of all *good* things', Deut. 6.11). where God would satisfy them 'with good as long as you live' (Ps. 103.5). Families could live in peace without fear, under their own 'vine and . . . fig tree' (Mic. 4.4). This description of the Promised Land reminds us of the Garden of Eden with its trees 'pleasant to the sight and good for food' (Gen. 2.9).

The people who inherit Yahweh's gifts of the *good* land, *good* cities and *good* homes, must show their love for Yahweh by using of these gifts according to God's will, by doing 'what is *right and good* in the eyes of the LORD' in the place where they live. Only thus will it *'go well'* (using the same Hebrew word usually translated 'good') with them (Deut. 6.18), '*for our good* always . . . preserve us alive' (6.24).

*Note*: Some people today may question God's fairness or justice in giving to the Israelites land already occupied by the Canaanites, plus cities and houses built by the Canaanites. The reason given in Deuteronomy 9.5 is that the Canaanites had lost the privilege of living on the land because of their wickedness. To put it in another way, the land had become sick and 'vomited out its inhabitants' (Lev. 18.25). If the Israelites did not do right and good, the land could do the same to them (Lev. 18.28).

## LOVE FOR OTHER GODS, 6.12–19

As in the garden of Eden with its forbidden tree of the knowledge of good and evil, there were, in the Promised Land, the forbidden gods of the peoples of the land (Deut. 6.14–15; see pp. 35, 37, 47–49, 50). We may call these 'culture gods': the values and practices of the dominant culture.

Throughout Deuteronomy there is a deep anxiety about the dangers of living in the midst of cultures which have different values and standards of behaviour, as we can see from the nineteen warnings against serving other gods (see note on 5.7). Prosperity (31.20), which is a gift of God, will tempt God's people to 'forget' (Deut.6.12) the command to love Yahweh alone. The good things of nature, society and home may draw the people away (13.13), deceive them (11.16) or tempt them (13.6) to worship other gods and participate in the 'abominable practices' of those who serve them (18.9).

### YOU SHALL NOT GO AFTER OTHER GODS

Some people may follow these culture gods, comforting themselves with the belief that God's Covenant love for them will protect them from any adverse results. This is the meaning of putting God 'to the test' (6.16; see Matt. 4.7; Luke 4.12 in which Jesus quotes this verse in His struggle against temptation in the wilderness). Putting God to the test is like a disobedient child trying to see how far he can go without getting punished.

Forgetting God and following other gods will arouse the 'jealous' anger of Yahweh (6.15; see pp. 15, 21, 23). Without the love for God and all that this means in home and community, the *natural environment* (land) He has given, with its crops and flocks, will be a ruin, and the water will be polluted (Deut.29.23; Jer. 4.26). The once beautiful *political, social and economic environment* (cities) will become places of violence and death (Isa.6.11). Bloodshed and the cries of the oppressed will replace justice and righteousness (Isa. 5.7). The poor will lose their pleasant *family environment* (homes) He has given, because of the covetousness of the rich (Isa. 5.8; Mic. 2.2).

Did God destroy the land, or did the Israelites destroy it themselves? Paul helps us to understand God's anger in this way: God 'gave them up to a base mind and to improper conduct' (Rom. 1.28). God allows humans the freedom to do wrong, to destroy their natural, social, and family habitat, so that they may return to Him (see Deut. 30.1–3). In Jesus's parable, the loving father allowed the prodigal son to waste all he had inherited, and waited for the boy to repent and return home (Luke 15.11–24).

## LOVE FOR GOD IN EVERY GENERATION, 6.20–24

*The third generation* is often a problem for Christian families. The first generation have come to believe in Jesus with fervent faith. The second generation does not have to struggle with the questions of faith, and their belief is less fervent. The third generation are likely to be very much affected by the surrounding culture and in danger of forgetting the faith of their grandparents.

There was a 'generation gap' in ancient Israel. The third generation ('children's children', 4.9,25; 6.2) in the Promised Land were especially vulnerable to the temptations of the culture gods of the land. They were far removed from the events at Mount Sinai/ Horeb, and the leadership of Moses. Some of them might inter-marry with the peoples of Canaan (7.3–4), and even entice God's people to follow other gods (13.6–10). They could be 'stubborn and rebellious' (21.18–20).

A vivid example of this generation gap was Rehoboam, grandson of David at the time when the northern tribes rose in revolt against the Jerusalem monarchy. Rehoboam rejected the good advice of the older men (second generation) who had been Solomon's counsellors, and followed the advice of the 'young men who had grown up with him'. His harsh reply made enemies of the northerners (1 Kings 12.6–16).

### OVERCOMING THE GENERATION GAP

To avoid this problem of the third generation, Deuteronomy emphasizes how important it is for parents to teach the command-ments to their children (Deut. 4.9–10; 11.19). Parents should 'recite' (6.7, NRSV) this Great Commandment to their children, explaining what it means in each new situation (see p. 7).

Deuteronomy 6.20–24 gives an example of such teaching in the form of a question by children and an answer by parents 'in time to come', that is, when the people would be living in the good land full of good things of all kinds. The question suggests doubts in the minds of later generations about 'the testimonies . . . statutes . . .

and ordinances' which were so important to their fathers and mothers. Such regulations don't seem to produce quick profit, and they obstruct the ambition of those selfish individuals who want to take advantage of others, especially the poor. Behind the question 'What is the meaning?' is the feeling that perhaps it is time for the third generation to declare their independence of the teaching given them by their parents or grandparents.

The parents, in their answer, try to help their children understand that they, and all later generations as well, were symbolically present at the first formative events of the past (see p. 7). Past events become present once again. Even though the parents themselves did not experience those events at first hand, yet they have learned from them, and try to teach their children that it is 'we', in each generation, who were slaves, were delivered, and received the land. They tell them that it is 'our eyes', that is, the eyes of parents, children and children's children, who saw the mighty acts of God, and heard the voice of God commanding 'us' to observe the laws for 'our' continued welfare in the land from the present ('this day') on into the future ('the time to come').

## THE GIFT OF RIGHTEOUSNESS, 6.25

The final word from the parents is that if each generation loves God fully ('if we are careful to do all this commandment') then this 'will be righteousness for us'. When Abraham believed the Lord, God 'reckoned it to him as righteousness' (Gen. 15.6). According to Deuteronomy, it is only complete love for God that He reckons as righteousness. Loving God means *participating* in God's righteous purposes and acts. For example, to act generously toward the poor is reckoned as 'righteousness to you before the LORD your God' (Deut. 24.13). The temptation for the Israelites was to boast that the good gifts of God are a *reward* for righteousness (9.4–5). But righteousness is not a reward for good deeds; it is God's gift of love to a Covenant partner who loves Him without restriction.

## NOTES

**6.1. The commandment**: The Hebrew word translated 'commandment' appears in the singular and plural form in Deuteronomy. In the plural form it is very much like the other commonly used words 'statutes and ordinances' (see 6.2; 8.11). The singular form appears 14 times in Deuteronomy, of which the most important are 6.1 and 6.25, where it refers to the command to love God in 6.5. Elsewhere it is related directly (11.22; 19.9) or indirectly to the command to love God (11.1,8; 30.11, 20), or by implication, to love our neighbour (15.5,7; 17.20; 26.13; 27.1, 16–25).

**6.4. The LORD . . . is one** A Jewish litany for the *Shema* is as follows:

'The LORD is one':—for us.

'The LORD is one':—for everyone in the world.

'The LORD is one':—in this world.

'The LORD is one':—in the world to come.

'And so Scripture says, "The LORD shall be king over all the earth. In that day shall the LORD be one and His name one" ' (Zech. 14.9).

**6.5. Heart:** The Hebrew word *leb* which is usually translated as 'heart', is also translated as 'mind' in five verses (4.9; 5.29; 28.28; 29.4; 30.1, RSV and NRSV). The heart represents the whole person as thinking, planning, and making decisions as well as experiencing and feeling. In Deuteronomy we find that it is the heart of a person or people which remembers (4.39) or forgets (4.9), knows (8.5) or is deceived (11.16), is obstinate (2.30) or obedient (30.2), is proud and self-confident ((8.14,17) or humble (10.16), turns away from God (29.18) or returns to God (4.29 30.10), is fearful ((1.28–29) or courageous (20.3), is grudging or generous toward a poor neighbour. Our hearts are open to God's inspection (8.2; 13.3). God's people must constantly try to cleanse ('circumcise') their hearts of self-seeking (10.16); but in the end, this is beyond human capability, and only God can cleanse ('circumcise') the heart (30.6).

## STUDY SUGGESTIONS

REVIEW OF CONTENT

1. What is the difference between 'the Commandment' (singular) and 'the Commandments' (plural) in Deuteronomy?
2. What are *three* meanings of the phrase 'Yahweh is one'?
3. What *six* expressions help us to understand the meaning of love for God?
4. What were the various aspects of daily life described in Deut. 6.6–9, in which God's people should practise love for God?
5. What does 'putting God to the test' mean?
6. What is the final gift of God's love?

BIBLE STUDY

7. Paul wrote that 'Love is the fulfilling of the law' (Rom. 13.10). How do the following passages explain this statement?
   (a) Luke 11.42  (b) 1 John 2.5,15  (c) 4.20–21

8. 'Hearing is an act of will, a choice which humans must make each day' (p. 47). What do we learn about 'deaf ears' from (a) Isa. 6.9–10, (b) 42.18–20, (c) Mark 8.18? What do we learn about 'opened ears' from (d) Isa. 29.18, (e) 50.4–5, (f) Mark 7.37?

9. Which of the following verses refer to (i) actions of the 'hands', and which refer to (ii) attitudes expressed by the eyes'? (a) 1 Kings 11.26–27 (b) Psalms 10.8 (c) Prov. 6.17 (d) Isa. 1.15 (e) 3.16 (f) 10.13 (g) Jer. 22.17 (h) Hos. 12.7?
How might these actions and attitudes change if the people concerned were controlled by love for God?

10. What do the following verses tell us about righteousness as God's gift? (a) Gen. 15.6 (b) Rom. 4.22 (c) Phil. 3.9 (d) Gal. 5.5.

## CONTEXTUAL APPLICATION

11. What are some of the things which make it difficult for us to hear God's commands?

12. Talk with someone of another religious faith. What do they believe about 'highest truth'? In what way are their beliefs similar to, or different from, what Deuteronomy teaches about the Creator and Saviour God?

13. Which of the following sorts of love is closest to your own understanding of 'love for God'? Give reasons for your choice.
    (a) The love between a bride and bridegroom.
    (b) The love of a daughter or son to parents.
    (c) Students' respect and love for a teacher.
    (d) The loyalty of soldiers to their commander.
    (e) The respect and admiration citizens may have for the ruler or rulers of the state.
    (f) The love of Christians for their Church.

14. Moses told the Israelites to write the words of God on the 'gates of their cities' where public meetings were held, and judgements given. What would be some ways of relating God's commands, and love for Him, to public life today, and what problems might result?

15. As with the forbidden tree in the Garden of Eden, there were in the Promised Land the forbidden gods of the peoples of the land (see p. 53). What, if anything, do you see as 'forbidden gods' and 'abominable practices' in the world today? What is likely to happen to people who 'forget' the command to love God only?

16. If 'love for God' is the highest value in your home, how does, or should, this affect each of the following? (a) Your family

God the Creator 'shows His love for the nations by giving lands to each for their welfare', wherever they are—from the rice-terraces of East Asia, as above in Indonesia, to the flat cornlands of the Americas where the 'harvesters' are giant machines.

devotional life, (b) Your way of solving problems as a family, (c) Your attitude toward strangers, (d) Your participation in community events

# 7.1–26
# An Alternative Society in the Promised Land

## OUTLINE

7.1–5, 25–26: Danger From the Dominant Culture.
7.6–24: Israel, God's Alternative Society.

## INTERPRETATION

One of the urgent questions facing Christians in the world today is their relation to the cultural background in which they live, whether it is traditional, or mixed with other influences, or, as in many places, changing very quickly. Should they reject or embrace the surrounding culture of their parents and grandparents, or of their younger friends, or try to sift out the true from the false values? Should they conform to the dominant practices and standards of behaviour of their society? What did Paul mean when he appealed to Christians not to 'be conformed to this world', but to 'be transformed by the renewal of your mind' (Rom. 12.2)? Deuteronomy ch. 7 can give us important guidelines as we try to answer these questions.

### DANGER FROM THE DOMINANT CULTURE, 7.1–5, 25–26

#### THE NATIONS: PART OF GOD'S CREATION

Before studying these verses in ch. 7, let us recall what we have already learned from Deuteronomy about the 'nations' as the cultural environment of Israel. As we have seen in ch. 4, God's creation of all human beings is the context of His Covenant with the Israelites at Sinai/Horeb (see p. 25). God the Creator shows His love for the nations, so the Israelites believed, by giving lands and appointing heavenly rulers to each nation for their welfare (see note on 4.19, pp. 26–27).

Because of the rebellion of the nations, God made a plan, which He had announced to Abraham (Gen. 12.3), to enable them once again to enjoy His blessing. According to Deuteronomy this plan meant that God's people should serve as a model for the nations by observing all the guidelines for life which God had given them through Moses. When the nations saw how Israel lived, they would know God's will for themselves (Deut.4.6 and note pp. 21–22).

In Deuteronomy ch. 7 we find a preliminary step in God's plan: those particular nations living in the land of Canaan and forming its dominant culture (7.1) had failed to live up to God's expectations and had become very wicked (9.5). For God's plan to succeed, God's people must survive in the midst of the dominant culture of Canaan without being overwhelmed by it. The danger was that the Israelites would imitate the practices of the dominant culture and reject God (7.4; see 20.18). This was the sort of danger Paul had in mind when he wrote to the early Christians in Rome, 'Do not be conformed to this world' (Rom. 12.2)

THE DOMINANT CULTURE

In the time of Moses, the dominant culture of Canaan lay on the western side of the Jordan River. Moses was warning the Israelites about the dangers awaiting them. In the time of the Narrator, the culture of Judah had been greatly influenced by Assyria. For about 100 years Assyria as the dominant power in Western Asia had kept close control of the economic, religious, and political life of its vassal state Judah. Assyria had chosen Manasseh, the royal grandfather of Josiah, to rule Judah. As a vassal, Manasseh had to swear to be loyal to the Assyrian god Ashur as well as to Yahweh.

Assyrian religion, with its worship of the male god Ashur and his female consort Ishtar (known as 'the queen of heaven' in Jer. 7.18, as Ashtoreth in 2 Kings 23.13, and as Venus in Roman mythology), and of the star gods ('all the host of heaven', 2 Kings 21.3) was common in Judean religious life, extending even into the Jerusalem Temple (2 Kings 21.5). The men speaking with 'an alien tongue' or 'obscure speech' to whom Isaiah referred in an earlier time (Isa. 28.11; 33.19) may have been Assyrian merchants, visiting officials, military troops, or perhaps an Assyrian commissioner to the court. Besides following the practices of Assyrian religion, Manasseh also returned to the Canaanite worship of Baal and Asherah which his royal father Hezekiah had suppressed (2 Kings 21.3,7,11). Manasseh practised human sacrifice (2 Kings 21.6) and 'shed much innocent blood' (2 Kings 21.16), perhaps in response to Assyrian pressure to control unrest in Judah.

RADICAL SEPARATION FOR SURVIVAL

At the time of Josiah's reform in 622 BC, the words of Moses in Deuteronomy 7 about danger from the dominant culture must have seemed revolutionary. They would be a call for a return to radical Yahwism, with an end to Assyrian and baalistic practices, including religious and political independence from Assyria.

The need *to survive as God's people* in the Promised Land helps us to understand the stern policy of no contact between the Israelites and the dominant culture of Canaan or Judah: no treaty or covenant, no mercy or pity (Deut. 7.2,16), no intermarriage (7.3), and the complete elimination of any idols or other cult objects (7.5,25). The people must choose between loving God which leads to blessing, or rejecting God which leads to destruction (7.9–10). On a first reading of the text it appears that the preferred way of choosing Yahweh is to eliminate the Canaanites, or, in the time of the Narrator, to declare independence from Assyria!

## IS RADICAL SEPARATION POSSIBLE?

Modern readers will find these instructions to 'utterly destroy' people with opposing views difficult to understand and impossible to accept. We know of tensions between religious groups such as Muslims and Hindus in India, Muslims and Christians in former Yugoslavia, Jews and Arabs in Palestine, Protestants and Catholics in Northern Ireland. There are also racial tensions between blacks and whites in South Africa and North America; ethnic tensions between dominant and minority groups; tensions between castes in India and between different nations, tribes and clans and classes in many parts of Africa and other regions of the world. There is no possibility of eliminating one or the other side. They must live together. Intermarriage cannot be ruled out. Must we, then, totally reject these instructions of Moses?

## CO-EXISTENCE?

A careful study of the text will help us look behind the words of violence and see a picture, not of immediate destruction, but rather of a period of living together. The words in 7.22 suggest a long period in which the Israelites as newcomers will have to live side by side in *co-existence* with the dominant culture (the seven nations). During that period Israelites and Canaanites must co-operate in order to preserve the land and protect both peoples from common problems of disease and dangerous wild animals. A new nation would take time to become a reality in the land ('little by little'). This verse describes a period of shared use of the land, looking forward to the future complete rule of Yahweh. We see this kind of picture in Judges 1.21,28–33.

If we put this matter in the context of God's plan for the nations He has created, we may see a hint of a period in which the attraction of Israelite wisdom and understanding (Deut. 4.6) and the benefits of God's blessing on them will grow stronger until the nations will want to become a part of God's people. Their national identities ('names') such as 'Canaanite' will be only a memory of the past (7.24).

As we know from the history of Israel, the Israelites did not either destroy or drive out the Canaanites and other peoples (see Judges 3.5). As early as the time of Samuel, 'there was peace . . . between Israel and the Amorites' (1 Sam. 7.14). During the reigns of David and Solomon the former Canaanites became a part of Israelite society. By the time of the Narrator there were no 'Canaanites', only Israelites or Judahites.

The Narrator did not write Deuteronomy 7.1–5 to provoke a civil war between 'Israelite' and 'Canaanite', but to urge a radical reform which would cleanse the land from all 'abominable practices' which were due to Canaanite or Assyrian *cultural influence*. These included ritual child sacrifice (12.31; see 2 Kings 21.6), consulting mediums (Deut. 18.10–14; see 2 Kings 21.6), dishonest business practices (Deut. 25.13–16; see Amos 8.5), and, in general, violation of the Ten Commandments (Jer. 7.9–10). Radical reform would create an alternative to the dominant culture.

Many Christians live in this situation today, waiting for the establishment of God's reign, but, in the meantime, trying to remain faithful to God, and co-operating with their neighbours to deal with common dangers and working for the welfare of the land. Jeremiah advised the Israelite exiles in Babylon to 'seek the welfare of the city where I have sent you into exile' (Jer. 29.7).

Studying the text in this way will help Christians to deal with the difficult theological problem posed by the Narrator's statement that the victories of Israel will be *according to the will and purpose of the Creator God*, who will Himself eventually remove the nations of Canaan from power (Deut.7.1,22) and give them into the control of His people (7.2,24). The danger of reading Deuteronomy 7 without proper care is that it could be used as an excuse for a 'crusade' or 'holy war' against an enemy who is considered to be an absolute evil.

We can say that God's people are to be the beginning of His long-range plan of 'salvation in the midst of the earth' (Ps. 74.12) for all nations. For this plan a transformed society is necessary, whether in Canaan of Moses's day, Judah of Josiah's day, or in our own time.

In New Testament terms, Canaanite ways were part of the 'old' which must 'pass away'. This is what Paul was saying when he wrote to the Christians in Rome, 'be transformed by the renewal of your mind' (Rom. 12.2) The transformed society of God's people is the 'new' which is coming into existence (2 Cor. 5.17).

## ISRAEL, GOD'S ALTERNATIVE SOCIETY, 7.6–24

In order to be 'transformed' rather than 'conformed', the people of Israel must remember five things about their relationship to God.

### 1. THE COVENANT WITH THE ANCESTORS

In bringing His people into the land, God was *keeping the Covenant* He had made with their ancestors (Deut. 7.8,12; see pp. 28–29 and Special Note D). This was the beginning of His long-range plan for the blessing of the nations.

### 2. 'A PEOPLE FOR HIS OWN POSSESSION'

The Creator of heaven and earth (4.39) chose His people 'to be *a people for His own possession*' (Deut. 7.6; 14.2; 26.18; see Exod. 19.5). They were to be His alternative society, the nucleus of His new creation in the midst of the dominant culture.

Many people criticize Jews and Christians for thinking of themselves as 'chosen' by God, and therefore 'better' than others. Here in Deuteronomy we see that God's way of working in the world is by choosing some people as His partners for the benefit of all. For example, God chose the patriarchs to begin His long-range plan for the good of all nations (Deut. 4.37; Gen. 12.3). Within Israel God chose the priestly tribe of Levi 'out of all your tribes' to keep the contact open between God and people, to mediate His blessing to the people and to help settle disputes (Deut. 18.5; 21.5). In the same way God chose one people 'out of all the peoples that are on the face of the earth' (7.6), in order to show all peoples His way of life (4.6).

However, God chose the smallest and weakest 'out of all the peoples' (7.6; 10.15) as His partner. This seems to be characteristic of God's way. Gideon was from the weakest clan of his tribe and he was 'least' in his own family (Judges 6.15). The Messiah will come from one of the 'little' clans of Judah (Mic. 5.2). The servant of the LORD is 'despised and rejected' (Isa. 53.3). God chooses what is 'weak', 'low and despised' (1 Cor. 1.27–28).

### 3. GOD'S YEARNING LOVE

God had '*set His love*' on His people (7.7; 10.15; NRSV 'set His heart on you'). This beautiful expression gives us a glimpse into God's heart. The Hebrew verb suggests a need, an incompleteness in God's heart. One writer has described this as Yahweh's 'yearning love' for His people. A modern poet has suggested that God created humans because He was 'lonely'. However, when God saw how wicked they were, He was 'sorry that He had made humankind on the earth, and it grieved Him to His heart' (Gen. 6.6 NRSV). God was 'lonely' again! So the Creator of humankind and Lord of 'heaven . . ., the earth with all that is in it' (Deut. 4.32; 10.14) came down to 'take a nation for himself from the midst of another nation', and spoke to them out of the fire so that they might love Him and become partners in His new creation (4.34,36; 6.5).

## 4. A HOLY PEOPLE

The people were *'holy to the LORD* your God' (7.6) . The word 'holy' means first a *holy separation* from the false gods and corrupt practices of the dominant culture (7.25–26; see Lev. 20.26). Here we think of the actions prohibited in the Ten Commandments (Deut. 5.7–21).

Second, holiness also means energetic *holy action* serving the holy God as partners in His new creation, by loving Him with all the heart and soul (6.5). We will see this theme developed in later chapters (14.2,21; 26.19; see 28.9).

## 5. GOD IN OUR MIDST

The LORD of heaven and earth who made covenant with the ancestors and chose the people of Israel was always *present with them*, 'in the midst of you' (7.21). God's presence in their midst meant four things:

(a) It was *the basis for courage* in their struggle against evil. With the God of the Exodus in their midst, there was no need to fear superior forces (Deut. 7.17–21).

(b) It meant *a promise of blessing* to those who keep His commandments. God would show them steadfast love, bless and make them prosperous in the land (7.13–14).

(c) It also meant *a potential danger*. If they conform to the corrupt practices of the dominant culture, God would punish them (7.4,10; see 6.15; 23.14; 32.51). As Amos pointed out, God holds His chosen people to strict account for their actions:

> You only have I known [chosen]
> of all the families of the earth;
> therefore I will punish you
> for all your iniquities. (Amos 3.2)

(d) It was *a call to witness*. The call to witness is hidden behind the words 'all the peoples' of the earth (7.6,14). The Creator and Liberator God chose Israel *from* these peoples, to be a witness *to* them (4.6). God's presence in their 'midst' became visible at the time of the Exodus liberation (Exod. 8.22). The phrase 'most blessed of peoples' (Deut. 7.14 NRSV) suggests that the nations will notice God's presence among the Israelites because of their prosperity. *Through the people of Israel then, God's presence will become visible 'in the midst of the earth' for all humankind to see*

(see Ps.74.12 and Isa. 40.5). Prophetic words tell of the time when God's presence will make His people 'a blessing in the midst of the earth' (Isa. 19.24). For Christians, Jesus Christ is the ultimate form of 'God in our midst' (see John 1.14; Matt. 18.20).

## NOTES

**7.2. You must utterly destroy them.** The Narrator underlined the extreme danger to God's people from the dominant culture by using the Hebrew term *hrm* (see Special Note C) at the beginning and end of ch. 7 with two different translations (Deut. 7.2,26). The Israelites must 'utterly destroy' (*haram*, 7.2) the seven nations mentioned in 7.1. The verb *haram* is a technical term meaning to remove all traces of the polluting influence, whether from a nation (7.2; 20.17) or from a city within Israel (13.15; see 17.2–6).

**7.26. You shall not bring an abominable thing into your house:** At the end of ch.7, Moses warns that if the Israelites covet and acquire any of the 'accursed' (*herem*) things, including the wealth (silver and gold, 7.25), of the dominant culture, they themselves will become 'accursed' (*herem*; 7.26) and liable to destruction.

## SPECIAL NOTE D: HEREM-DESTRUCTION

The Hebrew noun *herem* refers first to something which has been separated from ordinary use. A field declared 'devoted' (*herem*) to God (Lev. 27.21) could be used only by priests. No one else could touch it without suffering penalties. The same was true of first fruits of the soil (Num.18.13). It was 'taboo' to anyone else.

A second application was to objects which led the people away from faith in Yahweh. Such an object (usually an idol) would be 'devoted' (*herem*), that is, separated from ordinary use. In the words of Moses, 'none of the devoted things shall cleave to your hand' (Deut. 13.17). A *herem* thing was also called 'accursed' (7.26) because it was doomed to destruction. If any Israelite came into physical or social contact with a 'dedicated' or 'accursed' object, that person or group would also become 'accursed'. or doomed to destruction like it (7.26).

The verb derived from the noun *herem* means to remove something from ordinary use by destroying it. It is used in connection with the cities of Sihon and Og, as well as the peoples who lived in Canaan, who were 'accursed' by their contacts with idols. Those cities, including all inhabitants, would be 'utterly destroyed' (*herem*-ized), that is, doomed to destruction as *herem* objects (Deut. 2.34; 3.6; 7.2; 20.17). The same would happen to cities in Israel which turned away from Yahweh (13.15).

The reason for this cruel custom was the fear that 'they would turn away your sons from following me, to serve other gods', with the result that 'the anger of the Lord would be kindled against you, and he would destroy you quickly' (7.4). The fear was that those peoples would 'teach you to do according to all their abominable practices which they have done in the service of their gods, and so to sin against the Lord your God' (20.18). In other words, this custom was one way of making sure that the people would observe the first two commandments.

During the reigns of Hezekiah and his son Manasseh (see 2 Kings. 18.4 and 21.1–6), idolatry was a serious problem. The danger was that *herem* destruction would come on the entire nation because of the spiritual and social poison or pollution, resulting from the worship of idols. That is why both Hezekiah and Josiah carried out reforms. After the failure of Josiah's reform, in the days of King Jehoiakim, Jeremiah said that God would use Babylon to bring about a *herem* destruction of the land of Judah, 'because you have not obeyed my words' (Jer. 25.8–9).

## STUDY SUGGESTIONS

### REVIEW OF CONTENT

1. What evidence is there in Deuteronomy of God's love for the nations?

2. What were the dangers (a) in the time of Moses, and (b) in the time of the Narrator, which threatened the survival of God's people in the Promised Land?

3. (a) What is the meaning of the Hebrew word *hrm* or *herem* in 7.2 and 7.26?
   (b) What was the reason for the policy of no contact between the Israelites and the seven nations?
   (c) What evidence is there in 7.16 and 7.22 that the Israelites did not literally carry out the command of 7.2?

4. (a) In what way is Romans 12.2 related to Deuteronomy 7?
   (b) What *five* things will help the people of God to be 'transformed'?

5. What *four* things did God's presence mean for His people?

### BIBLE STUDY

6. Read Exod. 19.4–6, Deut. 7.6–8, and 1 Peter 2.9. What words appear in all three passages? What words are different? Does each passage say the same thing?

7. (a) What are the two meanings of the word 'holy' in 7.6?
   (b) What sorts of 'holy action' are described in Lev. 19.9–18?

8. What words or phrases in the following passages show God's need of partners in His new creation?
   (a) Jer. 2.2  (b) Ezek. 16.6  (c) Hos. 9.10
9. Which of the following verses tell us about (i) courage, (ii) blessing, (iii) warning, and (iv) a call to witness, that come to us because Jesus Christ is 'in our midst'?
   (a) John 3.19  (b) 10.10  (c) Matt. 5.3–10  (d) 7.26–27
   (e) Mark 10.29–30

CONTEXTUAL APPLICATION

10. Briefly describe the dominant culture in which you live, under the following headings: (a) religions, (b) politics, (c) customs, (d) education, (e) modernization, (f) justice. What are the main temptations in that culture which may lead God's people to forget, or even reject Him?
11. Deut. 7.1–5, 25–26 seems to contradict the command to 'love your enemies' in Matt. 5.44, and to feed an enemy in need in Prov. 25.21 and Rom. 12.20. Which of the following do you think is the way Christians should interpret this contradiction? Or is there an even better way?
   (a) We should relate it to Ecclesiastes 3.3, that there is 'a time to kill and a time to heal'.
   (b) We should reject Deut. 7.1–5 because it belongs to an old way of thinking which is no longer acceptable.
   (c) Deut. 7.1–5,25–26 refers to beliefs and practices rather than people. We can 'love' our enemies without believing what they believe or doing what they do.

# 8.1–20
# Love for God Applied to Economic Life

## OUTLINE

8.1–6, 15–16: Lessons from a Time of Want.
8.7–14, 17–20: Lessons for a Time of Plenty.

## INTERPRETATION

The great commandment to love God with heart, soul, and strength must be applied in particular situations. This chapter lays the foundation for applying love for God to economic life. God's will for His people and for all peoples is that there should be no lack of material things that support life for all in the land (8.7–9). Everyone should be able to 'eat and be full' (8.10).

The temptation for God's people, and for people today in all parts of the world, is to love technology and its material benefits instead of loving God as our highest good. The result is injustice, poverty and hunger, and destruction of the good land and the natural world.

This chapter begins with lessons on economic life which were learned at a time when there was no wealth, and continues with an urgent appeal to people living in a time of prosperity.

## LESSONS FROM A TIME OF WANT

The way for people who live in a time of plenty to avoid worshipping false gods of technology and wealth is to 'remember all the way which the Lord your God has led you these forty years in the wilderness' (8.2).

The Israelites' experience in that 'great and terrible wilderness', with dangers from snakes and scorpions, hunger and thirst (8.15), was like a journey through the 'valley of the shadow of death' (Ps. 23.4) in order to learn lessons for life. Moses helped them understand the meaning of that experience. They learned that God Himself had caused them to go through the wilderness. He had brought them low, or 'humbled' them, by hunger and thirst. When they were ready to die, God gave them manna from heaven and water from the rock, which they could not produce by themselves (8.2,3,15,16). God subjected them to 'discipline' (8.5) to train them for their mission as 'God's alternative society' in the Promised Land (see pp. 63–66). Moses tells them that God had three reasons for leading them through this experience of want.

1. *God was testing the Israelites* 'to know what was in your heart, whether you would keep His commandments or not' (8.2). God's tests show His intense interest in how people respond to His divine initiative (see Ps. 14.2; 33.13–15). God would test them again and again after their arrival in the Promised Land, whether by false prophets (Deut. 13.3), enemies (Judges 2.22; 3.4) or foreign envoys (2 Chron. 32.3).

God knows the hearts of all humans (see 1 Kings 8.39), and He knew the purposes forming in the minds of His people before they entered the land (Deut. 31.21). Yet He *did not know in advance* how they would react in situations of stress. When God created humans He took the risk of giving them freedom (4.34; see p. 25).

2. *God was revealing a different sort of knowledge* which neither the Israelites nor their ancestors had known before (8.3). This was not technical information about feeding cattle, shearing sheep, or

The Israelites' experience in the wilderness, as refugees from 'the house of bondage' in Egypt, resembled the experience of many present-day refugees in time of war or oppression, like these Bangladeshis returning to their homes after border clashes with India. But the Israelites' experience was also a time of testing and training for their future task as God's 'alternative society'.

planting wheat. It was theological knowledge learned by experience, that they 'might know' what their ancestors had not known: 'that man' (Hebrew: *Adam*, that is, human beings, see note on 8.3) 'does not live by bread alone but by everything that proceeds out of the mouth of the LORD'. *God's gift of His words came before His gift of the land* (8.7–10).

The experience of complete dependence on God's grace would teach His people the truth that humans are not self-sufficient, but are dependent on the Creator for life. This is the higher 'wisdom and understanding' which came to Israel in the wilderness, and which would be part of their witness to the nations (4.6).

3. *God desired His people's welfare.* The experience of hardship was to 'do you good in the end' (8.16). Liberation from slavery was only the *first stage* in the process of their salvation. Formation as a people through the Covenant at Sinai/Horeb was the *second stage* of the process. The 'evil generation' (1.35) who had perished in the wilderness (2.14) were evidence of the fact that this second stage was not enough (see p. 15). The time of hunger and humbling was necessary as the *third stage* of the preparation for finding life in the Promised Land (8.1).

The discipline of the wilderness period was for the people's own good. It made them recognize their own limitations so that they would be more ready to follow God's teaching. People who had been humbled or brought low in the wilderness (8.2–3) would understand the suffering of those humbled or brought low by misfortune or injustice (15.7–11; 'poor' and 'humble' are translations of the same Hebrew word). The later generations who remembered the wilderness experience would understand the words of God spoken by Isaiah to the rulers of Judah:

> It is you who have devoured the vineyard,
>    the spoil of the poor is in your houses.
> What do you mean by crushing my people,
>    by grinding the face of the poor? (Isa. 3.14b-15)

Poor people mourn when rich people scheme to 'seize the poor' to make a profit out of them (Ps. 10.9). They understand Amos's words about 'a famine in the land, not a famine of bread nor a thirst for water, but of hearing the words of the Lord' (Amos 8.11).

## LESSONS FOR A TIME OF PLENTY, 8.1–6, 15–16

'Beware lest you say in your heart "My power and the might of my hand have gotten me this wealth". You shall remember the Lord your God, for it is He who gives you power to get wealth' (Deut. 8.17–18; see note on 8.18 below). Power shared with and given by

God must be used responsibly by all who wish to find life in their 'promised land'.

## LESSONS ABOUT WEALTH

The production of 'wealth' is a co-operative enterprise between three partners: God, the land and humankind. (1) *God* shares productive power with humans. The land is under God's constant protective care (Deut. 11.12). (2) *The fertile land* with its abundant water supply (8.7; 11.11) puts forth 'vegetation, plants yielding seed, and fruit trees bearing fruit' (Gen. 1.11). (3) *Humans* apply their God-given productive skills to till the soil, tend the flocks and herds, gather the honey, mine the iron and copper to make utensils, tools, and weapons, build houses and cities, and use money to exchange goods and services (Deut. 8.8,12,13; 6.10; 7.13). With this three-way partnership between God, nature or natural resources, and humans with their God-given technological and management skills, there will be wealth for all. *There will be no poor in the land* (15.4) *if humans act according to the wisdom and understanding learned in the wilderness.*

The problem comes when humans as individuals or societies forget God and nature as partners in production of wealth. When they forget these partners, individuals do only what is right in their own eyes (12.8), instead of 'what is good and right in the sight of the LORD your God' (12.28). They think that their science, technology and management skills ('the might of my hand', 8.17) have produced their wealth. They are tempted to use their skills to oppress other people rather than to liberate them. They pollute the land, water and air in order to make money for themselves, without a thought for future generations. They forget God (Deut. 8.14). In the words of Amos, they 'are not grieved over the ruin of Joseph' (Amos 6.6). A stern warning follows: 'Like the nations that the Lord makes to perish before you, so you shall perish, because you would not obey the voice of the Lord your God' (8.20).

## LESSONS ABOUT PRIDE

We find many examples in the Bible of this sort of pride, not only in God's people but among powerful world rulers. The King of Assyria boasted, 'By the strength of my hand I have . . . removed the boundaries of peoples . . . plundered their treasures . . . found . . . the wealth of the peoples . . . gathered all the earth . . .' (Isa. 10.13–14). The King of Babylon 'made the world like a desert', in order to live in luxury in the hanging gardens of Babylon, and worshipped his military machine which brought him luxuries like a net full of fish (Isa. 14.17; Hab. 1.16). Ezekiel taunted the King of Tyre: 'You have said 'I am a God' . . . you consider yourself as wise as a god . . . by your wisdom and your understanding you have gotten wealth for yourself . . . gathered gold and silver . . . increased your wealth, and your heart has become proud in your wealth' (Ezek. 28.2–5). In many countries today the political leaders as well as the heads of business organizations are more interested in gaining fame and wealth for themselves, than in ruling wisely or improving the people's standard of living. Without wisdom and understanding gained in the 'wilderness', human skills in science, technology and management as well as material wealth will become idols.

## LESSONS ABOUT POWER

In this modern age too ('this day', Deut. 8.1,11,18,19), science, technology and management skills have enhanced human knowledge and power in ways that affect every aspect of our lives in all parts of our world. Humans are able to walk in space and split atoms, to manage genes that control physical and mental characteristics of plants, animals and humans, to manipulate and destroy life on a grand scale, to cause changes in our natural environment including the soil, forests, rivers, oceans, and even the atmosphere that protects us from the harmful radiation from outer space.

This enormous power, however, is not available to everyone. People who have this knowledge and power can use it to dominate others, to make money by exploiting natural resources like rain forests or minerals for quick profit, even though it leaves many homeless, hungry and sick. On the other hand those with this sort of knowledge and power can instead share it with ordinary people so that they will not destroy the environment by their ignorance or carelessness.

## THE NEED FOR WISDOM AND UNDERSTANDING

Laws must be made on the basis of the wisdom and understanding gained from a time of want, or from 'the wilderness experience', to protect the weak and helpless people from this sort of domination, and to equip them with knowledge and power of their own. Vast industrial empires carry on trade in the entire world. Some use their technological and management skills to cause devastating and life-threatening pollution of land, water and air. Their directors and stock-holders must come to understand that management skills, human labour, and the earth's natural resources are gifts from God. Those who use them are stewards accountable to the Creator of all. There are many who are powerless in our day, as in the time of Moses and the Narrator of Deuteronomy. Governments must accept the idea that the economic system should work for the benefit of all.

## NOTES

**8.3. Man:** The use of the Hebrew term 'Adam' twice in 8.3 (translated in RSV 'man', in NRSV as 'one') indicates that the lessons which the Israelites learned during the wilderness period were intended by God as a message of life for all humans: 'that He might make *you* know that *man* [Adam] does not live by bread alone, but that *man* [Adam] lives by everything that proceeds from the mouth of the LORD'. The words 'that *you* may live' (8.1) are expanded in 8.3 to mean 'that *all humans* [Adam] may live'.

**8.18. Power:** The Hebrew word translated 'power' occurs only four times in Deuteronomy. Twice it refers to the power of Yahweh in liberating His people from slavery (4.37; 9.29), and twice to Yahweh's power shared with humans to enable them to produce 'wealth' (8.17,18). The Hebrew word means the ability to accomplish something, whether liberation from slavery or freedom from want. The implication is that God's people should use the gift of power in imitation of the divine giver, that is, for liberation of the powerless from hunger and anxiety.

**8.17,18. Get:** The Hebrew word means to make or produce, rather than to acquire. It describes God's creative activity as the one 'who made heaven and earth' (Ps. 121.2; see Gen. 1.16,25,26). God's gift of the ability or power to produce wealth, means that humans are partners with God in the creative process.

**8.17,18. Wealth:** The Hebrew word here translated 'wealth' occurs three other times in Deuteronomy with different translations: (1) 'men of valour' (NRSV 'troops'), referring to well-armed soldiers (3.18), (2) 'army', referring to the military strength of Egypt (11.4), and (3) 'substance', meaning possessions or goods (33.11). From this it is clear that the Hebrew word in 8.17,18 implies strength or security, whether from possession of material goods or from strong armed forces. It means much more than a big bank account.

## STUDY SUGGESTIONS

### REVIEW OF CONTENT

1. What is God's will for all humans?
2. Where did God's people learn lessons for life?
3. What were God's three purposes in leading His people into the wilderness?
4. What are the three partners in the production of wealth?
5. What is the temptation that comes from the possession of skills in science, technology and management?
6. What should be the purpose of an economic system?

BIBLE STUDY

7. (a) Jesus quoted Deut. 8.3 in His struggle against temptation by Satan in the wilderness (Matt. 4.4). Does this mean that Jesus was against feeding the hungry?
   (b) Read Deut. 8.3,8–9 and John 6.27. Did Jesus mean that we should not work to produce food for ourselves and others? Give reasons for your answer.
8. Compare Deut. 8.10 with Matt. 14.20. In what way does the plenty at Jesus's feast reflect the plenty in the Promised land?
9. Read Luke 12.21 and Rev. 3.17–18. Use Deut. 8.3 and 18 to explain what it means to be 'rich toward God', or to 'buy gold refined by fire'.

CONTEXTUAL APPLICATION

10. In what ways could a study based on Deut. 8.3,18 help Christians in your country to resist the temptations of materialism?
11. In many countries today the rich are getting richer and the poor grow poorer. What if anything are the government, and other organizations, Churches, and individuals in your country doing in order to close the gap?
12. People have said that in South East Asia 'Child prostitutes are saving their families from hunger and destitution'. Some reasons suggested for this situation are:
    (a) The parents of the children are too greedy for money.
    (b) The rich tourists are too selfish.
    (c) The government encourages sex tours in order to gain income from abroad.
    (d) The economic system causes extreme poverty, and many poor families see prostitution as the only solution.
    (e) The public do not value children very highly.
    Which do you think is the most important, and what do you think should be done to change the situation?

# Special Note E
# The Shape of Deuteronomy

We have now come far enough in our study of Deuteronomy to get some idea of the general shape which the Narrator has given to the book. It tells us much about the history of the Israelites, and about the teaching which was to shape their development as a people. But it does not provide a simple chronological record of events, and much of the teaching is repeated again and again.

We may think of Deuteronomy as a long prose-poem to be recited before a congregation at festival times (see 31.10–11), like the recitals by traditional story-tellers who repeat tribal or clan ancestral history and myths. The epic tales of the *Ramayana* or *Mahabarata* contain teachings of Hinduism, recited or enacted in India and in puppet shows or dance dramas of South East Asia. Thai Buddhist monks recite the *Jataka* tales in the hearing of people gathered in the temples at the festivals of Visakabucha, Makabucha or Asalahabucha. Temple walls contain pictorial representations of various incidents from these tales as well.

As in those recitals, the poet-author of Deuteronomy (the Narrator) repeats themes like the people's frequent rebellion against God, blessing and curse, kindness to the poor, to make sure that the hearers or readers fully understand each point. In the final section of the prose-poem (chs. 31—34), the author brings each of the themes to a dramatic conclusion.

A second comparison: Deuteronomy is like drawings on a temple wall, or an illustrated Chinese hand scroll about 20 cm. wide and many metres long, depicting events in a story, a historical incident, or the life of a folk hero. Viewers may unroll one segment of the long scroll for study, then go on to the next segment, until reaching the final segment (chapters 31—34). In the first segment of the scroll Moses recalls events of history to the new generation of Israelites on the plains of Moab. We see vivid illustrations of defeat (1.26–33), victory (2.26—3.11), the fiery mountain (4.11), Moses interceding on the mountain for 40 days (9.25), a vision of the prosperous and the ruined land (ch. 28), and Moses gazing longingly at the Promised Land from Mount Nebo before his death.

We may also think of the Book of Deuteronomy as a musical symphony with several movements. Each movement introduces various themes which the composer develops in later parts. For example, one part would present in musical form the experience of the assembly at Mount Sinai/Horeb (ch. 4), followed by the giving of the Ten Commandments (ch. 5). In the final movement (chs. 31–

34), the composer brings the themes of the previous parts together in a great climax.

These comparisons help us to think of the Narrator as a skilful poet, or an artist or a composer of a beautiful piece of music. They also help us to see Deuteronomy as a unified work of art with many themes woven together to make a whole. In addition, the comparisons assume the presence of a community of people to be inspired by the music, learn from the recital of the poem, and gain understanding from the sequence of incidents in the hand scroll.

Of course the *content* of Deuteronomy is different in many ways from the literary or artistic works of other religions.

# 9.1—11.32
# Characteristics of Covenant Life

*Note*: In this final section of Part 2 of this Guide, and in the first seven sections of Part 3, we study several chapters of Deuteronomy together: Deut. chs. 9—11 (1 section), 12—16 (2 sections), 16.18—21.9 (3 sections) and 21.10—25.19 (2 sections). Instead of working through in the order of the Bible text, in each of these sections we consider particular *subjects* which appear in different parts of each group of chapters. You should, however, read right through the chapters in each group before starting on detailed study of them. Please also re-read Special Note E which explains how the Narrator has arranged Deuteronomy, with frequent repetition of themes.

## OUTLINE

9.1–8, 22–24: Rebellion.
9.9–21, 25–29; 10.1–5, 10–11: Intercession.
10.12—11.32: Interaction.

## INTERPRETATION

### THREE CHARACTERISTICS:
### REBELLION, INTERCESSION, INTERACTION

In this concluding section of Moses's presentation of the Primary Covenant made on Mount Sinai/Horeb, the Narrator focuses once again on the risk of the Covenant relationship to both God and people (see pp. 28–29). The basic problem of the Covenant relationship is the nature of the human heart: its wilful tendency to reject God's gracious guidelines for life. This problem is the reason for the frequent warnings in Deuteronomy about the terrible consequences of turning aside from the God of life to serve the gods of death. The people's very existence, as well as the purpose of God in choosing them, are at risk.

In a wider perspective this is also a general human problem. Moses's words to the Israelites at the border of the Promised Land that 'you have been rebellious against the Lord from the day that I knew you' (9.24; see 9.7), remind us of God's sad evaluation of humanity before and after the flood. God saw that 'the wickedness of man was very great in the earth, and that every imagination of the thoughts of his heart was only evil continually' (Gen. 6.5; see Gen. 8.21). Rabbi W.Gunther Plaut shows us a link between the two passages: 'Throughout the Torah' (i.e. Genesis - Deuteronomy) '. . . God's people Israel represent humanity as a whole. . . . Israel's defiance of God is but an acting out of what the Torah judges to be the general character of man'. Indeed, this 'general character' of humanity is one of the reasons for the emergence of many of the religions of the world. According to a Thai saying, religion is like a bit in a horse's mouth. It helps to control the wild nature of humanity.

In these chapters of Deuteronomy we find that *rebellion* closes off the people's relationship with God, and that *intercession* reopens the relationship, allowing for *interaction* between God and humans. These are the three themes we study in this section. In this process, two sorts of knowledge are necessary: *knowledge of God* and *knowledge of human nature*, as we see in the two commands introduced by the words 'know therefore . . .' in Deut. 9.3 and 9.6.


## REBELLION

### SELF RIGHTEOUSNESS (9.1–5)

The negative command 'Do not say in your heart . . . "It is because of my righteousness . . .".' (9.4), warns against a false claim to the land on the basis of superior moral achievements. This showed the people's ignorance of God and of their own human nature. In the time of the Narrator, people in Judah were saying that they were 'innocent,' and had 'not sinned' (Jer. 2.35), in other words, that they were righteous. They thought of themselves as righteous children of the righteous Abraham (Gen. 15.6), heirs of God's promise to Abraham and his descendants to give them the land of Canaan (Gen. 15.18). They felt secure because, in the words of Scripture, 'the righteous shall possess the land, and dwell upon it forever' (Ps. 37.29).

They did not understand that 'righteousness' is not merit earned by obedience to the Covenant commands, which would entitle them to win victory over their enemies and get possession of the Promised Land. It is not a claim on God as though God owes His people something. Righteousness is rather 'God's gift of love to a Covenant partner who loves Him without limit' (see p. 64). The land is not a reward for obedience, but a place for obeying God's Covenant teaching, and participating in God's righteousness for the well-being of all nations (see Deut. 4.6).

The 'wickedness' of the nations (9.4–5) refers to their 'abominable practices' arising from their worship of 'other gods'. However, the Israelites were also guilty of wickedness (9.27). As a psalmist had said (Ps. 14.3; see Rom. 3.10–12) this is part of human nature. Paul expressed this same idea: 'Are we' (Jews) 'any better off?' (i.e. than others who are not Jews) 'No, not at all; for we have already charged that all, both Jews and Greeks, are under the power of sin' (Rom. 3.9 NRSV).

## GOD'S ALTERNATIVE SOCIETY

If wickedness is universal, what is the meaning of the words 'it is because of the wickedness of these nations that the Lord is 'driving them out' (of power) 'before you' (Deut. 9.4,5)? Again we find a clue from Paul: 'Jews are entrusted with the oracles of God' (Rom. 3.2). God's rebellious people are chosen partners in His long-range plan for all nations which began with His call to Abraham (see Deut. 9.5), and continued with the call to form an 'alternative society' among the nations.

## SELF KNOWLEDGE, (9.6–24)

The imperative 'know therefore ..'. (9.6) is a call to true self-knowledge which comes to God's people by remembering their own stubborn rebelliousness against Him from the time of the Exodus until the arrival at the plains of Moab (9. 6,7,24). Certainly the Narrator extended the story of rebellion to the latter days of Judah and Jerusalem, when, in the words of Jeremiah, the people had 'a stubborn and rebellious heart' (Jer. 5.23; see Jer. 7.24). Psalmists reflected on the stubborn heart of Israel throughout its history (Ps. 78.17,37,40, 56–58). Ezra included references to it in his great confession (Neh. 9.6–37, esp. vv. 16,17,33–34)

## FIVE PAINFUL MEMORIES

Moses recalls five painful examples of past rebellion with disastrous consequences, which the people must never forget. The most important was the making of a calf-image at *Mount Sinai/Horeb* during Moses's absence on the mountain (Deut. 9.8–21; see Exod.

Because of their stubborn rebelliousness God's people are always in danger of destruction. Today many people would question whether God actually *causes* such plagues and disasters as epidemic diseases or volcanic eruptions, or the earthquake in Iran which destroyed the homes of these townspeople searching the rubble while a soldier guards against looting—though there was nothing left to loot.

32.1–35; Ps. 106.19–20). This would have reminded people in the Narrator's time of the molten image, probably of a calf, in the sanctuary at Dan while Moses's grandson and his descendants were priests (Judg. 18.30), and of the two golden calf images set up by Jeroboam in Bethel and Dan (1 Kings 12.28–29; see Hos. 8.5; 10.5; 13.2).

Ironically, this rebellion at Mount Sinai/Horeb occurred immediately after the solemn Covenant ceremony (Exod. 24.3–8), during which the people had bound themselves by oath, that 'all that the Lord has spoken, we will do' (Exod. 24.7, see v.3). The Covenant was sealed by the 'blood of the covenant' (Exod. 24.8, see v.6). Apparently the stubborn human heart was stronger than either oath or shed blood.

Three examples come from the wilderness journey. At *Taberah* the people complained because of the hardships of freedom, and felt the heat of God's anger (Deut. 9.22; see Num. 11.1–3; and Ps. 106.18). At *Massah* they doubted whether God was really in their midst, and put Him to the test (Deut. 9.22; see 6.16; Exod. 17.1–7). At *Kibroth-hattaavah* their greed brought on a terrible plague (Deut. 9.22; see Num. 11.31–34; Ps. 106.14–15).

The final example of their constant rebelliousness happened at what should have been the end of the wilderness journey, at *Kadesh-barnea* (Deut. 9.23; see 1.26,43; see pp. 15–16). Their rebellious disobedience prevented that entire generation from entering the Promised Land (1.35) and delayed entry for 38 years.

Paul said of these wilderness rebellions 'these things happened to them as a warning, but they were written down for our own instruction . . .' (1 Cor. 10.11). Because of their constant stubborn rebelliousness, God's people are always on the border between life and death, even in the Promised Land. They are always in danger of destruction (Deut. 9.14) by God who is 'not partial' (10.17). For this reason intercession is of critical importance.

INTERCESSION, 9.9–21. 25–29; 10.1–5, 10–11

### THE MODEL INTERCESSOR

Moses is the model intercessor in the Old Testament. His intercession on Mount Sinai/Horeb as reported in Deut. chs 9—10 is a pattern for all subsequent intercessions.

In each of the four incidents mentioned only by name (9.22–23), Moses's intercession caused a change in God's plans. At *Taberah* 'Moses prayed to the LORD and the fire abated' (Num. 11.2). At *Massah* 'The LORD said to Moses, "gather for me 70 men . . . and I will come down and talk with you there" ' (Num. 11.16–17). At *Kibroth Hattaavah* 'The LORD said to Moses "Pass on before the people, taking with you some of the elders of Israel . . . and go. Behold I will stand before you there on the Rock at Horeb" ' (Exod. 17.5–6). At *Kadesh-barnea* Moses prayed 'Pardon the iniquity of this people . . .' God replied 'I have pardoned, according to your word' (Num. 14.19–20).

Moses tells of two ascents to God's presence on the mountain. In the first (Deut. 9.9–13; see Exod. 24.18) he fasted for forty days and forty nights to prepare himself to receive the Covenant teaching. Then something else happened. God asked Moses to share His sorrow and anger over the corrupt (or self-destructive, see below, note on 9.2) action of the people in violating the second commandment (9.12). We can sense the depth of God's grief by the use of the expression 'blot out' (9.14), which recalls the story of the flood (Gen. 6.6–7; 7.4,23).

## GOD NEEDS INTERCESSORS (9.14)

Then comes God's strange request, 'Let me alone and I will destroy them . . .'. (Deut. 9.14 NJPS; see note on this verse). God was asking Moses to be a part of His own decision-making process. The possibility of preventing the self-destruction of the 'stubborn people' (9.13) was entrusted to the great intercessor! God in His grief was leaving the door of Israel's future open. It was with this immensely important responsibility that Moses 'turned and came down the mountain . . .' (9.15).

## PREPARATION FOR INTERCESSION

The Narrator focuses on Moses's second ascent of the mountain, as we can see from the fact that Moses mentions it three times (9.18,25;10.10), interspersed with other narrative material (9.21–24; 10.5–9). Once again it was a time of fasting for Moses ('as before,' 9.18; see 10.10), to clarify his thoughts and cleanse his will of all self-seeking (see 3.23–29). This time, however, Moses 'lay prostrate' (9.18,25) in a position of extreme humility as though to identify with his stubborn people. He saw clearly the dangerous position into which the people had brought themselves, and was 'afraid' for them (9.19).

## THE BOLD ARGUMENTS OF THE INTERCESSOR (9.26–29)

Moses's bold arguments for a reconsideration of the decision to 'blot out' (9.14) 'this people' (9.13) show his own understanding of the importance of God's people to God. His arguments are based on this understanding:

1. *Will God abandon His heritage among the nations?* (9.26). First and last, Moses places Israel's rebellion in the context of God's greater purposes of 'working salvation in the midst of the

earth' (Ps. 74.12). He reminds God (and himself) that Israel is not simply Moses's people ('your people,' Deut. 9.12), nor 'this (stubborn) people' (9.13), but God's people '*thy* people and *thy* heritage' (9.29). The term 'heritage' refers to the special on-going relationship between God and Israel (see 7.6; 10.15; 32.8–9; see p. 59). God might 'abhor' His heritage (Ps. 106.40), yet He could not 'abandon' it (Ps. 94.14) without giving up His plan for the nations (Deut. 4.6). The success of God's own purpose was at risk!

2. *Will God forget His purpose in calling the patriarchs?* The same wider context is implied by Moses's request that God 'remember' the patriarchs (9.27). God's first act of remembrance is to 'remember' all humans (Ps. 8.4, NEB), as defined in Genesis in 'their families, their languages, their lands and their nations' (Gen. 10.20,31). Moses was reminding God (and himself) not only of the divine promise of the land, but of God's long-range plan to bring blessing to many generations of the nations through the descendants of Abraham (Gen. 12.3).

3. *How will the nations know God?* Moses recalls to God what the Egyptians might say if the Israelites did not reach the Promised Land: that the Lord was 'not able to bring them into the land which He promised them', and that He really 'hated them' (9.28). Curiously enough, Moses's fears about the reaction of the Egyptians echo the rebellious doubts of the Israelites themselves at Kadesh-barnea (1.27)! Putting these two texts side by side suggests (a) that God's reputation or Name among the nations is at stake in the way He deals with the sin of His people, and (b) that the nations will never come to know the one true God unless His people trust Him and show their trust by obedience.

4. *Acknowledging sin, appealing to love.* At the heart of Moses's argument are the words 'Do not regard the stubbornness of this people, or their wickedness, or their sin' (9.27). The intercessor was frank to acknowledge before God (and to himself) the reality of sinfulness. At the same time he was affirming his faith in God's mercy and Covenant love (4.31) which is strong enough to turn divine attention away from the sins of this generation and to consider instead the wider context of His long-range plan which began with the patriarchs. Moses was asking God to 'blot out' the sin instead of the sinner (see Ps. 51.1)!

## THE INTERCESSORS AS GOD'S PARTNERS

When Moses 'stayed on the mountain', he was standing by God in His grief. The Narrator has purposely used the same Hebrew word as in Deut. 5.31 where God says to Moses 'stand here by me'. Intercessory prayer involves the intercessor. It implies an offer to co-operate with God. By interceding for his people, Moses was giving God his personal guarantee to teach the people to remember their identity (see 4.14), and return to God (4.30), in short, to choose blessing instead of disaster (11.26). He was pledging himself to be a partner with God in accomplishing this goal.

## EFFECTIVE INTERCESSION: NEW POSSIBILITIES

The effect of Moses's intercession was to open up new possibilities for the future. Moses reported that 'the LORD hearkened to me that time also,' (9.19). In the end 'the LORD was unwilling to destroy you' (9.19; 10.10). Because of Moses's intercession, God

(1) gave the people another copy of the tablets of the law (10.4);

(2) told Moses to make an ark as a portable reminder of the Covenant Teaching (10.2–3,5);

(3) appointed the Levitical priests to carry the ark and interpret Covenant Teaching (31.25–26), to help the people worship properly, and to keep the way open for the people to receive God's blessing (10.8–9);

(4) heard Moses's intercession for Aaron (9.20) and allowed him to die a natural death (10.6; see Num. 33.38); and

(5) commanded Moses to lead the forgiven people toward the Promised Land (10.11) with the Covenant Teaching and its interpreters at their head (see Num. 10.33; Josh. 3.3–4).

All of these opened up new possibilities for God's people. The two following examples show how this sort of intercession can provide new possibilities for Christians today.

At a workshop of women students from eight African nations, participants described fifteen problems faced by female students. For each problem they suggested possible solutions. Following Moses's model, anyone making an intercessory prayer for African female students would undertake to be a part of the solution to their problems.

A teacher living in a large city prayed for young people in a poor section of her country. The result was that she gave up her comfortable home and her job in the city, and went to live among those poor people. She established a school which brought blessings to many generations of those children and youth.

## INTERACTION

This section alternates between statements about the *knowledge of God* ('Know therefore . . .', Deut. 9.3) and the *knowledge of self* ('Know therefore . . .', 9.6), especially the obligations or ethical implications for God's people which follow from the knowledge of God (see p. 84). Interaction between these two sorts of knowledge creates both faith and faithfulness, and overcomes the stubborn self-will of the people.

KNOWING GOD

As *Lord of heaven and earth* (Deut. 10.14; see Ps. 24.1; Isa. 42.5), the God of Israel is not a tribal God, but the Creator who is concerned about 'all the peoples under the whole heaven' (Deut. 4.19; see pp. 26–28; 78), and about the harmonious relationship between humans and nature. The God who will subdue the peoples of Canaan under His people is also Creator of the nations (26.19). He will punish the nations (9.4–5), including His own people (11.16–17), for their wickedness which violates the standards of His design of creation.

*God is especially concerned about justice* for the weak and helpless. He is 'not partial' (10.17; contrast the false gods described in Ps. 82.2). Lavish gifts and bribes will not influence His judgement, nor bring favour to the givers (10.17; see p. 110 on bribes). God 'executes justice for the fatherless and the widow, and loves the sojourner, giving him food and clothing' (10.18).

*God is merciful.* He rescued His people from slavery, gave them the Covenant Teaching at Mount Sinai/Horeb, and taught them in the wilderness (11.1–7; see 8.5 and pp. 68–71)). God gave His people the beautiful fertile land which is always under His care (11.10–12; see 6.10–11; see p. 52), and will give rain, grass, grain, wine, oil and abundant food to a faithful people (11.14–15).

*God is Israel's 'praise'* (10.21). The Israelites are the people who praise God (Ps. 95.2), as a model for all the nations (Ps. 67.3,5; see 65.1). By their righteous life and God's resulting blessing, the Israelites will be 'a praise and a glory before all the nations of the earth, who shall hear of all the good' that God will do for His people (Jer. 33.9).

HOW SHALL WE RESPOND TO GOD?

Three things which God requires of His people deserve special mention here:

*Change your heart!* First is the command to 'circumcise therefore the foreskin of your heart', which is explained in the same sentence: 'be no longer stubborn' (Deut. 10.16; see note on 10.16). A modern version translates in this way: 'Cut away the thickening about your hearts' (NJPS). In other words, knowledge of God and of oneself should lead to repentance and openness to the possibility of a new beginning.

*Love your needy neighbour!* The second command is 'Love the sojourner, therefore, for you were sojourners in the land of Egypt' (10.19). Following on the statement about God in 10.18, this is a call to respond to God's love by loving our neighbour, whom God loves, and to practise justice because that is God's way.

*Bring integrity back to human relationships!* The third command is that 'by His name' (that is, not by the name of any other god) 'you shall swear' (10.20). Taking an oath was a religious act performed at shrines (Hos. 4.15; Amos 8.14; Zeph. 1.5). It was thus a confession of faith in God. Taking oaths by the names of other gods (Deut. 11.28) would lead to disaster. An oath taken in God's name was the mark of loyalty to God (see pp. 34–35 on the proper use of God's name). More important, it was an act of social responsibility used in making agreements or contracts. We may compare it to the custom practised in some 'Christian' countries of requiring witnesses in a law court to swear 'on the Bible' that the evidence they give will be true. It was a vital element in the health of a society, showing integrity, justice, and kindness in human relations.

All three of these commands came together in the words of Jeremiah when he told them that God's plan for the salvation of the nations will go forward when His people repent of their stubborn hearts, and change their society and their individual lives in the direction of 'truth, . . . justice, and . . . uprightness' (Jer. 4.2).

## THE CHOICE BEFORE US (11.26–32)

As the conclusion of his presentation of the Primary Covenant, Moses repeated the great commandment to love God with our whole selves (Deut. 10.12; 11.1,13; see 6.5), to fear Him, walk in His ways, serve and trust Him, and keep His commandments (10.12–13,20; see pp. 49–52). Observance of these commands in daily life, and teaching them to the younger generation (11.18–20; 6.6–9; see pp. 54–55) will make it possible for the people to continue living on the good land (11.8–9, 13, 21, 22).

There on the border between the wilderness (death) and the Promised Land (life), Moses set before his people a choice to be made 'this day' (11.2,26). Blessing and disaster would lie before them, not only on the border but each day in the Promised Land, where the people could see the hill reminding them of the blessing which follows from obedience (Mount Gerizim), and the other hill reminding them of disaster which follows disobedience (Mount Ebal; Deut. 11.29). This theme will appear again at the end of the presentation of the Moab Covenant (30.15–20). As Psalm 95.7–8 and 2 Corinthians 6.2 remind us, the day of decision confronts all those who read Deuteronomy in every generation.

## NOTES

**9.2. The Anakim:** See p. 15, note on 2.10,11,21. In Hebrew thought, the Anakim were descended from the Nephilim (Num. 13.33), who were legendary half-human, half-divine beings. The 'sons of the Anakim' with their three legendary hero-tyrants

Sheshai, Ahiman and Talmai (Num. 13.22; Josh. 15.14) were symbols of irresistible tyrannical power in pre-Israelite Canaan. They were located in or around Hebron until they moved to the sea coast (Josh. 11.22). They caused such terror among the Israelite scouts from Kadesh-barnea that the Israelites refused to attack (Num. 13.28,33). The result was a forty-year delay in their entry into the land (see p. 15). Joshua defeated them at Hebron (Josh. 11.21), and at a later time Caleb had to do it again (15.14; Judg. 1.20).

**9.3. Destroy . . . perish:** Each of these actions which apply in this verse to the powerful and well-armed nations in Canaan, also apply in other contexts to unfaithful Israelites. For the Hebrew word translated 'destroy' as applied to the Israelites see Deut. 4.26; 7.4; 9.8,14,19,20; 28.20. For 'perish' applied to the Israelites see 11.17 and 30.18.

A different Hebrew word also translated 'destroy' appears in 9.26 and 10.10. In 4.16,25; 9.12; 31.29 the same Hebrew word is translated 'act corruptly,' which means to act in such a way as to cause self-destruction.

**9.6. You are a stubborn people:** This call to self-knowledge is the basis of confession of sins found in Jewish and Christian worship services as, for example, in the Jewish service for the Day of Atonement: 'We are arrogant, brutal, careless, destructive, ego-centric, false, greedy, heartless, insolent, and joyless. Our sins are an alphabet of our woe'.

**9.14. Let me alone:** The only other occurrence in the Old Testament of this identical Hebrew expression is in the words of Jephthah's daughter when she asked for a period of time to prepare for her death: 'let me alone two months, that I may . . . bewail my virginity' (Judges 11.37). God's words to Moses must be understood in relation to Moses's role as intercessor. The translation '*that* I may destroy them . . .'. expresses purpose which is not self-evident in the Hebrew. Another translation is equally possible: '. . . *and* I will destroy them' (NJPS). It means that God will not act without hearing again from Moses.

**10.16. Circumcise . . . the foreskin of your heart:** Physical circumcision is a minor operation to remove some of the foreskin on the male sex organ, performed by some peoples to mark transition to adulthood. Except for the Philistines, all of Israel's neighbouring nations, including the Egyptians, practised circumcision. Many tribes in Africa still circumcise young males, and in some cases, females as well.

For the Hebrews, circumcision was the outward sign of an invisible truth: membership in the Covenant community with a special interactive relationship between God and people (see Gen.

17.10–13). When Jeremiah called Israel's neighbours 'circumcised but yet uncircumcised,' and said that 'all the house of Israel' was 'uncircumcised in heart' (Jer. 9.25–26), he meant that they no longer lived according to the inner meaning of circumcision. When Jeremiah pleaded with his people to 'circumcise yourselves to the Lord, remove the foreskins of your hearts' (Jer. 4.4), he explained the meaning of the expression in the previous verses: 'return to the LORD . . . remove your abominations . . . swear "As the LORD lives" in truth, in justice and in uprightness' (Jer. 4.1–2). When Jeremiah spoke of closed (literally uncircumcised) ears (6.10), he meant that there was no possibility of interaction with God because the people were no longer willing to listen (see Isa. 6.10).


# STUDY SUGGESTIONS

REVIEW OF CONTENT

1. What two sorts of knowledge are necessary if God's people are to maintain their relationship with Him?
2. For what reason is it wrong for Christians to boast that they are 'righteous'?
3. What were the *five* examples of the Israelites' past rebellion which had disastrous consequences?
4. In what way was Moses's second meeting with the Lord on the mountain different from the first meeting?
5. (a) In what ways are God's people different from 'the nations'?
   (b) What is the meaning of the word 'heritage' as applied to God's people?
6. What was God's long-range plan which began with the call of Abraham?
7. What were the effects of Moses's prayer?
8. What *four* things about God should the people remember?
9. What *three* obligations in addition to the obligation of love, result from the knowledge of God?

BIBLE STUDY

10. Which words in Exodus 32.8 and 1 Kings 12.28 are similar to some words in Deut. 9.12? Was the calf meant to be an image of another god, or an image of Israel's God?
11. Who are the intercessors in the following passages?
    (a) Ezra 9.6–15 (b) Neh. 9.32 (c) Job. 42.8 (d) Jer. 18.20 (e) Joel 2.17 (f) Amos 7.1–3,4–6 (g) Luke 22.31 (h) John 17.15,20–21 (i) Rom. 8.26–27

12. What can we learn from each of the following passages about why God forgives sin:
    (a) Isaiah 43.25   (b) Isaiah 48.9–11   (c) Psalm 51.1
    (d) 1 Kings 8.46–53   (e) Psalm 79.8–10   (f) Jer. 33.8–9
13. Is it possible for us to change ('circumcise') our hearts by ourselves? (see Deut.10.16 and 30.6). What did Paul say about circumcision (Gal. 2.7; 5.6; 6.15; Col. 2.11–13)?

CONTEXTUAL APPLICATION

14. Every religion must deal with the problem of evil in the human heart. Find out if you can, what some other religions teach about this problem.
15. Some people say that Christianity is too negative because it emphasizes people's sinfulness. What is your opinion, in the light of Deut. chs. 9–11, and of your answers to question 12 above?
16. God asked Moses to 'stand here by me' (Deut 5.31), and Moses stayed or stood by God while on the mountain (10.10).
    (a) Does this mean that God had not yet made up His mind about what to do? If not, what does it mean?
    (b) Does God expect us to pray for other people? In what ways, if any, can we help God by intercessory prayer?
    (c) If God is all-powerful, why does He need intercessors?
17. How would you respond to this statement: 'Intercession is asking God to do something about a problem. After I place the matter before God, I have done my part'?
18. Is fasting or other spiritual preparation (a) necessary, (b) important but not necessary, (c) unimportant, for effective intercessory prayer? Give reasons for your answer.

# PART 3: 12.1—16.22

# DIRECTIONS FOR LIFE:
# THE COVENANT IN MOAB

## INTRODUCTION

Deuteronomy 4.44—11.32 has been a review and interpretation of the Primary Covenant at Sinai/Horeb. Now in this third part of Deuteronomy, the Narrator shows Moses in Moab preparing the people for the renewal of the Primary Covenant.

In chs. 12—26 Moses gives the people an extended set of instructions on how to choose life: (a) by covenantal worship (12.1—16.22), (b) by covenantal justice in public life (16.18—21.9), and in family and social life (21.10—25.19). There follow (c) instructions for liturgical presentation of first fruits (26.1–11) and the payment of tithes in the third year for those dependent on the community (26.12–15), as a preparation for covenant renewal.

Then in chs. 27 and 28 comes (d) a review of the meaning of the Covenant; with (e) promises and warnings of what will follow obedience or disobedience to the Covenant stipulations (27.1—28.68); and in chs. 29 and 30.1–14 (f) the renewal of the Covenant (29.1–30.14).

Finally, (g) just as in 11.26–31 Moses was shown as closing his description of the Primary Covenant with an appeal to the people to choose life instead of death in the Promised Land, so in 30.15–20 he closes the presentation of the Covenant renewal in Moab with a similar appeal.

*Note*: Please re-read the Note on p. 76 and Special Note E. In this section and the six sections to follow we continue to study particular themes from each group of chapters, rather than working straight through each chapter in turn. First we select several themes from chs. 12—16 related to covenantal worship, which have already appeared in previous chapters.

In this third Part of Deuteronomy the Narrator shows Moses in Moab preparing the people for the renewal of the Primary Covenant, appealing to them to choose life instead of death.

Looking back across the Jordan at the deserts and mountains of Moab, a man riding his donkey up from the river seems dwarfed by the vast wilderness.

# 12.1—16.22
# Covenantal Worship (1)

## OUTLINE

Chs. 12—16 (selected verses): Holy Separation from Wrong Places, Customs and Practices of Worship.
Chs. 12—16 (selected verses): Holy Actions of Gathering and Offering.

## INTERPRETATION

The high point of Part 1 of Deuteronomy was the 'day of the assembly' at Mount Sinai/Horeb, when the people encountered the God of life (4.9–14). As we noted in studying that section: 'God's people live by making past experiences . . . become real again. . . . Each generation that followed must live through the same experience and pass it on to the next generation' (see pp. 54–55). Now, in the style of an artist or skilled craftsman, the Narrator shows Moses as emphasizing, for the new generation, the value of covenantal worship as a means of maintaining the holiness of the people and the health of society in the Promised Land. Moses calls once again for *holy separation* from the corruptions of the dominant Canaanite culture (see pp. 34–37, 47–49, 53–54 and 60–61). He also describes four *holy actions* of covenantal worship which will help to keep the original experience of encounter with the God of life fresh in the minds and hearts of the people.

### HOLY SEPARATION FROM WRONG PLACES, CUSTOMS AND PRACTICES OF WORSHIP

The basic fact which lies behind covenantal worship is the understanding that God set His people apart as 'children of the Lord your God . . . a people holy to the Lord your God' (14.1–2 NRSV; see 7.6).

### FORBIDDEN PLACES, CUSTOMS, FOOD

Chapter 12 begins with a theme already presented in ch.7: the importance of maintaining the people's identity as a means of survival in an environment full of temptations to forget their Covenant God (see p. 60). Their *first* step must be to *remove the sacred places* where the people of the Canaanite culture gathered to worship other gods. By this action the Israelites would also *remove the names* of these gods from their memories (12.2–3).

The *second* step must be to *avoid customs* (14.1, 21b) and particular sorts of *food* (14.3–19) associated with worship of those gods (see notes on 14.1 and 3).

## CORRUPTING INFLUENCES FROM WITHIN

*Thirdly* the people must constantly guard against any corrupting influences as though they were sources of infection or disease. Such influences might come from a false prophet in Israel, a member of one's own household, or even an entire city (13.1–18). The danger of such influences was that they would tempt Israelites to imitate the ways of the Canaanite culture by doing 'every abominable thing which the Lord hates', including child sacrifice (12.29–31).

The purpose of this holy separation was that 'all Israel shall hear, and fear, and never again do any such wickedness as this among you' (13.11).

## WHAT SORT OF SEPARATION?

Christians today find these commands troubling. In many countries today various religious groups vandalize or destroy places or objects sacred to each other's faith. Different groups who have lived together in peace for many years may become enemies and try to drive neighbours out of their territory so as to 'cleanse' it (see p. 61). In the conditions of modern life, killing a member of one's own family, no matter how 'wicked' (13.9–10), or completely destroying a city with its inhabitants, no matter how 'bad' (13.15–17), cannot be the right way to avoid 'the fierceness of' (God's) 'anger' (13.17), or to ensure obedience to His commands.

Jesus rebuked James and John when they asked permission to 'bid fire come down from heaven and consume' a Samaritan village, when its inhabitants would not allow Jesus to stay there overnight 'because his face was set toward Jerusalem' (Luke 9.53–54). Paul taught that we should 'not be overcome by evil, but overcome evil with good' (Rom. 12.21). These chapters of Deuteronomy tell us to eliminate wickedness from our lives, so as to preserve the holiness and health of our community. The way to do this is by covenantal worship which must replace wrong worship.

## HOLY ACTIONS: GATHERING AND OFFERING

The Narrator has already shown Moses as recalling the importance of the people's worship experience at Mount Sinai/Horeb (4.10; see p. 18). Throughout chapters 12—16 we find four holy actions that are involved in the human side of worship. The first two, *gathering* and *offering*, refer to the actual place, times, and practices of worship. The other two describe the people's inward attitudes of *rejoicing* and *remembrance*, which encourage compassion and justice in human relations.

## GATHERING ('GO . . .' 12.5)

*A place chosen by God.* As we have seen, God's carefully laid plan was to establish a new and holy 'alternative society' in the land of Canaan on behalf of all the peoples of the earth. For this plan to succeed there must be a special meeting-place where the people could gather for constant communication between Him and them. Just as Moses first gathered the people at the holy mountain for worship (4.10), so, in the Promised Land after his death, the people must gather in the place chosen by God as His habitation in their midst (12.5). Instead of the names of the many gods of Canaan (12.3), there would be the one name of Israel's God, Creator of heaven and earth (12.5; see 6.4).

When God's people gathered there for worship, they would (a) seek to restore their relationship with God through repentance and commitment, in hope of averting His anger and receiving His blessing. They would also (b) strengthen the *shalom* of the community, and (c) experience the power of the God who gives victory over the forces of evil (7.21–24), and is both 'jealous' and 'merciful' (4.24,31).

*An inclusive fellowship.* In God's presence all members of society were included. The people would gather as 'households' (12.7), including children and young people, as well as male and female slaves attached to the family (12.12). The disadvantaged members of society, 'the strangers, the orphans, and the widows resident in your towns' (16.14, NRSV) would join in worship. Levites resident in their towns but without land were also part of the worshipping community (12.12). We may assume that the poor would also be there (15.7). Covenantal worship would express the solidarity of the entire community.

*Times of worship.* The three annual pilgrimage festivals of the year were related to the agricultural seasons.

The *feast of Unleavened Bread* (16.3–4,8) came at the beginning of the barley harvest in March or April. This was combined with the *Passover* (16.1–2,4–7), commemorating the time when 'the Lord your God brought you out of Egypt by night' (16.1).

The *feast of Weeks* (16.9–12), seven weeks later in May or June, marked the completion of the wheat harvest.

The *feast of Booths* (16.13–15) in September or October brought the year to a climax with the 'ingathering from your threshing floor and your wine press.' Besides the annual feast of Booths, every seventh year was the 'Year of Release' (15.1,9; 31.10).

In addition to these annual community worship occasions, there would be regular weekly observance of the *Sabbath*, (5.12–15), and daily *worship in the home* (6.7; see p. 51). There were also *special worship occasions*, such as Hannah's visit to Shiloh with her son Samuel (1 Sam. 1.24).

*Festivals of other nations.* These agricultural festivals in ancient Palestine were similar to agricultural festivals of many societies and cultures today. For example, *Sòng Krant*, the traditional New Year festival in Thailand observed each April 13, is at roughly the same time as the Passover/Unleavened Bread festival of ancient Israel. *Khao Pannsa*, the beginning of the rainy season when Buddhist monks remain in their monasteries, comes at the time of the feast of Weeks. The feast of Booths corresponds to *Awk Pannsa*, the end of the rainy season when Buddhist monks are free to go about among the people again.

Christians who are a minority cannot simply use the principle of separation to refuse participation in such festival times which are part of the life of their own culture. If they accept the Christian festivals of Christmas, Easter and Pentecost as celebrated in other lands, without relating them to their own agricultural year, they may become uprooted from their own culture. At the same time, full participation in these festivals of the dominant culture involves the danger of worshipping other gods.

We can find help in dealing with this problem by following the example of the Israelites. They adapted local customs and festivals to new meanings related to their faith in God. They accepted the agricultural meaning but added historical connections, related to their deliverance from Egypt (16.3,6). For them the festivals were occasions to thank God for the blessings of the harvest, and to remember their own history (16.12; see note on 16.16).

OFFERING (12.13–14)

The Israelites knew that there were 'holy things which are due' to God from the members of the worshipping community (Deut. 12.26). For this reason the people should 'not appear before the Lord empty-handed; all shall give as they are able, according to the blessing of the Lord your God that He has given you' (16.16–17 NRSV). Chapters 12—16 describe the sorts of offerings the people should bring with them, as summarized in 12.6: 'your burnt offerings and your sacrifices, your tithes and your donations, your votive gifts, your freewill offerings, and the firstlings of your herds and flocks' (12.6 NRSV).

*The 'burnt offerings': symbol of repentance and recommitment.* The 'burnt offering' was a bull from the herd, a goat or sheep from the flock, or, in the case of a poor family, a turtle dove or pigeon

(Lev. 1.3,10,14). The altar fire consumed the entire animal (Deut. 12.27) as an offering wholly given to God. According to the Book of Leviticus a person making the offering was instructed to 'lay your hand on the head of the burnt offering' (Lev. 1.4 NRSV). This action symbolized a direct link between the worshipper's household and the life of the animal about to be sacrificed.

The inner meaning of this act of worship was that by offering the life of the animal, *the entire household was offering itself to God as a 'living sacrifice'* (Rom. 12.1). It symbolized the intention of the worshipping group to love God with their whole heart, soul, and might (Deut. 6.5). The importance of this sacrifice was not in the death of the animal but in the offering of the heart of the person or group making the sacrifice.

*The 'peace offering': strengthening shalom.* The 'sacrifices' could also be called a 'peace offering' (as in Deut. 27.7 and Lev. 3.1), or, in other translations, a 'sacrifice of well-being' (JPS, NRSV), 'fellowship offering' (NIV), a 'shared offering' (NEB), a 'communion sacrifice' (JB). The purpose of the peace offering was to (a) strengthen the condition of *shalom*, (b) heal divisions within the community, and (c) maintain covenantal bonds with God. Unlike the 'burnt offering', only the blood of the animal was offered to God, by pouring it out at the base of the altar. The flesh was eaten at a fellowship meal (12.27) in God's presence (14.23).

As in the case of the 'burnt offering', the worshipper making the offering laid hands on the head of the animal before killing it (Lev. 3.7–8). However, in the case of the peace offering, the worshipping group was symbolically *offering its own life for the well-being of the whole community*. The body of the sacrificial animal would become food which would strengthen *shalom* between them and make them whole (see Isa. 53.5). The 'peace offering' symbolized their intention to 'love your neighbour as yourself' (Lev. 19.18).

Strengthening *shalom* would mean concern for the poor. Besides being a part of the fellowship meal of the worshippers, some of the flesh of the peace offerings as well as the produce from the fields would go for the support of the poor people of the community and the landless Levitical priests (14.29; see also 18.1–5).

*The tithe.* The 'tithe' or tenth part of the produce of grain, wine and oil was also part of the fellowship meal at the sanctuary (14.23), but it had another function as well. Every three years tithe was kept in the towns and used in support of the Levites, resident aliens, orphans and widows who were the poor of the community (14.28–29; 26.12–13).

*Offerings.* 'Donations,' 'freewill offerings' or 'votive offerings' made in payment of a vow (see Deut. 23.21–23) consisted of grain, bread dough, or fruit which were eaten at the fellowship meal

(Num. 15.19–21; Deut. 16.14). The same was true of the flesh of
'firstlings', the first-born males of cattle or sheep (Deut. 15.19–
20,22).


## NOTES

**12.1. Statutes and ordinances:** These opening words of Part 3
leading up to the renewal of the Covenant in Moab, have appeared
in earlier chapters (e.g. 4.5,8; 6.1) as an advance reference to the
requirements of the Covenant as renewed in Moab.

**12.5. The place which the LORD your God will choose:** This might
mean the *only* sanctuary for all the tribes. This was the interpretation used by King Josiah and the reformers, as we can see from his
destruction of all other shrines (2 Kings 23.8,13,15,19). The
cleansed Temple in Jerusalem was then the only authorized place
for the worship of God.

In the Book of Deuteronomy as we have it, however, 'the place'
may well have meant a *central* sanctuary, not necessarily the *only*
one. In favour of this interpretation are references to altars in
general (Deut. 16.21), an altar on Mount Ebal (27.4–7), and a
sanctuary in the territory of Zebulun (33.18). Elsewhere we learn
that God made His name 'dwell at first' at Shiloh (Jer. 7.12), and
'the people of Israel' went to worship (1 Sam. 2.28) where the altar
of the LORD stood (Josh. 22.29; see vv.9,12). Other sanctuaries
were at Gilgal and Bethel (Amos 4.4; Hos. 4.15).

**14.1. You shall not cut yourselves or make any baldness on your
foreheads for the dead:** These were mourning customs of other
peoples (see Jer. 47.5; 48.37). They were forbidden to Israelites
(see also Lev. 19.27–28; 21.5), but some Israelites practised them in
the time of Jeremiah and the Narrator (Jer. 41.5). Here are some
suggested reasons for this custom, based on the fact that blood
which flows through the body constantly, and hair which always
grows, were both symbols of life. So, by gashing themselves and
cutting their hair (a) the mourners may have desired to make it
clear that they had not wished or caused the death, thus avoiding
revenge from the spirit of the dead. Or (b) the mourners may have
been showing their grief by offering symbols of life as a gift to the
spirit of the loved one. In either case the custom was based on a
recognition of the power of the spirits of the dead, and a belief in
the power of the dead. It was thus a participation in the sin of
'necromancy,' or consulting the dead (Deut. 18.11; see Ps. 106.28;
Isa. 8.19).

**14.3. You shall not eat any abominable thing:** This refers to certain
kinds of food which were 'taboo', i.e,. forbidden for the 'people
holy to the LORD' (14.2). We do not know why these particular

animals (14.7–8), fish (14.10), birds (14.12–18) and insects (14.19) were regarded as 'unclean'. We do know from archaeological excavations that pigs (14.8) were used as sacrificial animals in Canaanite worship, and were sacred in Babylon, Cyprus and Syria. In the period after the return from Exile in Babylon, idolatrous Jews would go to a garden shrine at night to join in a sacred meal composed of 'swine's flesh . . . and mice' (Isa. 66.17) and a 'broth of abominable things' (65.4).

From these examples we may assume that the peoples of Canaan in early days, and idolatrous Jews in later times, used 'unclean' animals in sacrifices and in sacred meals in worship of other gods. Such worship practices would mean coming under the influence of the 'other gods' and would lead God's people to follow the 'abominable practices' of the Canaanites in the service of their gods' (Deut. 18.9; 20.18; see 12.31). These animals were considered 'unclean' not because their flesh was poisonous or unhealthy, but because they were associated with the worship of other gods and with the evil practices that resulted.

Sacred meals may have been included in the worship practices in the northern kingdom after the fall of Samaria (2 Kings 17.10–11) and in Jerusalem (Jer. 7.17–18). Many centuries later, Jesus did not agree with the laws of Deuteronomy 14 and Leviticus about unclean food. He distinguished between the food itself, which is good by creation, and the evil things which 'come from within and . . . defile a person' (Mark 7.23 NRSV), thus making 'all foods clean' (Mark 7.18–19).

**16.16. Three times a year:** The Israelites adapted the three major agricultural festivals of the Canaanites to their own worship of Yahweh the God of Life. They connected the agricultural feast of *Unleavened Bread* with the people's hasty departure from Egypt (Exod. 12.17–20,34,39), and connected it with the Passover (Exod. 12.21–27). At the feast of *Weeks*, they gave thanks to God not only for the wheat harvest, but also for their freedom from slavery and the gift of the land (Deut. 26.1–11). In later years, after the destruction of the Temple, this festival became a celebration of the giving of the Covenant Teaching at Mount Sinai/Horeb. The feast of *Booths* was originally associated with the time of harvest of the olive orchards. People would stay overnight in shelters of branches and vines, and join in dances like the one described in Judges 21.19–21. The Israelites made this festival also a remembrance of the Exodus, 'that your generations may know that I made the people of Israel dwell in booths when I brought them out of the land of Egypt' (Lev. 23.42). From Deuteronomy 31.9–13, we see that every seven years the feast of *Booths* was also a celebration of the renewal of the Covenant.

## STUDY SUGGESTIONS

### REVIEW OF CONTENT

1. Why did Moses tell the people to destroy the sacred places of the people of Canaan?
2. What were the three sorts of temptations common in Israelite society, which could cause Israel to forget their covenant God?
3. Why was it necessary for the Israelites to separate themselves from the dominant culture of Canaan? What was the purpose of the principle of separation?
4. What *four* actions or attitudes are necessary for covenantal worship?
5. (a) Why did God choose a central place for worship in Canaan?
   (b) Which groups of people were included in the worshipping community?
6. What were the *three* annual festivals in ancient Israel?
7. What was the inner meaning, in each case, of (a) laying hands on the head of the animal to be sacrificed, and (b) the 'burnt offering'?
8. What was the purpose, in each case, of (a) the 'peace offering' and (b) the 'tithe offering'?

### BIBLE STUDY

9. Read Romans 14.13–21 and 1 Corinthians 8.4–13. What reason does Paul give for *not* eating certain foods? In what way does Paul's teaching differ from the teaching of Deut. 13 and 14? What sorts of food, if any, do you think Christians should avoid today, and for what reasons?
10. Read Ezekiel 11.19–20 and Romans 12.1–2. What must a worshipping group do to ensure that their worship of God is to be 'in Spirit and in truth'?
11. Read Malachi 3.8–10. In what way were the people 'robbing' God? In what way would to 'rob' God be the same as to 'oppress the hireling . . . the widow and the orphan' (Mal. 3.5 and see Deut. 14.28–29)?

### CONTEXTUAL APPLICATION

12. In what circumstances, if any, do you think that Christians should participate in the rites of another religion?
13. Read Deuteronomy 12.5, John 4.20–24 and Matt. 18.20. Discuss the following interpretations of the words of Moses and Jesus.
    (a) Christian congregations do not need a special place or

church building for worship. God chooses to be present wherever Christians gather to worship Him.

(b) A special place is essential for God to come and meet His people. Without it we might be meeting with other gods and not know it.

What is your own opinion on this subject?

14. As described in Deuteronomy, the Israelite worshippers were to be 'an inclusive fellowship' (p. 93). How inclusive is the worshipping fellowship of your Church? What sorts of people, if any, would your congregation *not* welcome at its worship services, and why?

15. (a) Compare the three Christian festivals (Christmas, Easter, Pentecost) with the three festivals of ancient Israel. What events does each commemorate? What does each teach about God? What continuity, if any, do you see between the festivals in each case?

(b) Compare the three Christian festivals with any major festivals observed by other religions in your country. Does the celebration of Christian festivals include any of the same elements as the festivals other religions? Do you think Christians could adapt any aspects of other festivals to Christian meaning without worshipping 'other gods'?

16. Compare the fellowship meal which was part of the 'peace offering' (see p. 95) with Christian Holy Communion, or other present-day Christian 'fellowship meal'. What elements in each are like or unlike elements in the other? Who should contribute food for such fellowship meals? (b) What takes the place of the death of the animal in Holy Communion? (c) In what ways does Holy Communion strengthen *shalom*?

# 12.1—16.22
# Covenantal Worship (2)

## OUTLINE

Chs. 12—16 (selected verses): Rejoicing and Remembering as Holy Actions.

Chs. 15, 16 (selected verses): Compassion and Justice as Fruits of Worship.

# INTERPRETATION

## HOLY ACTIONS: REJOICING AND REMEMBERING

### REJOICING

*Joyful Thanksgiving.* 'You shall rejoice before the Lord' (12.12,18; 16.11; see 27.7). Joy in worship is an enthusiastic expression of thanks for 'all the good which the LORD your God has given to you and your house, you and the Levite and the sojourner who is among you' (26.11). God's blessings have been described before in concrete terms (e.g. 6.10–14; 7.13; see also 28.3,5).

*Joy in Work.* Rejoicing at worship also expresses a joy in work well done as a continuation of God's own work (see 5.13 and p. 35). At worship there would be a prayer for God's blessing 'in all that you undertake' and 'in all your produce and in all the work of your hands' (12.7, 16.15). Such rejoicing was an acknowledgement that God gives 'power to get wealth' (8.18). When the people do 'what is good and right in the sight of the LORD your God' (12.28), rather than 'all of us according to our own desires' (12.8 NRSV), they will be God's partners in the production of wealth for the *shalom* or well-being of all.

*Joy with Others.* 'You shall rejoice in your feast' (16.14). An important part of rejoicing was the act of eating a communal meal in God's presence, to strengthen *shalom* (12.18; 14.22–26). The presence of the 'the strangers, the orphans, the widows' (16.11,14 NRSV) meant that food was shared with the poor and disadvantaged, so that they too could rejoice in God's gifts.

A prophet in later times may have been thinking of this joyful feast when he wrote of God's feast 'for all peoples' in the time to come (Isa. 25.6). Jesus continued this idea when He spoke of the time when 'people will come from east and west, from north and south, and will eat in the kingdom of God' (Luke 13.29 NRSV).

*Selfish Joy.* We know from the history of Israel, however, that some sorts of rejoicing could be a cover-up for selfishness. Gathering for worship, offering sacrifices, and sharing fellowship meals became an 'abomination' to God who 'cannot endure iniquity and solemn assembly' when there was injustice and oppression in human relations (Isa. 1.11–13; see Amos 5.21–24; Jer. 7.9–10).

### REMEMBERING

'Remember that you were a slave in Egypt; and diligently observe these statutes' (Deut. 16.12 NRSV). Worship is not only a rejoicing in God's present blessings. It also involves the act of remembering the past (see p. 18). In chs 12—16, however, there is a special sort of remembering: *a recollection of the people's former status as slaves in Egypt* (15.15; 16.12) from which God delivered them (16.3). The conscious act of remembering will encourage those gathered in worship at God's chosen place to 'love the stranger' (10.19 NRSV), and be generous to the poor (15.10, 13–14), so that they may rejoice with the others (16.11–12). In this way those rejoicing in their own well-being and remembering past suffering will learn 'to fear the LORD your God always' (14.23).

## COMPASSION AND JUSTICE AS FRUITS OF WORSHIP

### COMPASSION

The Narrator has placed ch. 15 which deals with release from debt (15.1–3), poverty (15.7–11) and slavery (15.12–18), between chs. 12 and 16 which deal directly with worship itself. This arrangement suggests that compassion is a natural fruit of covenantal worship. The people who gathered in worship to offer sacrifices, rejoice at a communion feast, and remember the past, would also learn to fear and love God with their hands, their eyes, and their hearts. They would be able (a) to relax (the basic meaning of 'release') the grip of their hands on the poor (15.11), (b) to see their neighbours with new eyes (i.e. not 'hostile,' 15.9), and (c) to treat slaves and debtors with favour and generosity (15.10,12).

*Open your Hand* (Deut. 15.8). The expressions 'release' (15.1–3), 'open your hand' (15.8, 11) 'let him go free' (15.12,13,18), all involve giving up what is one's own, whether debts owed by the poor, or financial advantage from slave labour at half the price of a hired worker. In addition, there should be a generous gift to freed slaves. Such acts of generosity will save 'neighbours' (15.2) or 'brothers' (15.2,3,7,9,11,12) from the misery of poverty, oppression and debt, and enable them to escape from the burden of debt, emerge from poverty, and go free once again.

*Organized Compassion* for the poor was part of the structure of the ideal society according to legislation found in Deuteronomy and Leviticus. *Every week* there would be a reminder of their ancestors' past slavery which would encourage the people not to overwork their own slaves and servants (5.14). A similar recollection at the central shrine would encourage generosity to the poor (15.10). *The annual festivals* were an occasion to welcome strangers, orphans and widows in their midst (16.11–12). *In every third year* the tithe would be given to the poor (14.28–29). *Every seventh year* would be 'the year of Release' (15.1) at the festival of Booths (31.10) when debts were forgiven and slaves set free. *Every fifty years* (Lev. 25.8–17) there would be a Jubilee year when family and social relationships would be celebrated and renewed to ensure justice and *shalom* for all.

*There willl be no poor among you* (Deut. 15.4). Active compassion towards the poor was essential if the Israelites were to receive the blessings promised in 7.13–14. '*Because for this* the Lord God will bless you in all your work . . .' (15.10; see 14.29; 15.18; 23.20; 24.19). The words 'there will be no poor among you . . . if only you will obey the voice of the LORD your God' (15.4–5) mean the same thing in another way. Compassion will help the poor get free from poverty. Poverty was widespread 'on the earth' (15.11 NRSV). So the Israelites' example in removing poverty by compassionate help will be a guiding light to the nations.

## RIGHTEOUSNESS AND JUSTICE

*Justice in a context of worship.* The Narrator has placed the administration of righteousness and justice (16.18–20; see note on 16.20 below) between references to covenantal worship and wrong worship (16.16–17 and 21–22). Hc has sct it appropriately at the end of the section on the vital importance of worship (chs. 12—16), and at the beginning of the section on the need for integrity in public life, i.e. government service (chs 17.1—21.9). Righteousness and justice in public life are essentially a reflection of God's own righteousness and justice (10.18;32.4). They are both the fruit of covenantal worship, and the basis for a peaceful society (16.20).

*Public officials.* As we have seen, Moses instituted the offices of 'judge' and 'officer' as well as 'commander' at Mount Sinai/Horeb to help him administer justice during the journey through the wilderness (1.9–18). At Sinai/Horeb the tribes chose their leaders and Moses appointed them (1.13). In Moab Moses commands the people, when they come into the land without him, to appoint their own judges and officers 'throughout your tribes, in all your towns' (16.18 NRSV).

*A society that pursues righteousness and justice.* The collective pronoun 'you' to referring to the people in 16.19–20 shows that, by judging 'the people with righteous judgement' (16.18; see 1.16) these leaders ('they') will help the people ('you') to maintain a righteous society. In practising covenantal worship both people and leaders will learn of God's nature (10.17–18) and will try to reflect that nature in public life. By trying to reflect God's justice (10.18; see Exod. 23.6; Deut. 24.17; 27.19), leaders will ensure that aliens, orphans and widows as well as the poor receive the proper justice due to them. There will be no favouritism toward the rich and powerful. There will be neither giving nor taking of bribes. The pursuit of 'justice and only justice' will be the task of all (16.20).

When Moses appointed judges and officers he expected them to help the people to maintain righteous relationships with God and with their neighbours: 'You shall not take the name of the Lord in vain . . . Neither shall you bear false witness against your neighbour'. Many Christian countries today stress these commandments when appointing judges and calling witnesses to testify in court. This woman being posted as a Supreme Court Judge in the USA swears on the Bible to uphold justice and truth.

## NOTES

**16.20. Justice and only justice.** The Hebrew word here translated 'justice' is *tsedeq*. It is usually translated as 'righteousness', as in 1.16, where judges are to judge 'righteously'. In 25.15 it refers to 'just' weights and measures. In this sense it refers to the relationship between humans. The feminine form of the noun is *tsedaqah*, also translated as 'righteousness', which in 6.25 and 24.13 is a quality of life given by God to an obedient, loving people (see pp. 51, 55). In this sense 'righteousness' refers first to our relationship with God, and then to human relationships. God's people can never boast of their own 'righteousness' (9.4–6). *Tsedeq* in 16.20, when considered in the context of chs. 12—25, carries both meanings, and we translate it as 'righteousness and justice', the fruit of covenantal worship. Those who are 'righteous' by God's gift, will follow 'righteousness and justice' in their conduct of life (see Micah 6.8).

## STUDY SUGGESTIONS

### REVIEW OF CONTENT

1. What *three* sorts of joy should be expressed in covenantal worship?
2. What were the Israelites to 'remember' during their worship services?
3. What are the two fruits of right worship mentioned in Deuteronomy 12—16?
4. In what way does the placing of ch. 15 between chs 12 and 16 help us to see the relationship of covenantal worship with care for debtors, slaves and poor people?

### BIBLE STUDY

5. Compare Deuteronomy 16.12 with Ephesians 2.12–16.
   (a) What was to be remembered in each case?
   (b) What would be the result of remembering in each case?

### CONTEXTUAL APPLICATION

6. In what ways can Christians as individuals help to make a nation or a world in which 'there will be no poor among you' (Deut. 15.4)?
7. Righteousness and justice in public administration are fruits of right worship. In what ways, if any, could prayers, sermons or other parts of Christian worship be related more closely to justice in public administration in your country?

8. You shall lend to many nations, but you shall not borrow; and you shall rule over many nations, but they shall not rule over you' (15.8). How should this verse be understood in the context of the relationships between rich and poor nations today: (a) In the giving and receiving of 'aid'? (b) In negotiating trade agreements?

# 16.18—21.9
# Righteousness and Justice in Public Life (1)

## OUTLINE

18.13: The Goal: A Society where God Rules.
Chs. 17—19 (selected verses): Leaders and Officials of a Society where God rules.

## INTERPRETATION

The Narrator has arranged chs. 12.1—25.19 in a way that binds worship and social teaching together. In his conclusion to the section on worship he emphasized righteousness and justice as the fruit of covenantal worship (16.18–20). The same passage is also the introduction to detailed teaching on the application of righteousness and justice to public life and family and social life (chs. 16.18—21.9 and 21.10—25.19).

## A SOCIETY WHERE GOD RULES

### BLAMELESS BEFORE GOD

Striving for righteousness and justice in public life (16.20) is an expression of the 'righteousness' that is 'God's gift of love to a Covenant partner who loves without restriction' (6.25; see p. 55). The goal is not that this stubborn people (9.4–6) should boast of their own 'righteousness', but that they may be accepted as 'blameless (Hebrew *tamim*) before the LORD your God' (18.13; see note). They should model their society upon God whose 'work is perfect (*tamim*) . . ., a God of faithfulness and without iniquity, just and right is he' (32.4). This does not mean that the Covenant society could ever achieve perfect righteousness and justice. But to be 'blameless' the people must constantly renew their efforts to apply '*the* Commandment' to love God in public as well as private life ('when you walk by the way' (6.7) with humble dependence on God.

The practice of righteousness and justice in public life requires (a) social and political organization, i.e. the appointment of religious and secular leaders, (b) the development of laws and institutions to preserve justice, (c) laws and institutions to purge evil which destroys justice and righteousness, and (4) rules for the conduct of war.

## LEADERS AND OFFICIALS OF SOCIETY

In a society where God rules, there should be a *balance of power* as a way of guaranteeing that righteousness and justice prevail. Power should be shared by elders, judges, kings, priests, and prophets.

### ELDERS

In each of the cities and towns there would be a council of elders (*chosen by the people*, 19.12), who were responsible for teaching (27.1; 29.10–13) and enforcing accepted rules of conduct. They would examine cases in the open space inside the gates of the town (21.19; 22.15; see Ruth 4.1), where the words of Deuteronomy 6.4–5 would be inscribed (6.9). At the tribal level, a number of them (perhaps six) would represent the people as 'the elders of your tribes' (Deut. 31.28). Together they would form an inter-tribal council of 'all the elders of Israel' (31.9).

### JUDGES AND OFFICERS

At the local level certain elders could be appointed as judges (*chosen by the people*, 16.18), to 'judge the people with righteous judgement' (16.18; see also 1.16), knowing that the right decision would be from God (16.17; see 10.17–18). In cases needing more detailed knowledge of the laws, the elders or judges could go to the high court at the central sanctuary, where a judge at the national level would give a final decision in the case (17.8–9). See note on 16.18 regarding officers.

### PRIEST

The Levitical priests (*chosen by God*, 18.5) would serve as guardians of the Covenant Teaching or *Torah* (17.18) along with the council of elders (31.9). At the Covenant Renewal festival every seven years the priests would read and interpret the Torah as guidelines for making righteous judgement (31.11). At the local level (19.17), or at the central sanctuary (17.8–9), they would join the judges in deciding cases (19.17), thus making the decisions binding (21.5).

## KINGS

The Narrator has arranged these chapters so that the discussion of the office of king (*chosen by God* 17.14–20) is surrounded by references to elders, judges, priests and prophets. This arrangement emphasizes *the covenantal nature of the Israelite kingship* in which the king shared responsibility for government with elected officials and people. The king and elected officials would be responsible to God. This was very different from the ideas about government in 'all the nations that are round about' them (17.14), where all power rested with the king alone. Four differences stand out.

1. *God Himself*, the Creator of all human beings (4.32), the 'God of gods, and LORD of lords, the great, the mighty, and the terrible God who is not partial and takes no bribe' (10.17) *would choose the king*, and therefore exercise authority over him. A king who seized the throne with no authority from God, would acknowledge no limitation to his power. 'They made kings, but not through me. They set up princes, but without my knowledge' said God through Hosea (Hos. 8.4).

2. The king must be *'one of your own community'* (Deut. 17.15 NRSV), one with the people in memory and tradition, who would share the Covenant ideals of righteousness and justice in government. He would rule with the consent of the governed, for the people would make him king.

3. The king must exercise covenantal *restraint in the use of power*. He must limit *military power* ('horses') to national self-defence. He must limit *economic power* by not enriching himself at the expense of the people. He must limit his *political power* by not making alliances through marriage with women of other peoples (17.16–17).

4. He must get from the Levitical priests *his own personal copy of the Covenant Teaching or Torah* for daily study and meditation (17.18–19), just like ordinary Israelites (6.7–8; see Josh. 1.7–8). Such meditation would protect him from temptations to consider himself superior to his people, or to follow 'the abominable practices of those nations' around him (18.9). In short, the king should be a model for, and a blessing to his people (17.20).

These verses would remind readers of the description of 'the ways of the king' according to the ideas in other nations (1 Sam. 8.11–17). Without the guidance of the Covenant Teaching, the king would be tempted to confiscate property and land from the people, and to make slaves of them. Readers would think of certain kings who violated the Covenant ideal. The most obvious was Solomon, who bought horses in Egypt (1 Kings 10.28–29), built many chariot cities (9.17–19), accumulated great wealth (10.14–22), had many wives (11.1–3), and laid heavy burdens on his people (12.4). These were evidence of his neglect of the Covenant Teaching or *Torah* and caused the division of the kingdom (11.4–11; 12.16). Readers in the last days of Jerusalem would dream of the future king promised by Jeremiah:

> Their prince shall be one of themselves,
> their ruler shall come forth from their midst;
> I will make him draw near, and he shall approach me;
> for who would dare of himself to approach me?
> says the Lord.
> And you shall be my people,
> and I will be your God. (Jer. 30.21–22)

## PROPHETS

Prophets (*raised up by God*, Deut. 18.15,18) were essential to the administration of righteousness and justice. Elders, judges, priests and kings were all dependent on the written Covenant Teaching or *Torah* for their guidance. Prophets had direct access to God through dreams or visions (Num. 12.6) or even, in Moses's case, 'face to face' (Deut. 34.10; Num. 12.7–8 NRSV). They would be responsible for communicating the will and plans of God for the present and future to the leaders of Israel. The God of the Covenant would Himself raise them up in every age (Deut. 18.15,18). They would carry God's Covenant words, and speak them to the Covenant people (v.18), with the authority of God Himself (v.19).

## FALSE PROPHETS

One problem was that there were *false prophets*, who *claimed* to speak in the name of the Covenant God, or of other gods (Deut.18.20; see 13.1) 'a word which the Lord has not spoken' (18.22). According to Deuteronomy 18, they were so dangerous that they must be removed by death (18.18–20). The problem was how to distinguish these false prophets from true ones. The two tests suggested in Deuteronomy both have to do with the *results* of the prophets' speaking.

1. The first sort of test could not be applied immediately. It required patience to wait for a later outcome. If what a prophet says 'does not take place or prove true' (18.22 NRSV) his words are not from the Covenant God. For example, Hananiah, claiming to be a spokesman for the Covenant God, predicted the defeat of Babylon and the restoration of the Davidic monarchy in Jerusalem within two years. Jeremiah predicted the destruction of Jerusalem and the

end of the monarchy (Jer. 28.2–4, 11, 14–17). Only Jeremiah's words proved true.

2. The second test was this: Do the words of the prophet lead the people away from their Covenant God (Deut. 13.2,5)? Jeremiah saw false prophets leading the people astray, strengthening the hands of evildoers, prophesying lies which the people wanted to hear, planning to make the Covenant people forget the name of the Covenant God (Jer. 23.13.14,27,32). This is what the 400 prophets of King Ahab's court did when they promised that Ahab would be victorious in battle. They were merely saying what the king and people wanted to hear. Only the true prophet Micaiah ben Imlah told the unwelcome truth, that the king would die in battle and the armies of Israel and Judah would be defeated by Syria (1 Kings 22.6, 13, 17, 34–36).

From these tests we can formulate a general rule: we should avoid making absolute judgements about people who claim to be able to tell about the future. We must wait, like the Rabbi Gamaliel, for the future to show us the truth (see Acts. 5.34–39).

In modern times we hear many voices inviting us to follow this or that way. Here are some ways in which we can test these voices to know whether they come from God or not.

(a) Do the voices call us to practice righteousness and justice, especially in our relations to the weak and needy, or do they encourage us to be more selfish?

(b) Do the voices call us to loyalty and love for the one true God, or do they lure us to follow the idols of wealth, material possessions or power, whether personal, family or economic?

## FORTUNE TELLERS

According to the covenantal ideal, prophets like Moses were to replace the fortune tellers, sorcerers, charmers, augurs, and mediums of Canaan. Immediately preceding the discussion of the office of the prophet, the Narrator has listed seven techniques including human sacrifice, magic, incantations, spirit possession, or reading signs in nature (Deut. 18.9–12; see note on v.12). The peoples of Canaan in the time of Moses, and the Canaanized Israelites in the time of the monarchy, used such methods to contact the unseen world in order to predict or even control future events. These and other similar practices were widespread in the world of West Asia and North Africa. In fact they are common today, and form an important part of the life of many societies in Asia, Africa, Latin America, and the islands of the Pacific.

These practices were very tempting to the Israelites throughout their history. Magic and prediction, however, had nothing to do with covenantal demands for righteousness and justice (16.20).

King Ahab, under the direction of the foreign Queen Jezebel and her 'sorceries' (2 Kings 9.22), confiscated the land of Naboth and had him executed in a typical miscarriage of justice (1 Kings 21.1–14). The evil king Manasseh supported five of the seven practices (2 Kings 21.6).

## NOTES

**16.18. Officers:** See p. 10 for the duties of officers. In addition to the duties described there, the officers may have been court recorders and legal scholars in the period of the monarchy. According to 20.5–9, they had an important role in time of war.

**16.19. Pervert justice:** Readers in the time of the Narrator would remember the words of the prophets about evil judges, priests, kings and prophets who pervert justice, show partiality, accept bribes, and oppress the poor. See e.g., Micah 2.8–9; 3.1–3, 9–11.

**18.12. Whoever does these things:** Verses 10–11 refer to seven sorts of magical practice. People believed that these would enable them to predict the future, and even influence events, by calling on the spirits of the dead, or pleasing the gods of the Canaanites. As far as we know these acts were as follows:

1. To make 'a son or a daughter *pass through fire*' (18.10, NRSV) probably refers to a method of trying to discover the will, or influencing the actions, of the Ammonite god Molech. People would cause a child to pass through fire as a part of the ceremony. Death may have resulted. We find references to this practice in the reigns of Ahaz and Manasseh (2 Kings 16.3; 21.6), and of Jehoiakim and Zedekiah in the days of Jeremiah (Jer. 7.31; 19.5; 32.35).

2. *Diviners* may have shaken marked arrows from a quiver (Deut. 18.10; see Ezek. 21.21). The first arrow to fall would show the decision of the god. In the same way fortune tellers in many countries today scatter bones or marked stones, or shake pieces of wood shaped like a half banana, as a way of forecasting events or advising about actions. There were diviners in the northern kingdom (2 Kings 17.17), as well as in the Jerusalem court in the days of Isaiah (Isa. 3.2), Micah (Mic. 3.6–7), Jeremiah (Jer. 14.14; 27.9) and Ezekiel (Ezek 22.28). They were advisers to the king like the white-robed Brahmin *hone* in traditional Thai drama. In an earlier period of Israelite history priests used the same method for finding out the will of Yahweh by casting the Urim and Thummim (see note on Deut. 33.8).

3. *Soothsayers* (18.11) were common in Jerusalem during the reigns of Ahaz, as described by Micah (Micah 5.12), Manasseh (2 Kings 21.6), and Zedekiah as mentioned by Jeremiah (Jer. 27.9).

'Prophets would communicate God's will to the leaders of Israel.' In modern times many voices call us this way and that way. But do they call us to love God and our neighbours, or do they 'pervert justice' by luring us to try and increase our power by following magical and 'occult' practices? Diviners and sorcerers were as widespread in the ancient world as spirit-mediums, astrologers and fortune-tellers are today, like this one in Zambia with his magic 'charm' necklace.

We do not know what methods they used to predict the future. The Hebrew word may refer to the hoarse sound of the soothsayer's voice when he or she gave the oracle. The English word 'soothsayer' comes from the Old English word 'sooth' meaning 'truth.' Only later did the word 'soothsayer' come to mean one who predicts the future.

4. *Augurs* (Deut. 18.10) may have interpreted natural phenomena like the flight of birds, or atmospheric changes, as omens of good or bad fortune. They practised their arts in the Northern Kingdom (2 Kings 17.17 RSV 'sorcery') and during the reign of Manasseh (21.6). Many sorts of magic and witchcraft similar to these, such as 'Obeah' or 'Voodoo' in Caribbean culture, continue to be widely practised in spite of being condemned as evil by Churches, or ridiculed as 'trickery' by many other people. Today even in the 'scientific' culture of the West many people regularly consult 'astrologers' who base their predictions on the movement of the stars.

5. *Sorcerers* (18.10) practised their magical arts in the time of Queen Jezebel (2 Kings 9.22), Ahaz (Mic. 5.12), Manasseh (2 Chron. 33.6), Zedekiah (Jer. 27.9) and in Babylon in the time of Deutero-Isaiah (Isa. 47.6). We do not know what method they used, but they probably resembled those still used in parts of Africa and Asia at present.

6. Those *who cast spells* (18.11 NRSV) claimed to influence events by tying magical knots, or composing spells or incantations (see Isa. 47.9,12).

7. Those *who consult ghosts or spirits or seek oracles from the dead* (18.11 NRSV) claimed to be able to contact the spirits of the dead for information or power. They were active in the days of Saul (1 Sam. 28.3,7,9), Ahaz (Isa. 8.19; 29.4) Manasseh (2 Kings 21.6) and Josiah, who removed them (23.24). We may compare them to modern 'spiritualist mediums' who seek to communicate with people who have died. In the Greek translation of the Old Testament these are called 'ventriloquists'.

**18.13. Blameless before the Lord your God:** The Hebrew word translated 'blameless' is *tamim*. We find *tamim* in only one other passage in Deuteronomy where it describes God's work as 'perfect' (Deut. 32.4). In Leviticus, the word *tamim* refers to an unblemished animal to be used as a sacrifice (Lev. 1.3). 'Blameless' in this sense would mean, in the words of Paul, 'holy and acceptable to God' (Rom. 12.1). *Tamim* can refer to 'men of integrity' (Prov. 2.21; see 28.18). The probable meaning is to conform the life of an individual or a people to God's will.

For the Israelites to be *tamim*, therefore, they must fulfil God's will by trying to be like God in doing justice, being faithful and doing what is right. When Jesus said 'You therefore must be perfect as your heavenly Father is perfect' (Matt. 5.48), He meant that the disciples should be even-handed like God. Paul also counselled Christians to 'be imitators of God' (Eph. 5.1), and so to be 'holy and blameless before Him (1.4).

**18.15. A prophet like me**: The NRSV margin gives the collective meaning of the word 'prophet' by the alternative translation: 'prophets'. Similarly, the term 'king' (17.14) has a collective sense of a succession of kings. Because of its association with the false prophets of every age, the promise here means a line of prophets in the Mosaic tradition. On the basis of this verse, Jews wait for a Messiah-Prophet. For Christians Jesus is the prophet like Moses (see John 6.14; 7.40; Acts 3.22; 7.37).

## STUDY SUGGESTIONS

REVIEW OF CONTENT

1. What does 'blameless before God' mean?
2. (a) What *five* sorts of officials helped to maintain a balance of power in the administration of righteousness and justice?
   (b) Which of the officials were chosen by the people and which by God?
3. Where should the judges go for a decision if a case was too difficult for them?
4. In what *four* ways did the covenantal ideal of a king differ from ideas about kingship in other nations?
5. (a) In what way did prophets differ from elders, judges, priests and kings?
   (b) What were the two tests which would show whether a prophet was true or false?
6. What *seven* ways of foretelling the future or calling on spirits were practised in ancient Israel?
7. Which passage in Deuteronomy do Christians interpret as a reference to Jesus?

BIBLE STUDY

8. Which kings besides Solomon violated the Covenant, and in what ways, according to the following passages?
   (a) 1 Kings 21.25–26   (b) 2 Kings 21.1–16   (c) 2 Kings 23.36,37   (d) Jer. 22.13–14, 17–18
9. How far is it possible for any society to be 'blameless before the Lord' or 'perfect' like God? Consult Jeremiah 17.9, Deuteronomy 6.25; 9.4–6; 30.1–6; 31.26–29 and Matthew 5.38.

CONTEXTUAL APPLICATION

10. Which of the following ideas from Deut. 17—19 are taken seriously by the government of your country? (a) balance of powers, (b) participation by the people in choice of officials, (c) moral restraint on the powerful, (d) responsibility of officials to a higher power.
11. Give examples of public officials, laws and institutions in your country which (a) promote justice or (b) obstruct justice.
12. How would you apply today the two tests as to whether someone is a true prophet or not, to such people as (a) a popular evangelist, (b) a political speaker seeking votes, (c) advertisers on TV or radio, (d) a school teacher.
13. What is your attitude as a Christian towards consulting horoscopes or fortune tellers or using any form of magic? Do you agree with the warnings in Deuteronomy 18.9–14? Give reasons for your answer.


# 16.18—21.9
# Righteousness and Justice in Public Life (2)

## OUTLINE

Chs. 17—20 (selected verses): Laws and Institutions to Preserve Justice.
Chs. 17;19; 20.1–8 (selected verses): Laws and Institutions to Purge Existing Evil.


## INTERPRETATION

### LAWS AND INSTITUTIONS TO PRESERVE JUSTICE

Some laws erect a 'fence' around members of the Covenant society, to prevent the outbreak and spread of evil actions. These 'protective' laws would guard against the ways of death.

1. *In Covenant society there will be no seizure of land belonging to a neighbour* (19.14). Under the Covenant, all are 'neighbours'. The land of each is an 'inheritance' from God 'which the men of old have set'. This may be a reference to the land allotment described in Joshua 13—19, which 'Moses the servant of the Lord gave them' (Josh. 13.8). Land rights among the Israelites were different from the laws prevailing among 'all the nations' (Deut. 17.14), where the

rights of the king were absolute (see the words of Jezebel to Ahab, 1 Kings 21.7).

This law applies the eighth commandment to land theft. Removing 'your neighbour's landmark' means more than shifting the position of a stone marker. It means taking your neighbour's entire field, an action that brings divine punishment ('curse') on the offender as well as the land (Deut. 27.17). The chief targets of this law were the powerful landowners who would 'remove the landmark' of their poorer neighbours (Hos. 5.10; see Prov. 22.28), 'add field to field until there is no more room' (Isa. 5.8), and 'covet fields and seize them, houses and take them away' (Mic. 2.2 NRSV). They would drive out 'the women of my people' and take inheritance from 'their young children' (Mic. 2.9; see Prov. 23.10–11).

2. *In Covenant society there is no room for revenge* (19.21). The stern injunction 'life for life, eye for eye, tooth for tooth, hand for hand, foot for foot' (Exod. 21.23–25; Lev. 24.17–20), was to be administered strictly by the judge: this was to protect an offender from unlimited revenge that could wipe out an entire tribe for the murder of one member, or kill many in revenge for a slight wound. The revenge sought by Lamech (Gen. 4.23–24) has no place in Covenant society. Samson, though classed as a judge, was no model for Israelites in his thirst for vengeance (Judges 15.4–8, 15; 16.28). In the Covenant society there must be exact retribution according to the damage caused by the offender, with no thought for revenge. Another way of stating this law is that 'the punishment must fit the crime'.

3. *In Covenant society there should be no wanton destruction of creation* (20.19–20). Among the rules of conduct in time of war was a law which prohibited the use of technology ('an axe') to destroy the trees which are good 'for food' (v. 20; see Gen. 2.9,16). The natural resources of God's good creation are God's gifts for the benefit of all. The trees of the field are not 'human beings that they should come under siege from' humans (Deut. 20.19 NRSV). In other words, human beings should not make war on nature! This law is witness to the interdependence of creation, humanity and God. The 'dominion' over the earth's resources which God gave to humans (Gen. 1.28) is that of stewards who are responsible to the Creator to whom 'the earth . . . and all that is in it' belongs (Ps. 24.1 NRSV). This law limits not only the conduct of war, but also the unchecked use of technology to destroy creation for selfish gain.

## AN INSTITUTION TO PROTECT THE INNOCENT, 19.1–10

The administration of righteousness and justice in any society requires institutions as well as laws. The cities of refuge (19.2) were designed to maintain the health of the new society, by keeping innocent people from being killed and so protecting the land from evil and destruction (19.10).

*Blood guilt.* The ancient Israelites believed that the violent death of a human person created in the image of God polluted the land (Num. 35.33). Their view was that the only way to cleanse the land from 'the guilt of bloodshed' (Deut. 19.10) was by the blood (i.e. death) of the murderer (Num. 35.33; see Deut. 19.13). The common custom was that the nearest of kin of the slain person, called 'the avenger of blood' (Deut. 19.6) would avenge that death by killing the murderer, thereby cleansing the land of blood guilt (Num. 35.19).

*Accidental murder.* In the case of an accident in which a death occurred, the killer was both guilty and innocent - guilty because he had shed innocent blood, and also innocent because he had not intended to kill. A woodcutter's axehead might fly off the handle and kill his helper (Deut. 19.5), or a stone innocently dislodged might crush a fellow worker (Num. 35.22–23). In present day legal language, that person would be a 'manslayer' (Deut. 19.4) rather than a 'murderer' (Num. 35.16; the same Hebrew word is used in both cases, and in Deut. 5.17). If the avenger of blood took the life of the one who did not intend to kill his neighbour, the chain of bloody violence could spread without limit like a cancer, so that 'murder follows murder' (Hos. 4.2) and the Covenant society would weaken and destroy itself.

## A LEGAL SANCTUARY

The cities of refuge were a way to halt the spread of such violence in the land given to them by God (Deut. 19.1,10; see 4.41–43). They were part of God's plan to 'do you good in the end' (8.16), established 'for you' (19.2). The manslayer who 'did not deserve to die because he was not at enmity with his neighbour in times past' could find refuge from the 'hot anger' of the avenger of blood (19.6). The elders and judges, as well as the Levitical priests in the city of refuge (see note on 19.2) would protect the manslayer while his case was investigated to determine the truth of his report (see Num. 35.12 and Josh. 20.4). If he was found to be a 'murderer' he would be turned over to the elders of his city for action (Deut. 19.12).

## LAWS AND INSTITUTIONS TO PURGE EXISTING EVIL

From the point of view of Moses and the people waiting on the border of the Promised Land, there were cases where the land and people would be in danger of poisonous infections from the surrounding society. In the time of the Narrator the land was already full of such evil practices, which must be purged away if a healthy society was to survive. The Narrator selected three cases as examples which would be typical of others. They relate to three of the Ten Commandments.

## EXAMPLES OF EVIL

1. The first case (17.2–7) is a violation of the first commandment, by *worship of the astral gods* of Assyria (17.3) as in Samaria (2 Kings 17.16) and Jerusalem under Manasseh (2 Kings 21.3,5). Josiah cleansed Jerusalem of this sort of worship (23.4–5,11), but it was revived in the time of Jeremiah and Ezekiel (Jer. 8.2; Ezek. 8.16).

2. The second case is a violation of the ninth commandment against *bearing false witness* in order to do violence to a neighbour (Deut. 19.15–21). The most famous example of this is that of the two 'base fellows' hired by Jezebel. They brought a false charge against Naboth that resulted in his death (1 Kings 21.8–14). The Psalms too refer to 'malicious witnesses' who speak 'against those who are quiet in the land', and falsely claim to have seen the crime committed (Ps. 35.11,20,21). Behind their smooth speech there was 'violence and strife in the city' (Ps. 55.9; see Ezek. 7.23, describing Jerusalem). They wear violence 'like a garment' and 'speak with malice' (Ps. 73.6,8 NRSV). Micah also spoke of the inhabitants of Jerusalem with strong words:

> Your rich men are full of violence;
>  your inhabitants speak lies,
> and their tongue is deceitful in their mouth.
> (Mic. 6.12)

3. The third case relates to the sixth Commandment against *murder*, when the murderer is not known (Deut. 21.1–9). In ancient Israel, a dead body was considered unclean. Touching it, or even being in the same house with it made a person ritually unclean for seven days (Num. 19.16). An unclean person who did not perform the proper cleansing ceremony would make the entire people unclean. That person would be expelled from the community (Num. 19.13).

The shedding of blood (murder) of an innocent person polluted the land, bringing the threat of God's judgement (see Deut. 27.24). Like the blood of Abel, this neighbour's blood would cry out to God from the ground (Gen. 4.10).

## PROCEDURES

In each case there was a prescribed procedure. In the case of an unsolved murder, the law involved the elders and judges of the city nearest to the corpse (Deut. 21.3) and the Levitical priests from that city or the central sanctuary (21.5). The purpose was to absolve the nearest city from blood guilt. The procedure in other cases was meant to guard against injustice to the accused before he was proved guilty. The judges must make a careful inquiry to find out whether or not the charges were true (17.4; 19.18; 21.2). There must be two or three eye-witnesses before a sentence was given (17.6; 19.15). If guilt was established, the sentence would be carried out in public ('in the gates', 17.5). In cases of the death penalty, the witnesses must acknowledge their responsibility by casting the first stones, followed by the 'hand of all the people' (17.7).

These procedures were necessary because of the danger that some zealous reformers would take matters into their own hands. For example, priests, prophets and the common people wanted to put Jeremiah to death (Jer. 26.8,11). People wanted to stone Moses (Exod. 17.4), Joshua and Caleb (Num. 14.10), David (1 Sam. 30.6), Jesus (John 10.31–33) and Paul (Acts. 14.19). Some might even use reform as an excuse for taking revenge against a personal enemy. The result would be more Covenant violations by the shedding of innocent blood.

## RESTORATIVE PUNISHMENTS

In each case the purpose of the punishment was to 'purge the evil from the midst of you', that is to restore health and blessing to the Covenant community by preventing the poison from infecting the whole people (17.7; 19.19; 21.9; see 13.5; 22.21,22,24; 24.7). Punishment is a way of administering righteousness and justice in a land where God rules.

Today we find the practice of execution by stoning unacceptable. We should ask what system of punishment for crimes (whether by imprisonment, death or other means), will best serve to protect our society from evil and injustice.

## NOTES

**19.2. Set apart three cities**. In Joshua, all six 'cities of refuge' are named (Josh. 20.7–8). Each of them was also a city set aside for the Levites, according to Joshua 21. Resident Levitical priests would have an important role in welcoming a refugee.

**21.2. Him that is slain.** In most cultures there are customs related to the treatment of the bodies of the dead. In north Thailand, people think it is bad luck if a corpse is carried in front of their house. They prefer to carry a corpse out of a house through a temporary opening in the wall rather than to carry it out by the door, and a coffin with a body in it cannot be carried by ordinary rail, bus, or air transportation.

## STUDY SUGGESTIONS

### REVIEW OF CONTENT

1. What evils did the three 'protective' laws try to prevent?
2. What was the purpose of the cities of refuge?
3. (a) What were the cases given as examples of violation of the first, sixth and ninth commandments?
   (b) What were the procedures for punishing the wrong-doers in these cases?

### BIBLE STUDY

4. Read Hosea 4.1–3. What violations of the Covenant do these verses reflect? What was the effect of these violations, (a) On society? (b) On the environment?

### CONTEXTUAL APPLICATION

5. The purpose of judicial action in ancient Israel was 'to purge the evil' from society (p. 118). What laws are there to purge and protect society from 'evil actions' in your country today? What other evils, if any, do you think need to be purged from your society, and how could judicial actions in the courts purge them?
6. In some countries today, rich individuals or trading companies are buying more and more land for commercial purposes. In what ways does this affect the lives of the original owners or users of the land? In what ways do big landowners in your country today show respect or disrespect for the eighth commandment?
7. How far can the Church be a 'city of refuge' for victims of injustice in society today? Give some examples of the sort of injustice from which your congregation would welcome 'refugees'. Are there any sorts of people to whom the Church should *not* give sanctuary? Give reasons.

# 16.18—21.9
# Righteousness and Justice in Public Life (3)

## OUTLINE

20.1–18: Guidelines for the Conduct of War against Evil Powers.

## INTERPRETATION

Chapter 20 presents serious problems to readers today. It describes war as a divinely approved means of dealing with enemies, with God as the warrior and commander (20.4). It commands Israel to make the people of neighbouring cities do forced labour if they accept terms of peace (20.11; see note on forced labour) or, if they refuse such terms, to slaughter all males (20.13), and absorb women and children into Israelite society (20.14; see note on the word translated 'enjoy'). The command was to exterminate entire cities, sparing 'nothing that breathes' (20.16–17; see 7.2,26 and Special Note D). Do these commands make modern warfare with its mass destruction of innocent civilians acceptable because it is 'biblical'? Do they teach us to be self-righteous (see pp. 104–05), and to regard enemy tribes or nations as demonic agents of Satan? Do they contradict Jesus's teaching about peace-making? We must look more closely at this chapter.

## GOD'S STRUGGLE FOR A NEW CREATION

Many of the Old Testament writers describe God's warfare against evil powers. They use symbolic language to describe His struggle against these powers of death at the time of creation (Isa. 51.9; Ps. 74.12–14). In the Exodus God fought against Pharaoh and 'all the gods of Egypt' (Exod. 12.12), took 'a nation for himself from the midst of another nation, by trials, by signs, by wonders, and by war ..' (Deut. 4.34). Old Testament writers also tell of God's purpose in the struggle: to 'create new heavens and a new earth' (Isa. 65.17). His purpose in the Exodus was to give the Israelites a new way of life (Deut. 5.6–21) in a 'good land' (6.18). This was God's way of beginning a new creation, where righteousness and justice should prevail (16.20), where there would be no poor (15.4), and from which the peoples of the earth could learn the ways of wisdom (4.6; see Isa. 2.2–3; Mic. 4.1–2).

### THERE WILL ALWAYS BE ENEMIES

We also learn from Deuteronomy 20 that the practice of righteousness and justice in a Covenant society will always be in the presence

If enemy cities refused terms of peace the Israelites were to slaughter all the men there, and take women and children and everything else as booty. In some cities they were to 'save alive nothing that breathes'. Do these commands make modern warfare acceptable, with its mass destruction of innocent civilians—as here where soldiers in South-East Asia, advancing to capture a village, discover a child hiding in the bushes?

of opposition, or 'enemies' (Deut. 20.1,3,4,14) both outside and inside the bounds of the Promised Land (Deut. 20.15). Israel was to be God's 'bulwark . . . to still the enemy and the avenger' (Ps. 8.2). God would fight with and on behalf of His Covenant people against enemies of righteousness and justice (Deut. 20.4). However, if His Covenant people should cease to practise righteousness and justice, God would not go with them into battle (see Deut. 1.42), but would struggle against them (8.19–20; 11.17; see Isa. 63.10).

## FOUR RULES

A careful reading of this chapter, which contains so much that is difficult for us to understand or accept, will show four rules to guide the struggle of God's people against the powers of evil. (Please see again the lessons of defeat and victory in the wilderness, pp. 13–14, 70–73).

1. The first rule is that *Covenant faithfulness, or the practice of righteousness and justice is more important than the size of armaments*. 'Horses and chariots and an army larger than your own' (20.1) are no cause for fear. These words echo the words of David to Goliath (1 Sam.17.45) and those of Isaiah: 'Woe to those who . . . rely on horses, who trust in chariots because they are many and in horsemen because they are very strong, but do not look to the Holy One of Israel or consult the LORD'! (Isa. 31.1). They also recall the words of the psalmist, 'Some boast of chariots, and some of horses; but we boast of the name of the LORD our God' (Ps. 20.7). There is no room for self-righteousness. According to this rule, God gives victory to His faithful people when they practise righteousness and justice (Deut. 28.7).

In our day many countries spend more on building up modern armaments than they do on practising righteousness and justice in their land.

2. The second rule is that *the purpose of war is not to gain power over the enemy, but to maintain a place of abundant life and righteousness and justice for all*. The three exemptions from military service listed in Deut. 20.5–7 show the importance of newly-built homes which have not yet been occupied, of newly-planted vineyards which have not yet come into bearing, and newly-engaged couples who have not yet married. Homes, agriculture, and family are basic values in Covenant society. If these are destroyed, wars become pointless.

Modern warfare destroys many of the values of life for both victors and defeated. In that case, has war lost its valid purpose?

3. The third rule is that *enemies should be invited to become a part of the wider Covenant fellowship of peace (shalom) as an alternative to war*. At first reading, the actual 'terms of peace'

(20.10–11) sound like terms of surrender, and will seem very harsh to us today. They probably describe a vassal relationship common in those times, by which 'forced labour' was required of a defeated 'enemy' people.

Behind the word 'peace', however, we may see the ideal of an enlarging area of *shalom*, where, in the words of Amos, there was to be a 'covenant of brotherhood' (Amos 1.9) among nations united under David's rule (see note on Deut. 20.15). According to this understanding of the 'terms of peace', possible enemies could become neighbours. The Israelites, remembering their own forced labour in Egypt (Deut. 15.15; 16.12; see note on 20.11), would apply the laws about the sabbath (5.12–15), and treatment of neighbours (1.16; 24.14–15) to these new neighbours in the Covenant society.

This ideal of former enemies living together in peace continued after the end of the Jerusalem kingship. A prophet wrote to the Judean exiles in Babylon that many peoples would come over to join the exiled Covenant people (Isa. 44.5), and would admire God's people because of His blessings (Isa. 45.14; 49.7). Such peoples would confess that they had found healing and wholeness through God's servants (Isa. 53.5). Another prophet wrote that nations and kingdoms would be attracted by God's light shining from Israel, and would enter the open gates of Jerusalem to contribute their riches and serve God's people with joy (Isa. 60.3, 10–11). There would be an end to all war (Isa. 2:4).

## SOME PRACTICAL PROBLEMS

We may see some of the practical problems of waging war by recalling that David killed two thirds of the Moabite men after his victory over them (2 Sam. 8.2). Joab, David's army commander, killed all the Edomite adult males following the defeat of Edom (1 Kings 11.16). On the basis of the usual understanding of this third rule, the historian remarked that 'the Lord gave victory to David wherever he went' (2 Sam. 8.14). Yet the same historian, reflecting on Solomon's failure to live up to the ideals of the kingship, commented that God 'raised up' adversaries against Solomon from those same peoples that David had treated so cruelly (1 Kings 11.9–11,14,23).

According to the inner meaning of the third rule, David and Solomon had not really offered 'terms of peace (*shalom*)'. We should put the Israelite kingship in the perspective given by a psalmist. God's will was that all 'human beings on earth' (Deut. 4.32 NRSV) would 'bless themselves by him' (the Israelite king), 'all nations call him blessed' (Ps. 72.17). But killing the adult males of Moab and Edom had not made these defeated peoples a part of the covenant of brotherhood. On the contrary, this action had laid seeds for a long-term hatred and enmity. These peoples were given no opportunity to observe the 'wisdom and understanding' of God's people, or learn what a difference the 'statutes and ordinances' of the Covenant would make (Deut. 4.8). The divine purpose was frustrated by the failure of the kings to live up to the Covenant ideals.

This third rule reminds us that whoever our enemies are, we all have to live together on Planet Earth. Victors should not impose terms that make future wars inevitable. They should not forget God's purpose of *shalom* for all, including our enemies.

4. The fourth and final rule is that *dangers from enemies within are more serious than dangers from the outside*. The rules differentiate between cities outside Canaan, which were potential allies (see note on Deut. 20.15) and cities in the land which could destroy Israel from within. We have already noted the problem of corruption in Israelite society. Amos began his prophecies by pointing to the sins of the neighbouring nations, but then turned his most biting attacks on Israel itself (beginning with Amos 2.6–16).

Nations find it very difficult to apply this rule today. To mobilize public opinion and energies against external enemies is easy. To purge internal evils like corruption, dishonesty, prejudice, violence and oppression is much more difficult.

## NOTES

**20.11. Forced labour:** The Israelites knew the meaning of forced labour from their bitter experience in Egypt. They had suffered from 'taskmasters' (literally, foremen of the forced labour gangs) over them (Exod. 1.11), who gave them no rest from their burdens (5.4–5), until their spirit was broken (6.9). Moses became very angry when he saw the suffering caused by forced labour (2.11). God saw their oppression (3.9) and showed His power by bringing the forced labourers to freedom (6.6–7). The tribe of Issachar in northern Canaan had been 'a slave at forced labour' (Gen. 49.14–15) long before the Exodus from Egypt.

There is no evidence of the use of forced labour in Israel before the monarchy. David put the Ammonites to forced labour (2 Sam. 12.31), and must have had other peoples in his labour gangs as well, since he and his son Solomon appointed an official in charge of forced labour (2 Sam. 20.24; 1 Kings 4.6; 5.14). In Solomon's time foreign peoples served in labour gangs at work on the royal construction projects (1 Kings 7.1–12; 9.15). When this supply of cheap labour became inadequate, Solomon made his own people serve at forced labour (1 Kings 5.13).

This use of forced labour gangs from his own people was a fatal weakness (injustice) in Solomon's administration. The northern tribes so resented it that they stoned the taskmaster to death (12.18), and made Jeroboam, the former overseer of the forced labour (11.28), king over the Northern Kingdom (12.20). The principle of 'one law for the sojourner and for the native' (Lev. 24.22; see Num. 15.29; Josh. 20.9) was a warning that oppression of foreigners would lead to oppression of God's people themselves.

**20.14. enjoy.** The Hebrew word translated 'enjoy' means literally to 'eat', hence the meaning of 'absorb'. The same word is translated as 'destroy' in 7.16.

**20.15. The cities which are very far from you.** Deut. 20.13–14 suggests a reference to neighbouring peoples who were once part of David's kingdom, but had later become traditional enemies of Israel: Philistia, Edom, Moab, Ammon, and Syria. We have seen that three of them had received territory allotted to them by God (2.5, 9–11, 19–21). All five of these peoples invaded the land of Israel during the period of the Judges. David conquered them and made them a part of his kingdom (2 Sam. 8.1–14), but they revolted from Solomon. In the seventh century BC there were calls for a recovery of these lands in a renewed Davidic kingdom which would be once again independent from Assyria. References to Moab, Edom and Philistia in Psalm 60.8–9 (and see Ps. 83.7–8), and in Zephaniah 2.4–9 probably apply to this sort of independence movement. The rules for conduct in time of war described in Deuteronomy 20 may well have been related to such a political independence programme.

## STUDY SUGGESTIONS

### REVIEW OF CONTENT

1. What is the purpose of God's 'warfare'?
2. What are four rules of war for God's people that we can discover from careful interpretation of Deuteronomy 20?

### BIBLE STUDY

3. Read 2 Kings 3.18–19, and compare the words of Elisha with Deut. 20.19–20. What is the chief difference between them? Which of the following reasons for the difference do you think is most likely, and why? (a) Elisha did not have a copy of Deuteronomy in his possession; (b) the words in Deuteronomy were written down long after those of Elisha; (c) the words of Deuteronomy represent an attempt to reform the rules for waging war so as to include the protection of nature.

CONTEXTUAL APPLICATION

4. Choose one of the four 'rules of war' and describe how it could be applied today in your country.
5. In what circumstances, if any, can victory in war be regarded as proving the 'righteousness' of the victor?
6. Should victorious nations today follow the rule given in Deut. 20.14 to take 'the women and the little ones, the cattle and everything else in the city . . . as booty for yourselves'? If not, why not?
7. What 'enemies', if any, exist within your own country which may be more dangerous than the armies of foreign nations? What can be done to overcome them?

# 21.10—25.19
# Righteousness and Justice in Personal Life (1)

*Note*: In 21.10—25.19 the themes of family and social life are woven together in an alternating pattern in a way similar to that in chs. 12—16, and 17—20. So we again group themes together rather than following the sequence of verses as they appear in the Bible text.

## OUTLINE

23.1–8: The Assembly of Righteousness and Justice: Barriers to Membership.
Chs. 21—25 (selected verses): Righteousness and Justice in Family Relationships.

## INTERPRETATION

Righteousness and justice must be practised according to responsible procedures with specific results, not only in official and public life but in family and social life as well. In interpreting the rules and procedures laid down in these chapters, we must keep in mind that they reflect the conditions of society in ancient Israel, which in many ways differed from those in some nations and cultures today. For example, Mosaic law in Deuteronomy *permitted* both slavery (Deut. 15.12) and polygamy (21.15), which are now forbidden in many countries, though still practised in others, either explicitly or implicitly.

Jesus affirmed the importance of ethical guidelines, but gave a new interpretation of these laws of Deuteronomy by pointing out the *intention* or purpose of the legislation. 'You have heard that it was said to those of ancient times . . . but I say to you . . .' (Matt. 5.33,34 NRSV). In order to find God's word for today we should distinguish between the wording or *letter* of the regulations found in Deuteronomy 21—25, and the *intention* behind them.

God's threefold purpose in the proper ordering of family and social life is that 'it may go well with you' (22.7), 'that the Lord your God may bless you in all that you undertake' (23.20); and 'that your days may be prolonged in the land which the Lord your God gives you' (25.15). In the words of Isaiah, 'the effect of righteousness will be peace, and the result of righteousness quietness and trust forever' (Isa. 32.17). Laws and regulations for administering justice are an expression of God's love for His people.

As we have seen, God also has a wider purpose. When His people practise righteousness and justice in family and social life, they will be a model for the well-being of the nations and peoples of the world (Deut. 4.6–7). Peace will spread to the whole world.

## THE ASSEMBLY OF RIGHTEOUSNESS AND JUSTICE

### THE HUB OF A WHEEL

The Narrator has carefully placed a reference to 'the assembly of the Lord' in the centre of chs. 21.10—25.19 as the hub of a wheel. This expresses well the idea that when the people gather at the centre, i.e. before God, to make decisions, the result will be that both family life and social life will run smoothly in accordance with God's will. Actions in these two areas are not matters of individual taste or preference, but are part of the common life of the Covenant community as a whole.

### AN ASSEMBLY OF ADULT MALES

In four other instances, the term 'assembly' refers to the gathering of the people at Mount Sinai/Horeb (5.22; 9.10; 10.4; 18.16). Once the term refers to 'the assembly of Israel' (31.30). Six times in 23.1–8 and nowhere else in Deuteronomy is the term 'assembly of the LORD' used in reference to the gathering of the people in the land of Canaan. There is some question as to whether this 'assembly of the LORD' was as inclusive as the worshipping community at the annual festivals (16.11). It was probably a gathering of adult males, as we may judge from the reference to a eunuch (23.1 see note) and to 'all your males' (16.16).

## BARRIERS TO MEMBERSHIP IN THE ASSEMBLY

In order to protect the special character of this gathering, four classes of people were excluded from the 'assembly of the LORD'. 1. *Physical barriers.* At that time 'blemished' people were regarded as unfit to come into the Lord's presence. Anyone who was blind, lame, or disfigured, and also the eunuchs who served as court or temple officials (see note on 23.1), were considered to be blemished (see Lev. 21.17–20; for blemished animals see Lev. 22.24–25)). 2. *Social barriers* were meant to preserve the holiness of the assembly. Those excluded were children born of irregular unions, for example the offspring of Temple or ordinary prostitutes, or of incestual relationships ('bastards'). The reason for this may have been social prejudice, rather than standards of righteousness and justice. Descendants of such people were excluded for ten generations (Deut. 23.2)! 3. *Historical barriers* were also related to the holiness of the assembly of the Lord. Moabites and Ammonites (see note on 23.3) had been enemies of Israel in the time of the Exodus from Egypt and were associated with the worship of foreign gods in the reign of Solomon (1 Kings 11.7). Again, the factor of prejudice seems to have been more important than righteousness and justice, as we see in the regulation stating that they were to be excluded forever (Deut. 23.3–6)! Ezra, quoting this law, saw intermarriage with the Moabites and Ammonites as a threat to the purity of the 'holy race' (Ezra 9.1–2). 4. *Temporary barriers.* Two peoples could be admitted to the assembly after only two generations of exclusion: the Edomites who, though enemies, had kinship ties with Israel, and the Egyptians, who had shown kindness to the family of Jacob before the oppression (Deut. 23.7–8).

## AN ASSEMBLY WITH NO BARRIERS

A later prophet called these restrictions too narrow. He said that eunuchs and people of other nations *who observed the Covenant regulations* were welcome in the assembly of the Lord, and called the Temple a 'house of prayer for all peoples' (Isa. 56.3–7). Jesus quoted Isaiah 56.7 when He cleansed the Temple (Mark 11.17). He healed the blind and lame in the Temple, making them eligible for full participation in Temple worship (Matt. 21.14). He also said that 'the tax collectors and the prostitutes are going into the kingdom of God' before the chief priests and elders of the people (Matt. 21.31 NRSV). He spoke of other sheep 'not of this fold' (John 10.16), which recalls the words about 'yet others' (Isa. 56.8). Paul agreed that qualifications for entering God's presence

should not be external. 'He is not a real Jew who is one outwardly
. . . He is a Jew who is one inwardly' (Rom. 2.28,29).

Christians today still need to understand the *intention* of these
barriers, but will wish to reinterpret them. Physical handicaps,
social status, past enmities, nationality, political views cannot be
barriers to membership in the Christian community. Holiness is a
matter of the heart and of right relationships.

## RIGHTEOUSNESS AND JUSTICE IN FAMILY RELATIONSHIPS

Laws about righteousness and justice in family relationships were
necessary because of what Jesus called 'hardness of heart' (Mark
10.5), and what Deuteronomy calls the 'stubbornness . . . wickedness or . . . sin' of God's people (Deut. 9.27). These laws were
related to the *fifth* commandment concerning parents and children,
and the *seventh* commandment about adultery. They are concerned
with (a) women captives who are taken as wives (21.10–14), (b) the
rights of children of different wives (21.15–17), (c) rebellious
children (21.18–21), (d) marital unfaithfulness (22.22–24), (e) rape
(22.25–29), (f) incest (22.30), (g) prostitution (23.17–18), (h)
divorce and remarriage (24.1–4), guilt of parents for sins of their
children, or of children for sins of their parents (24.16), and
childless widows (25.5–10).

'Hardness of heart' still causes problems where there is a lack of
righteousness and justice in family relationships today. What can
we learn from these laws in Deuteronomy?

### FAMILY STABILITY

The intention of the laws was *to uphold the value of the family* as the
basic social structure in Israelite society. For example, the unfaithfulness of a wife was such a serious threat to the stability of the
family that the law prescribed the death penalty for her and her
lover (22.22–24). The law required a childless widow to bear a son
by her brother-in-law in order to preserve her husband's name and
property (25.5–6). Temple prostitution (23.17–18, see note) was
forbidden for the sons and daughters of Israelite parents because it
would corrupt their families.

Today there are other ethical problems that endanger family
stability, such as prostitution as a means of escaping poverty, single
parent families, family violence, destructive marriages, the effects
of AIDS on family life.

### A PATRIARCHAL SOCIETY

The family system in ancient Israel was *conditioned by the culture of
the time*. It was a patriarchal systems and the laws of Deuteronomy
reflect and even reinforce some aspects of this patriarchal structure

The intention was to uphold the value of the family as the basic social structure, and encourage a loving relationship between husband and wife, and between loving parents and their children, like that of this young Christian family in East Africa. In spite of the changes in practice which have occurred, happy family relationships remain the intention of marriage laws in most countries of the world.

of society. The husband and father was considered as the owner of his wife, with complete authority over her and her children (see note on 21.13).

Women appear in these laws as passive rather than active. Men take, marry, let go, send out, seize, lie with, humiliate, violate, and even stone women to death (21.11,14; 22.24,25,28,29; 24.1,3).

Men had rights and privileges not allowed to women. For example, a husband could divorce his wife if she didn't please him (24.1), but she had no such right. He could accuse her of 'shameful conduct' (22.14), but she had no such right. Chastity was not considered necessary for men, but if a man raped a virgin, he had to marry her and live with her for the rest of his life, regardless of her feelings (22.28–29). Parental authority over their children was absolute, even to enforcing the death penalty. This authority was upheld by the court (21.18–21).

## THE RIGHTS OF WOMEN

In spite of the harshness of some of the family laws, however, we can detect in some of them *an attempt to humanize the system*, especially in the matter of rights for women.

*A female prisoner of war* taken by an Israelite soldier (21.10) must be treated as his wife, not a slave (21.10–11). The law required him to respect her dignity by allowing her a month to grieve for her separation from her parents, and to prepare herself for her new status by getting a new set of clothes in place of her captive's garb, changing her hair style, and manicuring her nails (vv. 12–13). However, in case she did not please him, he could send her away according to custom (see 24.1), but he could not return her to slave status liable for sale, which would be the fate of prisoners of war. He had to give her the status of a free and independent woman, able to go wherever she wanted, and to remarry if she chose (see 24.2). The reason was that she had suffered injustice from him because he had 'forced her to have intercourse' with him against her will (21.14 TEV).

*A wife falsely accused of pre-marital unchastity* had the right to a trial before the elders of the city, with her father and mother as co-defendants. When her innocence was demonstrated, the husband who slandered her was flogged and made to pay a fine to her father. In order to protect her name he was forbidden to divorce her (22.13–19).

The other side of this case was that if the (male) elders of the city determined that a woman was not a virgin before marriage because of lack of evidence of blood stains on the wedding sheet, she would be stoned to death as a whore (22.21). The woman could not defend herself. Nothing is ever said about the chastity of the husband before or after marriage. From a New Testament perspective, this law denies righteousness and justice to women. Jesus called it into question when He challenged any male who was without sin to cast the first stone at the woman caught in the act of adultery (John 8.7).

*An engaged woman who was victim of a rape* in the open country where her cries for help could not be heard was protected by the law, while her attacker suffered the death penalty (Deut. 22.25–27). She was free to marry her fiancé. We may wonder whether the fiancé would accept her under those conditions, and whether righteousness and justice would not require more assistance to the rape victim.

*A virgin victim of rape* would receive protection of the law by marriage to her attacker who then had no right to divorce her (22.28–29). In that society, marriage was preferable to desertion and a life of disgrace (see 2 Sam. 13.1–20).

*A wife divorced by her husband* had the right to a 'bill of divorce' (24.1), which was a legal document stating that 'she is not my wife, and I am not her husband' (see Hos. 2.2). This protected her from any claim he might have on her, so that she was free to marry again (Deut. 24.2).

*A childless widow* whose brother-in-law refused to serve as surrogate husband had the right to a public hearing at the city court (the gate), so that she would be cleared of guilt and be free to marry again (25.5–10).

From these examples we can understand the important function of laws in enlarging the rights of women to righteousness and justice.

## LOVING RELATIONSHIPS

As we study these laws, we should remember *the positive picture of happy family life* which we find in Deuteronomy. A newly married man was allowed a full year's exemption from military service or other responsibilities that would take him away from his home, so that he might 'be happy with his wife' (24.5). This expresses the companionship and bonding between husband and wife as 'one flesh' which was God's intention when he 'created human beings on the earth' (4.32 NRSV; Gen. 2.24), as affirmed by Jesus (Mark 10.6–8). We find a similar view of the relationship between marriage partners in the advice of the wise: 'Rejoice in the wife of your youth, a lovely deer, a graceful doe . . . may you be intoxicated always by her love' (Prov. 5.18–19 NRSV).

In addition to this picture of a loving relationship between husband and wife, we have already seen the picture of loving parents teaching their children the ways of the Lord (Deut. 4.9–10; 6.7; 31.13; see pp. 26, 54–55).

The following four points will be of help to us as we think about ethical guidelines related to family life today.

1. We should focus on the *intention* of biblical legislation rather than the 'letter'. This will help us to see how we should apply laws for our own time.

2. We should look at the *cultural background* of these biblical laws as well as the background of the laws and customs of our own country. In recent years the way people live has changed enormously in many countries, and we need to study these changes as well as older customs in the light of God's will for men, women and children. We should consider what it is that makes some people's family life unstable and even violent, devalues women and children, or turns sex into a profit-making business.

3. We should follow the example of ancient Israel by *supporting laws or influencing attitudes that will 'humanize' the way families live and work*, so as to protect the weak from oppression by the strong, and encourage honest, fair, loving and life-giving family relationships. We should listen to the complaints of families who are victimized or oppressed by present day conditions, and look for ways of promoting righteousness and justice for them.

4. Following the example of the ancient Israelites (Deut. 24.5), families should *allow time for the growth of family ties* between husband and wife, parents and children. In this way families can be a part of God's 'alternative society' in the secular world as examples of His new creation. In these centres of righteousness and justice, love, and right relationships, everyone will be valued and enjoyed, and find encouragement to become fully human persons.

## NOTES

**21.13. Be her husband:** The Hebrew term means literally to 'be her master', from the root 'to rule over'. To 'marry' means literally for the man to 'lord it over' (24.1). To be 'wife of another man' (22.22) means literally to be 'lorded over by another lord'). The noun form of this word means 'husband' (baal, 24.4). Elsewhere in the Old Testament 'baal' is the name of a Canaanite god, as in 1 Kings 18.26.

**21.18. A stubborn and rebellious son:** It is important to see this shocking example of family discord and iron discipline in the context of the rest of Deuteronomy. In this passage (21. 18–21) we can see the family as a sort of mirror for all Israel. The son who rebels against his father and mother in spite of their 'discipline' (21.18 NRSV), mirrors Israel the son (1.31) who is rebellious against God (9.7,23,24) in spite of God's 'discipline' (8.5). As the parents and the elders condemn the son to death (21.21), so God will bring the full weight of the covenantal punishment on the rebellious Israelites (28.15–19). When this 'evil' is 'purged' from one family, all Israel is cleansed.

Most present-day readers will not wish to resolve family conflicts by means of beatings or sentence to death. People now understand that parents may be at fault as well as children.

**22.18. A glutton and a drunkard:** This expression comes from 'wisdom' language (see Prov. 23.21; 28.7). Jesus was accused of this same sort of behaviour in Matt. 11.19.

**22.5. A woman . . . a man:** In a traditional society, as in many areas today, clothing or other articles worn by men were different from those worn by women. Society gave fixed roles to each sex. A change of clothing would mean a change of role, a custom known as 'transvestism', in which men masquerade as women and vice versa. The practices behind this law may have been related to Canaanite rites where worshippers changed clothing to identify with a male or female divinity. This would explain the use of the term 'abomination' for this practice. Scholars do not agree as to whether or not this is a reference to homosexuality (see Lev. 18.22). Today some men seeking homosexual partners disguise themselves by putting on women's clothing and using cosmetics.

**22.22. Lying with the wife of another man:** Sexual relationships between a man (married or not) and a married or engaged woman were common in ancient Israel, as we can see from warnings given to young men (Prov. 2.16–17; 5.3; 6.24; 7.18–20), and from the example of David (2 Sam. 11.2–5).

**23.1. Testicles . . . crushed:** This is a reference to eunuchs who served in high positions in Samaria under Jezebel and in Jerusalem under Jehoiakim, Zedekiah and the Babylonian court and temple (2 Kings 9.32; Jer. 38.7; 41.16; Dan, 1,3). The Hebrew word is translated as 'official' or 'officer' in references to Ahab's court in Samaria and the Jerusalem court (1 Kings 22.9; 2 Kings 24.15; 25.19).

**23.3. No Ammonite or Moabite:** Although God gave these two peoples lands of their own (Deut. 2.9,19), they tried to block the passage of the Israelites on their way to the Promised Land. Moab's alleged refusal of food and water (23.4) is contrary to the statement in 2.28–29 that the Moabites did make food and water available. This law in Deuteronomy was the basis for separation of the Israelites in the restored community from 'all those of foreign descent' (see Neh. 13.1–3).

We find different evaluations of Moabites and Ammonites elsewhere in the Old Testament. Ruth, a Moabite woman, was David's ancestor (Ruth 4.17). 'Naamah the Ammonite', one of Solomon's wives, was mother of King Rehoboam (1 Kings 14.21

NRSV). Later writers spoke of God's sympathy for Moab's sufferings (Isa. 15.5; 16.11; Jer. 48.31–32) and His concern for the Ammonites (49.6). One writer urged Israel to accept refugees from Moab (Isa. 16.4).

**23.17–18. Cult prostitute . . . hire of a harlot . . . wages of a dog:** Ordinary prostitution was tolerated, though discouraged for men (see Prov. 5.3; 6.26; 7.10; see Gen. 38.15; Josh. 2.1). However, the law was firmly opposed to the Canaanite custom of Temple prostitution (Deut. 23.17–18), by which either men or women were Temple devotees to serve worshippers in a sexual way (1 Kings 14.23–24; 2 Kings 23.7; see Hos. 4.13–14).

**24.4. After she has been defiled:** This does not mean that her second marriage 'defiled' her. It meant that as far as her first husband was concerned, he was banned from further relations with her. If her second husband should divorce her or die (v.3), her first husband was not free to take her again as his wife (v.4). The reason was that the union ('one flesh') created by her first marriage had been completely broken by his action in divorcing her. Her marriage to another man had created a second union. Return to the first union would make a mockery of marriage, and bring 'guilt upon the land which the Lord your God gives you for an inheritance' (24.4).

## STUDY SUGGESTIONS

### REVIEW OF CONTENT

1. What are three beneficial results of the practice of righteousness and justice in family life?
2. (a) What evidence suggests that the 'assembly of the Lord' was composed of adult males?
   (b) What four groups were excluded from the assembly of the Lord?
3. (a) What was the main intention of the laws related to family life?
   (b) What was the difference between the roles of men and women in these laws?
4. What were the rights of victims of rape according to these laws?
5. For what reason was a newly married man exempt from military service for a year?
6. What was the difference between an ordinary prostitute and a Temple prostitute?

### BIBLE STUDY

7. Read Deut. 24.1–4, Matt. 5.31–32, Mark 10.2–12, Luke 16.18.
   (a) What difference was there between the *intention* of the law

of divorce as interpreted by Jesus and the *letter* of this law in Deut. 24.1? (b) Does Jesus rule out 'hardness of heart' as a sufficient reason for divorce?

8. Read Eph. 5.21–32. (a) What are the similarities and differences between Paul's advice given there to wives and to husbands? (b) What is the *intention* of this advice for the relationship between husband and wife? What are the main differences between Paul's teaching and the rules laid down in Deut. 22.13–30?

9. Read Eph. 6.1–4. What are the duties of (a) children and (b) parents in a family situation? What additional duties of parents were given in Deut. 4.10, 6.7 and Prov. 4.1–5? Now read Deut. 21.18–21, and suggest reasons which a son might give for his rebellion against his parents.

## CONTEXTUAL APPLICATION

10. Which, if any, of the following sorts of people would your Church probably bar from membership? For what reasons? Do you think it would be right to do so? What would Jesus's attitude be? (a) A person who has been cured of leprosy, (b) a person with AIDS, (c) a homosexual (either man or woman), (d) a prostitute, (e) a dishonest money lender. What other sorts of people, if any, would *you* bar from Church membership and why?

11. Some people say that Paul's teaching in Eph. 5.23 means that God intends all women to be subordinate to their husbands. Others say that it merely reflects the status of women in the Roman Empire at that time. What is your opinion and why? Is Paul's teaching or the teaching in Deut. 22 closest to the general status of women in your country today?

12. Many Christian denominations allow for divorce and remarriage. Find out what reasons they give for doing so. Do you agree with them? Give reasons.

13. What patterns of family life are chiefly found in your country? Which of them are (a) traditional (b) modern, (c) becoming more widespread, (d) becoming out of date? Which do you think is most suitable for your country and why?

14. Imagine that a woman member of your Church went to another country to earn money to help her parents, but found the 'work' offered there was prostitution. If she accepted the work but later returned and wished to renew her Church membership, do you think she should be allowed to do so? What, if anything, would you as a fellow Christian do to help her?

15. In what chief ways can Christian families become centres of 'God's alternative society'?

# 21.10—25.19
# Righteousness and Justice in Personal Life (2)

## OUTLINE

Chs. 21.10—25.16 (selected verses): Social Relationships.
Chs. 21.10—25.16 (selected verses): Ecological Relationships.
25.17–19: The Need for Constant Vigilance.

## INTERPRETATION

### SOCIAL RELATIONSHIPS

The laws laid down in these chapters deal with much the same relationships as those in Deut. 8.11–20 and ch.15. This set of laws, mostly related to the *eighth* commandment against stealing, were meant to overcome the hardness of heart of the strong toward the weak (see 15.7). The laws placed limits on selfishness so as to protect the poor from losing the justice due to them (24.17). Observance of these laws would also keep powerful people from 'sin' (24.14–15), and protect their homes from 'guilt of blood' (22.8). Keeping these laws would open the whole community to the gift of 'righteousness' from a just and compassionate God (24.13).

### LAWS FOR NEIGHBOURS

*The obligation to help a neighbour in trouble* (22.1–4). The case described is that of a neighbour whose animal goes astray. Contrary to popular wisdom which says 'finders keepers, losers weepers', Covenant law instructs the finder to return the animal to its owner even if he lives at some distance, or is not an acquaintance of the owner (22.2). The law is then extended to refer to 'anything else that your neighbour loses and you find' (22.3 NRSV), and to any situation where a neighbour needs help 22.4). Withholding help would be like stealing from neighbours. This law is reflected in Jesus's parable of the Good Samaritan (Luke 10.29–37).

*The obligation to give fair treatment to employees* (24.14–15). The case is that of an employer who selfishly holds back the wages of a poor and needy day labourer, regardless of whether the labourer is an Israelite or a guest worker from another land. To keep the wages until a later day would be like stealing 'their livelihood' (v.15 NRSV). Fair wages promptly paid are part of the Covenant ethic. Today we would call this a 'labour-relations' law. We would want to ask about the relationship of this law to unemployment which deprives people of the right to work.

*The obligation to be honest in business* (25.13–16; see Amos 8.5, Micah 6.11). The case is that of a merchant who has two sorts of weights and measures for pricing his goods. Cheating customers with false weights and measures is like stealing from them (see pp. 41–42 for other forms of dishonesty in business). This law reminds us that honesty and service are important in maintaining good relationships between buyers and sellers, who should not only look for profit. This is reflected in modern 'fair-trading' laws.

*The obligation to protect others from accidental injury or death* (22.8). A person who is careless about safety precautions when building a new house, perhaps in order to save money, will be guilty of causing the death or injury of anyone who falls from his roof garden. Today we would call this a 'liability' law.

*The obligation to respect the dignity of a neighbour who is sentenced to punishment* (25.1–3). The officials responsible for carrying out a court-ordered sentence of punishment must not demean fellow human beings by excessive punishment. The guilty too are made in God's image (see p. 55). This law would apply to torture or other kinds of inhuman or degrading practices in the prisons of today in many countries.

*The obligation to respect the freedom of a neighbour* (24.7). Kidnapping someone to enslave or sell them into slavery violates the eighth commandment so seriously that it calls for the death penalty for the kidnapper. A common form of this crime today is the kidnapping of children for forced labour in factories or use in the sex or pornographic business. Young women may be lured to big cities with promises of good work, only to be enslaved in prostitution.

*The obligation to give freedom and dignity to escaped slaves* (23.15–16). This law probably referred originally to foreign slaves escaped from foreign masters. Israelites who had themselves escaped from slavery must welcome escapees and help them to find a place to live in their towns without fear of oppression. Today we would apply this law to refugees from oppression.

## LAWS FOR LENDERS

*The obligation to lend money without interest* (23.19–20). Poor borrowers are often exploited by rich lenders. This law implies that giving a loan should not be seen as an opportunity to profit from the suffering of other people, but a way of helping them in their time of great need. In the ancient world as in many lands today money-lenders charged very high rates of interest, often increasing monthly. Failure to repay a loan could result in creditors taking the children of debtors as slaves (2 Kings 4.1; see Amos 2.6), or confiscating their land (Isa. 5.8; Micah 2.2,9). An interest-free loan

Honesty and service are important in maintaining good relationships between buyers and sellers. An Afghan customer buying vegetables in the market watches carefully as they are weighed out for him. Cheating customers with false weights and measures—or wrongly-set computers—is the same as stealing from them.

could make the difference between slavery and freedom. Today credit unions can help borrowers to get loans from a central fund created by the borrowers themselves.

*The obligation to show compassion in taking pledges.* In ancient Israel borrowers had to hand over a piece of movable property (a pledge) to the lender as security. In a covenant society, lenders should not take as pledge any articles necessary for the livelihood of the debtor, such as the mill on which the daily meal was ground (24.6), or a poor widow's only garment (24.17). They should return a poor person's cloak at nightfall so that he might 'sleep in his cloak and bless you' (24.13). The lender should respect the dignity of the borrower by waiting outside the house until he brings out the pledge (24.10–11). This kind of covenantal relationship between lender and borrower would result in a more stable society, lessening the gap between the rich and poor. Most countries today have laws regulating the loans given by banks, building-societies and pawnshops.

## LAWS ABOUT SHARING WITH THE POOR

*Travellers' rights.* In a rural society, the owners of an orchard or field should allow passing travellers to pick fruit or grain to satisfy their hunger (23.24–25). On the other hand, the travellers must not take advantage of the owner by bringing baskets or other means of carrying off the produce for themselves.

*Gleaners' rights.* Remembering the time when they themselves were the underclass of Egyptian society, owners of orchards and fields must share part of their harvest with foreigners, orphans and widows who were the most vulnerable members of the Covenant society (24.19–22). Only then could all members of the Covenant society rejoice before the Lord (16.11,14). These laws remind us that sharing of material goods is important to the meaning of life.

### RIGHTEOUSNESS AND JUSTICE IN ECOLOGICAL RELATIONSHIPS

The Covenant society is one in which people respect the integrity of creation as expressed in the mutual relationship between human society and 'the good land' (6.10–11; see p. 52). We have already noted a reference to the care of fruit trees as part of the natural environment (20.19–20). In this section of Deuteronomy there are additional laws dealing with ecology.

*The obligation to respect the distinction between the use and the conservation of natural resources* (22.6–7). Humans may take young birds for food, but the mother bird must be protected so that there may be future flocks of birds. An ox treading the unhusked grain has its rights to food (25.4), as well as to the Sabbath rest

(5.14). Many people today look on nature, including non-human life, as something to be controlled, dominated, and exploited for more and more consumption and profit. A Covenant society will limit consumption in order to conserve and care for the natural environment as stewards for the Creator God.

*The obligation to keep the land and society free from pollution.* Careless human acts can damage the natural environment. In ancient Israel sanitation for armies on the march (as well as in towns and villages) was a specific concern of God, because God 'walks in the midst of your camp'. Anything dirty or 'indecent' would be offensive to Him, and might spread disease from one area to another (Deut. 23.9–14). Dead bodies should be disposed of properly (21.22–23). Public health was important. People with diseases should follow prescribed procedures (24.8–9), like the quarantine laws laid down by health authorities in many countries today.

Today there are many human activities which not only endanger the integrity of creation but threaten its eventual destruction. These include the effects of industrial pollution, acid rain, deforestation, drift-net fishing, emissions of nuclear radiation and of other poisonous substances and gases into the atmosphere, waterways or oceans, destruction of animal habitats and wetlands. Such pollution is partly the result of our worshipping the false gods of technology, material goods and military power. Purging these sorts of evil from our world is a task that cannot wait for future generations.

In addition to these destructive practices which contaminate the good earth, wrong relations between humans also endanger the health or holiness of the land. We find in this section specific examples of moral pollution which must be purged from society: the breakdown of relations between parents and children (21.18–21), sexual immorality (22.21–22), and kidnapping (24.7). Hosea said that violations of the Commandments would make the land 'mourn' (see Hos. 4.1–3).

## THE NEED FOR CONSTANT VIGILANCE

The surprising conclusion to this section is a warning not to forget the Amalekites (25.17–19; see note). At the time of the Exodus, Moses concluded the narrative of Israel's victory with these words: 'The LORD will have war with Amalek from generation to generation' (Exod. 17.16). The comment in Deuteronomy 25.18 that the Amalekites 'did not fear God' identifies them as perennial enemies of righteousness and justice. God will always oppose such enemies (see p. 65 on God's enemies). In the time of the Narrator when there were no surviving Amalekites, the double command to 'blot out the remembrance of Amalek' and yet not to forget them

(Deut. 25.19) was perhaps meant as a warning that in every generation enemies *like* the Amalekites would rise to turn justice into bloodshed and righteousness into cries from the oppressed (see Isa. 5.7).

## NOTES

**22.8. A parapet for your roof:** The flat roof of a house in Palestine is commonly used to entertain guests. A railing (parapet) around the edges would protect them from falling.

**22.9–11. As second kind of seed . . . plow with an ox and a donkey . . . wear clothes made of wool and linen'** (NRSV). We do not know the original reason for these laws. They represent attitudes at that time concerning what was proper according to the created order.

**23.19. Lend upon interest:** The Hebrew word translated 'interest' means literally 'bite'. This was imposed in advance. For example, if the loan was for £100 or $100, the lender would take out 20% or 30% in advance. The borrower would receive 80% or 75% but had to repay the full 100%. The prophets condemned this sort of practice (Ezek. 18.8, 17). This law applied only to members of the Covenant society. In the other nearby lands high interest rates were common. Thus, loans to 'foreigners' as distinct from resident aliens or sojourners, would follow the generally accepted practice.

**25.3. Forty stripes:** Jewish law in the Mishnah limited the maximum number of lashes to 39 so that a mistake in counting might not lead to excessive punishment.

**25.4. Muzzle an ox:** See 1 Cor. 9.8–11 for Paul's interpretation of this law. See also 1 Tim. 5.17–18.

**25.17. What Amalek did to you:**   The Amalekites were enemies of Israel at the time of the Exodus, the period of the Judges, and during the reigns of Saul and David (Exod. 17.8–16; Num. 14.43–45; Judges 3.13; 6.3,33; 7.12; 1 Sam 15.1–33; 2 Sam. 8.12). No Amalekites are mentioned in the Old Testament as existing after David's reign. Haman, the chief enemy of the Jews in the story of Esther, is called the 'Agagite' (Esth. 3.1), linking him to Agag, the Amalekite king spared by Saul but killed by Samuel (1 Sam. 15.32–33).

## STUDY SUGGESTIONS

REVIEW OF CONTENT

1. What were *seven* laws for neighbours?
2. What were *three* laws for lenders?
3. What were *two* laws about sharing with the poor?

4. What were *two* laws regarding justice in ecological relationships?
5. Why was sanitation specially necessary in a military camp?

BIBLE STUDY

6. Read Matt. 10.5–11, Luke 10.1–9 and 1 Cor. 9.3–11. In what way does each passage relate to Deut. 25.4? What difference, if any, do you see between the teaching of Jesus and that of Paul in these passages?
7. Read Exod. 17.8–16 and 1 Sam. 15.1–33. What sort of forces in the world today do the Amalekites symbolize?

CONTEXTUAL APPLICATION

8. On the basis of Deuteronomy 22.1–4 suggest some present-day situations in which the teaching of these verses would apply, and say what you would do in each case.
9. Imagine you are an employer with ten employees. Your business is not doing well and you cannot afford to pay adequate wages. What course of action would you take in the light of Deut. 24.14–15?
10. Read Deut. 22.8. What laws, if any, exist in your country to protect people who have been injured because of inadequate safety precautions (a) by their employer, (b) by a government agency, (c) by a private individual? In what way, if any, do you think those laws should be improved?
11. Read Deuteronomy 25.1–3, with special attention to the word 'degraded'. For what offences are people in your country sent to prison? Are the conditions there likely to degrade the prisoners, or affirm their dignity? In what ways, if any, can the Churches help to affirm the dignity of prisoners?
12. Read Deuteronomy 23.19–20. Who are the money-lenders in your area, and do they charge fair rates of interest? What, if anything, should your Church do to help break the power of dishonest money-lenders, and to free people from the burden of permanent debt?

# 26.1–19
## Liturgies For Covenant Renewal

### OUTLINE

26.3, 16–18: This Day.
26.1–11: A Liturgy for First Fruits.
26.12–15: A Liturgy for the Tithe.
26.16–19: A Liturgical Summary of the Meaning of the Covenant.

### INTERPRETATION

In chs. 12—25 the Narrator has shown Moses applying the Primary Covenant to worship and its results in public, family and social life in the Promised Land. In ch. 26 Moses returns to the subject of worship and gives the people two liturgies which will prepare them for Covenant renewal. Three phrases show the close relationship between ch. 26 and chs. 12—16. The first two are related to the liturgy for First Fruits: (1) 'the place which the LORD your God will choose to make his name to dwell there' (26.2; see 12.5; 16.2); (2) 'You shall rejoice' (26.11; see 12.7; 16.11). The third is related to the liturgy for the Tithe: for giving help to 'the Levite, the sojourner, the fatherless, and the widow' (26.12,13; see 14.29; 16.11,14).

These liturgies have important lessons for new beginnings — whether in the Promised Land after Moses's death, in Judah at the time of Josiah's reform, in the land after the people's return from the Exile, or today wherever new beginnings are made.

### THIS DAY

In Deuteronomy past, present and future generations merge with each other (see Special Note A). Each generation has its 'today'. Each 'today' of offering first fruits (Deut. 26.2) would recall 'the day of the assembly' (10.4; 18.16), when 'you' (meaning each new generation of readers) 'stood before the LORD your God at Horeb' (Deut. 4.10). Each 'today' when they received the teaching of the priests would also recall past 'todays' of instruction (4.40; 5.1 NRSV) reflection (11.2), and decision for life or death (11.26 NRSV). Each 'today' of Covenant renewal (26.17–19 NRSV) would recall the memory of 'the most important day' of Covenant-making at Mount Sinai/Horeb.

The 'today' of Covenant-making at Sinai/Horeb and the 'today' of Covenant renewal and instruction at Moab would again become 'today' in the land of promise. The effect of recalling the 'days of old' (32.7) in the 'today' of worship, would be long life for the living and future generations in the land 'as long as the heavens are above the earth' (11.21).

Future generations would also have their 'today', as we can see from the reference to Covenant renewal 'not only with you who stand here with us today . . . but also with those who are not here with us today' (29.14–15 NRSV). For readers of Deuteronomy in the time of King Josiah, and in each new generation from then to the present day, the word 'today' would have fresh meaning. So a psalmist appealed: 'O that today you would listen to his voice' (Ps. 95.7 NRSV), to which the author of Hebrews, after quoting this verse (Heb. 3.7), added 'as long as it is called "today" ' (Heb. 3.15).

## A LITURGY FOR FIRST FRUITS, 26.1–11

### GRATITUDE FOR PLACE AND SPACE, 26.2–3

The liturgy begins with the offering of 'some of the first of all the fruit of the ground which you harvest from your land'. The words to be spoken by the worshippers give this liturgy its importance: 'Today . . . I have come into the land that the LORD swore to our ancestors to give us' (26.3 NRSV). The purpose of this statement is not to give God information, as people of other nations might inform a village guardian spirit about the departure or arrival of a member of the community. The liturgical words express joy and gratitude that God's promise made centuries ago has now come true: the promise to give His people an area of their own in which to make a natural, political, social, economic and family living place and space. We might compare this to the joy of a homeless person who has received the gift of a house and land for home and family after having lived in a cardboard shelter in the slums of a big city.

### THREE WORDS FOR PLACE AND SPACE

Three words refer to God's gift of place and space: 'land', 'ground' and 'inheritance'.

1. *Land* (Hebrew *erets*) means 'a place for security with justice, space for freedom and opportunity' (see p. 8). Three uses of the verb 'give' help us to understand God's gift.

(a) It is *a planned gift*. God's promise 'to give' a specific place for security and space for freedom reveals His plan of love for His people (26.3).

(b) It is a gift which *has already been given*. God has 'given' this particular land to His people as place and space for responsible living.

(c) It *continues to be given*. God is engaged in a long and

Each offering of first fruits would recall the day of covenant-making. *Shavuot*, the 'Festival of First Fruits', celebrated (*above*) with joy and gratitude by schoolchildren in Israel, also commemorates God's giving of the *Torah* to Moses. Before the Liturgy for the Tithe, worshippers were to hand over ten per cent of their harvest, like these members of an Indian Christian congregation, bringing bowls of grain for the priest to give to the poor.

complicated process of 'giving' an environment or homeland to His stubborn and rebellious people (26.1,2). The process began with the call of Abraham, and continued with liberation from slavery, the wilderness period, and the Covenant at Sinai/Horeb. It comes to a climax with the people's entry into the land, but will continue beyond that. Even though the people become landless because of disobedience, God is always ready to give the land to them again when they return to Him.

2. Part of the 'land' is the *ground* (Hebrew *adamah*, 26.2) or 'soil' (30.9 NRSV). With the gift comes the task of cultivating and harvesting crops for food to sustain life. Fertile soil for cultivation is God's gift to humans in all habitable parts of the earth. The soil produces vegetation such as trees, grass, plants, 'wheat and barley . . . vines and fig trees and pomegranates . . . olive trees and honey' for food, wine, oil and bread (Deut. 8.7–8; see 26.9; Gen. 1.11–12; 2.9; Ps. 104.14–15). God gives His blessing to all humanity and all living beings by renewing 'the face of the ground' (Ps. 104.30).

The particular piece of ground which God gives to the Israelites is very fertile, flowing 'with milk and honey' (Deut. 26.9; 31.20), and will produce all the crops and fruit they need.

3. Place and space are an *inheritance* (26.1) lent by the owner (God) to a tenant or steward (Israel) to manage ('possess') for Him. According to Deuteronomy 32.8 (RSV) Yahweh gave an 'inheritance' to each of the nations to manage for Him. For example, Esau (Edom), Moab and Ammon each received its own inheritance (2.5,9,19). Israel's inheritance was a special example of His gracious concern for 'all nations that he has made' (Deut. 26.19; see 'The Nations, part of God's creation' pp. 59–60).

In the New Testament, the 'special' inheritance of Christians, besides the living place and space God gives them, is a spiritual one (Col. 1.12), and refers to a future salvation reserved in heaven (1 Peter 1.4). However, Deuteronomy reminds Christians of the importance of living space and place for all people here on earth.

## GRATITUDE FOR GOD'S 'AMAZING GRACE' 26.4–9

The second part of the liturgy of first fruits is an affirmation of faith. Some people called it Israel's earliest creed. Before bowing down to offer the first fruits (v. 10), or rejoicing in the bounty of the land (v.11), the worshippers recall God's love and power in bringing His rebellious people to a place of their own. The liturgical words give a series of 'once . . . but now' contrasts, similar to the words of the hymn *Amazing Grace*: 'I once was lost but now am found'.

Once we were homeless and landless like Jacob, but now we live in a beautiful land of our own (26.5).

Once we were aliens in a strange land but now we live in a place of our own and can welcome strangers into our community (26.5,11).

Once we were few in number (see 7.7), but now we are 'a great nation, mighty and populous' (26.5 NRSV; see 4.7; 7.7).

Once we were slaves but now we are free (26.6).

Once we were helpless but when we cried to the Lord, He 'heard our voice . . . saw our affliction . . . brought us out . . . with a terrifying display of power . . . brought us into this place and gave us this land' (26.7–9 NRSV).

The words 'once . . . but now' in this statement of faith give hope to future generations. God who saw the landless, oppressed people and gave them land of their own, would gather the landless exiles in Babylon and bring them back to their own land again (30.1–5). Not only that, but God cares about all who have had to leave their land and wander as refugees among the nations. He cares about all landless people, and wills to give them a land of their own. Amos said that God brought the Philistines from Crete ('Caphtor' see Jer. 47.4 and Deut. 2.23), and the Syrians from Mesopotamia ('Kir') to Damascus. A psalmist expressed this well: 'God gives the desolate a home to dwell in; he leads out the prisoners to prosperity' (Ps. 68.6).

A once landless people, who have been given place and space to live in, should work with God to help displaced people find a place for security and space for freedom.

## A LITURGY FOR THE TITHE

### GIFT MUST PRECEDE LITURGY, 26.12

The purpose of this liturgy is to guard against forgetting the poor. Before reporting to the priest on the tithe, the worshippers must actually hand over ten per cent of their harvest for the use of the poor. From 14.28 we see that there was some kind of food bank in which to deposit the tithe, so that it would be available to the poor over an extended period of time, with no damage to their dignity. Today various organizations like Churches or self-help groups provide 'rice banks', 'food pantries', and 'cattle banks' to help the poor or guard against famine.

### 'I HAVE REMOVED . . . GIVEN', 26.13

In the first words of the liturgy the worshippers affirm that they have actually set aside one tenth of the grain, wine and oil produced in each third year. They must consider it as 'sacred', that is, set aside for Yahweh. Some Christians will set aside a tenth of their income each month or each year and keep it for contributions to the Church or for helping others.

## 'I HAVE NOT EATEN . . . OR OFFERED ANY OF IT TO THE DEAD', 26.14

The second affirmation is that the worshippers have not used this produce for themselves or offered any part of it in a forbidden religious ceremony, such as contacting the dead (26.14; see 14.1; 18.10–11; Isa. 8.19; 65.3–4). To use the tithe in such ways would be like 'robbing' God (see Mal. 3.8).

The liturgy for tithes does not emphasize the annual feast together as in 14.22–26, but rather the triennial gathering of the tithe offerings for the poor in the towns of Israel (26.12). This focus on our obligation to help the poor has been a frequently repeated theme in Deuteronomy. In this final and most important reference, caring for the poor is a summary of the 'entire commandment' (26.13 NRSV; see 6.1,25). Paul, quoting Leviticus 19.18, expressed the same idea: 'For the whole law is summed up in a single commandment, "You shall love your neighbour as yourself" ' (Gal. 5.14).

## PRAYER FOR BLESSING, 26.15

The Narrator's arrangement shows that only *after* the people have fulfilled their obligation to the poor, and made the required report to Yahweh, will they have the privilege of asking for God's continued blessing of fertility of the soil and cattle, and prosperity of the nation. Jesus taught that we must be reconciled with our neighbour before we approach God in worship (Matt. 5.23–24).

## A LITURGICAL SUMMARY OF THE MEANING OF THE COVENANT

The position of this summary, following the two liturgies of thanksgiving for God's gifts of the land and nationhood, and a declaration of care for the poor, suggests that it was intended to be part of a liturgy of preparation before entering the Covenant. Although the exact translation of 26.17–18 is difficult, the meaning is quite clear: entering the covenant means acceptance of mutual obligations, both by the people and by Yahweh.

*God's people agree*: (1) to accept Yahweh as their God and be loyal to Him (26.17); (2) to be 'a society where God rules' by walking in Yahweh's ways (26.17), that is by conducting their personal lives and their society according to His will, and by observing His statutes and ordinances, with all their heart and soul (26.16,17,18); (3) to live as an example and witness to other nations, so that the nations will praise Him, know His name, and give Him glory (26.19).

*Yahweh agrees*: (1) to accept the Israelites as His 'treasured people' (26.18; see 7.6; 14.2 all NRSV); and (2) to bless His people so that other nations will know about Him (26.19).

## NOTES

**26.15. Look down from your holy habitation, from heaven (NRSV):** In the ancient world people thought of God as living above the sky, which they believed to be a heavenly dome enclosing the earth. Today astronomers and physicists have learnt about outer space, which makes it difficult to imagine a particular location for God's dwelling. But behind these words we can see two important truths about God. (1) God is outside the process of human history, and is able to judge and to save when our human efforts fail. (2) God observes all human behaviour (see Ps. 33.13–15), and is deeply concerned about justice and injustice, oppression and freedom, violence and peace (see Ps. 33.13–15, 18–19; 102.19). God sees human misery, knows suffering, comes down to deliver through His chosen agents (Deut. 26.7; see Exod. 3.7–8,10). Although God 'lives' in heaven, the Israelites believed that humans could be 'near God' (Ps. 73.28).

**26.19. High above all nations that he has made, in praise and in fame and in honour:** One way of interpreting this phrase is that the nations would praise and honour *Israel* because of God's gifts of wisdom and understanding (4.6), as well as the blessings of a fertile and peaceful land. Another explanation is that Israel's example would cause *other nations* to praise God, to know of His fame, and to honour Him. The second view is preferable because the phrase 'all nations that he has made' suggests that God has a purpose for them. Psalm 86.9 expresses this clearly: 'All the nations you have made shall come and bow down before you, O LORD, and shall glorify your name' (NRSV). Jeremiah used the same three Hebrew words, here translated 'praise', 'fame' and 'honour' to describe Israel's mission to the nations (see Jer. 13.11 and 33.9).

## STUDY SUGGESTIONS

### REVIEW OF CONTENT

1. What *three* phrases show the close relationship between ch. 26 and chs. 12–16?

2. What different times does the phrase 'this day', or 'today' refer to?

3. (a) What *three* words refer to God's gift of place and space?
   (b) What is the specific meaning of each?
4. What were *five* contrasts between past and present that formed the basis for the Israelites' gratitude to God?
5. (a) What is the most important way of obeying the Great commandment?
   (b) What three actions would guard worshippers against forgetting the poor?
6. What obligations do God and people accept when they enter the Covenant relationship?

BIBLE STUDY

7. Compare the meaning of the word 'inheritance' in (a) Eph. 1.18, (b) Col. 1.12, and (c) 1 Peter 1.4 with its meaning in Deut. 10.9 and 26.1. What are the differences? Do the New Testament references mean that living place and space on earth are unimportant? Give reasons for your answer.
8. What do the following passages teach about love for God? (a) Deut. 26.13 (b) Gal. 5.14 (c) 1 John 4.20.
9. What does Hos. 4.1–3 tell us about the effects on the environment of *not* loving God and our neighbours?

CONTEXTUAL APPLICATION

10. God gives His people 'a place for security with justice, space for freedom and opportunity' (see p. 145). If this is God's will for *all* peoples, how does He help those who work for justice and freedom, even though they do not know or believe in Him?
11. Every year hundreds of tons of God's gift of fertile soil (Hebrew *adamah*) are lost as a result of erosion, deforestation, and new built-up areas. What, if anything, is being done in your country to prevent this loss? What part can the Churches play in helping to keep the land fertile?
12. Make your own list of 'Once . . . but now' happenings, to describe your experience as a Christian or as a human being.
13. (a) What sort of people in your country today would correspond to the 'Levites', 'aliens', 'widows', and 'orphans' mentioned in Deuteronomy?
    (b) Describe some of the ways in which (i) the government, (ii) the Churches, (iii) people generally, and (iv) you yourself are helping such poor or oppressed people? What more do you think could be done?

# 27.1–26
# The Promised Land, Vision or Nightmare? (1)

## OUTLINE

27.1–8: A Vision of Eden: Eden as Gift.
27.9–10: Eden's New People.
27.11–26: Eden at Risk: A Litany of Warning.

## INTERPRETATION

God's gift of the 'land flowing with milk and honey' (26.9; 27.3) was like a restoration of the Garden of Eden as a complete natural environment to provide abundant life for God's people. Just as the original Garden of Eden was God's gift to the first human beings, so this restored Eden is a sign of His good will for all peoples.

Continuing the theme of 26.19 (cf. 11.27), chs. 27 and 28 both start with a vision of a restored Eden as God's blessing for those who love Him according to the Covenant Teaching (27.1–10; 28.1–14). And reversing the theme of 26.19 (cf. 11.28), each chapter warns of the nightmare of doom which is God's judgement on those who do *not* live according to His Covenant Teaching (27.11–26; 28.15–68). Furthermore, the consequences of Israel's obedience or disobedience will reach far beyond the borders of Israel to 'all the peoples of the earth' (28.10, 25,37).

## EDEN AS GIFT

As we have seen, when God gave Israel a good land with goodly cities, full of good things (6.10,11,18), He also gave them two special gifts which set them apart from other nations and peoples of the earth: (1) the Covenant Teaching, and (2) nearness to Himself (4.7–8). These two gifts would enable them to preserve their Eden-like environment for future generations.

At this point, just after the conclusion of the Covenant, the Narrator shows something new happening. Moses, knowing that He himself would not be able to enter the land (3.23–29), placed the elders and priests at his side for the first time (27.1,9). By this act He *shared his authority with them*, so that they could continue to instruct and serve the people in the new land.

The *priests* would guard the Teaching, and minister at the altar. Moses had already instructed the *elders* in their responsibilities for administering righteousness and justice in the new land (19.12; 21.2,3,6,19–20; see 31.9). After Moses's death, the elders shared

Joshua's responsibilities and, after Joshua's death, they preserved the memory of Moses's teachings (Josh. 7.6; 24.31). Two monuments of stone firmly set on the soil of the new land (27.2–8) would serve as a permanent reminder to later generations of the crucial importance of maintaining the two distinctive marks of God's people: the Covenant Teaching and the nearness of the Covenant God.

## THE COVENANT TEACHING ON STONE

The first act of the Israelites in Canaan would be to set up these large stones, cover them with plaster, and write 'very plainly' on them 'all the words of this law', i.e. the Covenant Teaching (27.2–3, 8). In the Eden-like land, the Covenant Teaching would no longer be confined exclusively to the ark and the priesthood or even the elders. It would be on permanent public display, so that not only the Israelite people, but all the people of Canaan, whether Israelite or alien, as well as people of other nations passing through the land could know it. According to Jewish legend, the Covenant Teaching was first written in seventy languages, so that the non-Jewish nations might have the opportunity of learning and living by this Teaching.

## THE STONE ALTAR

The second act in the new land would be to erect an altar of natural, or 'unhewn', stones (27.6) as a sign of the people's need to maintain and strengthen their relationship to their Covenant God through covenantal worship.

## EDEN'S NEW PEOPLE

Just as God created a new humanity to care for the first Eden, so now the Levitical priests join Moses in proclaiming the good news that the Israelites have become a new people who must care for the restored Eden. The fact that the Levitical priests join with Moses indicates that these words are to be part of a liturgy of Covenant renewal in the Promised Land. 'Keep silence and hear, O Israel! This very day you have become the people of the LORD your God' (27.9 NRSV).

The good news was that God had accepted 'the wilderness generation', in spite of their constant rebellion (9.7,24), as His 'treasured people' (26.18 NRSV). They would be His partners in creating a new society in the new land. This good news lies behind all the promises and the warnings that follow in these two chapters. It is the beginning to which God's people can always return (see Hos. 2.23; 1 Pet. 2.10). This proclamation comes *before* the words

The word 'curse' may be applied to many 'abominable practices'—like the abuse of narcotic drugs making people vulnerable to disease and even death, and causing them to turn to crime and violence. In the crowded streets of Amsterdam in the Netherlands a Chinese drug-dealer demands huge sums in cash for heroin he has smuggled in from Hong Kong.

'therefore obey . . .'. (Deut. 27.10). Becoming God's new people is not a *reward* for past obedience, but the *result* of God's gracious act of new creation. Obedience to the Covenant Teaching is the way of partnership with the Creator in restoring the earth.

## EDEN AT RISK: A LITANY OF WARNING, 27.11–26

Unlike the Ten Commandments (5.6–21) which make little reference to the consequences of disobedience, this litany makes the consequences clear. Each act of rebellion will bring a curse to the land, that is, it will weaken the individuals who disobey, cause the break-up of society, and destroy the natural environment.

This list of twelve actions is symbolic, i.e. not meant to cover all acts of disobedience. However, the words 'in secret' which describe idolatry and murder (27.15,24) suggest the special nature of these particular acts. People could also do other destructive acts without public knowledge, dishonouring father or mother (v.16), moving a neighbour's landmark (v.17), misleading a blind man (v. 18), denying the justice due to the weak and vulnerable (v. 19), accepting bribes (v. 25), violating codes of sexual conduct (vv. 20–23). Such acts, whether in private or public, will put Eden at risk. A wisdom teacher in Israel agreed with this litany: 'For God will bring every deed into judgement, with every secret thing, whether good or evil' (Eccles. 12.14).

## NOTES

**27.3. Write upon them all the words of this law:** According to the Narrator Moses wrote the entire set of Covenant Teaching 'in a book' and gave it to the Levites and elders before his death (31.9,24), so that they could write it on stone and continue to interpret it in the Promised Land.

**27.5. An altar to the LORD your God:** We cannot tell whether the Narrator thought of this altar on Mount Ebal as additional to the one in 'the place where God has chosen' (12.26–27), or as the altar at which worshippers presented the first fruits of their harvest (26.4; see note on 12.5).

**27.6. Unhewn stones:** Some scholars have suggested that the command to use only 'unhewn' stones reflected a Canaanite custom of carving images of a god on their altar stones. See Judges 3.19,26.

**27.8. Write . . . very plainly:** The Hebrew verb here translated 'write plainly', was also used in ch.1, where Moses 'expounds' (NRSV) or 'explains' (RSV), i.e. 'opens up' the meaning of the Covenant Teaching (see note on 1.5). By using the same verb, the Narrator suggests that future leaders must follow Moses's example by explaining the meaning of the Covenant Teaching to each new generation. This is what the Levitical priests did in the time of Nehemiah. They 'helped the people to understand the law' (Covenant Teaching) '. . . so that the people understood the reading' (Neh. 8.7–8)

**27.14. The Levites shall declare . . . with a loud voice:** The Narrator may have found this litany among the records of an ancient liturgy which was held between Mount Ebal and Mount Gerizim at Shechem and included it here. According to Jewish tradition the original litany included twelve acts which would bring blessing, as a parallel to the twelve acts bringing disaster. Joshua himself 'read all the words of the law, the blessing and the curse'. between Gerizim and Ebal (Josh. 8.34).

**27.15. Cursed:** The word 'curse' in Deuteronomy 27—28 causes problems of interpretation. The word may remind us of present-day witch-doctors or spirit mediums, who, some people believe, can cause evil to happen to someone by a curse. Christians may ask whether our God can be like that. Again, why would God 'curse' anyone, let alone the 'people of His own possession' (7.6)? Didn't God change Balaam's curse against Israel into blessing (23.5)?

In the sense used in these two chapters, 'cursed' refers to the disastrous consequences that result from certain sorts of action, because they violate God's design of creation. In other parts of the Bible the word 'cursed' applies to individuals (Ps. 37.22), the family (Prov. 3.33), social life (Deut. 28.16,19), the soil (Gen. 3.17–18), the land (Jer. 23.10), even the whole earth (Isa. 24.6). When individuals or groups, whether members of the 'nations he has made' or God's own people, violate His design of creation, they threaten the well-being of creation as well as human society. The result is disaster, i.e. a 'curse'.

We may think of Miriam, who with Aaron challenged Moses's leadership in the wilderness (Num. 12.1–2). Their envy and ambition were causing division and threatened a break-up of the community. Miriam's skin disease was like the deathly consequence (Num. 12.12) of envy and ambition. Both Aaron and Moses prayed for her recovery and the recovery of health for the whole society (Num. 12.11–13). Only after she returned to the restored community could they move on toward the Promised Land (Num. 12.15–16).

The word 'cursed', as a description of disastrous effects of certain actions, may be applied to use of narcotic drugs which take away the strength of people's bodies and minds, making them vulnerable to disease and even death. Widespread use of drugs can weaken whole communities, by causing people to turn to crime and violence, causing social disintegration.

## STUDY SUGGESTIONS

### REVIEW OF CONTENT

1. What is the meaning of ' vision' and 'nightmare' in relation to these chapters in Deuteronomy?
2. (a) What are the two things that set God's people apart from others?
   (b) What two stone monuments pointed to those two distinctive things?
3. What is the 'good news' that underlies the promises and warnings of Deut. 27—28?
4. What makes the twelve actions in 27.11–26 alike?

### BIBLE STUDY

5. Psalm 19.12 refers to 'hidden faults'. Jesus spoke of things that are 'secret', but will eventually be made public (Mark 4.21–22). Which of the secret sins mentioned in Deut. 27.5–26 are most common in the society where you live? Which are most destructive?
6. Read Deut. 27.9–10 and Rom. 5.6–11. In what ways are these passages (a) alike, (b) different?

### CONTEXTUAL APPLICATION

7. How would you explain Deut. 27.15–26 and 28.15–19 to a friend who does not like the idea that God 'curses' people when they do wrong? Read the note on Deut. 27.15 before you answer.

# 28.1–68
# The Promised Land: Vision or Nightmare? (2)

## OUTLINE

28.1–14: Eden Preserved: A Blessed Society.
28.15–68: Eden Ruined: A Doomed Society.

## INTERPRETATION

### EDEN PRESERVED: A BLESSED SOCIETY

Chapter 28 starts with a clear picture of the results of God's blessing for a people who live by the Covenant Teaching. The people will succeed in everything they do, both in the home and in public ('when you go out;' 28.6; see 6.7). The phrase 'the work of their hands' refers to what they will do to make the Great Commandment a reality in their cities and fields, by organizing economic life for righteousness and justice (implied in the term 'your basket'), and by producing and distributing food and other necessities of life for the good of all (implied in the term 'your kneading bowl').

God's blessing will give them healthy children, increase of flocks and herds, abundant produce from the fields (28.4,11), and freedom from debt (28.12). God will also give them victory against oppressors (28.7).

Such a blessed society would show neighbouring peoples the benefits of obedience to the Covenant Teaching (see 4.6). God's blessing could then spread from His people to 'all the families of the earth' in fulfilment of His promise to Abraham (Gen. 12.3).

## EDEN RUINED: A DOOMED SOCIETY

The disasters described in the second part of ch. 28 are the opposite of the blessings, with more vivid details added to make this one of the grimmest parts of the Old Testament. These disasters are much more severe than the hardships in the wilderness, which had been a sort of 'discipline' for the people's own good. The sad refrain 'until you are destroyed' (28.20, 24, 45, 61), and similar phrases (28.21, 22, 48, 51) emphasize the end result that will follow the many disasters.

The ruin of *this* restored Eden is especially serious. Instead of being 'high above all the nations of the earth' (28.1; see 26.19), and fulfilling their mission of being a source of blessing, God's people will become 'a horror to all the kingdoms of the earth' (28.25, see 28.37).

This helps us to understand the difficult words in 28.63 that God will 'take delight' in bringing His beloved people to ruin. Amos put it in other words:

> You only have I known
> of all the families of the earth;
> therefore I will punish you
> for all your iniquities. (Amos 3.2).

Yahweh's basic purpose is always to do people good (Deut. 28.63; see 8.16). This means that the ruin and destruction will be temporary until He can again 'take delight in prospering' them (30.9), so that they can demonstrate to the nations the good way of life.

*Doomed Cities* (28.16) will be a return to Cain's city (Gen. 4.17). We may fill in some of the details from present-day experience. Cities will be places of violence, terror, homelessness, and injustice. Because the people who live in the inner cities are poor and powerless, society will forget them. In doomed cities, the rich will lord it over the poor, power stations, factories and motor-vehicles will pollute air, water and soil. Children will die early, young people lose hope, the homeless wander the streets without protection or help. In a word, cities will become zones of death.

*Doomed Fields* (Deut. 28.16) will return to the state described in Genesis 3.17–18. Crops will fail because of drought, blight and mildew (Deut. 28.22), infestations of locusts, worms (28.38–39) and cicadas (28.42 NRSV). Flocks and herds will grow sick (28.18). The people who work on the land will not own it but work for oppressors (28.30–31). What was once fertile land will become desert (28.23–24).

Today in many countries fields are ruined by excessive use of chemicals and unwise agricultural methods, and by international trading companies whose chief aim is to increase profits. Forests are destroyed, causing flooding and loss of top soil. Village life breaks down because there is no cultural vitality or economic base for community.

*A Doomed People.* 'Severe and lasting afflictions and grievous and lasting maladies' (28.59 NRSV) will drain the strength of the people. One of these illnesses would be a deadly pestilence (28.21) like that which attacked Pharaoh and his people (Exod. 9.3,15). Festering boils like those which afflicted the Egyptians (Deut. 28.27, 35; see Exod. 9.9–11) will cause great physical agony. Today we think of epidemics like cholera, AIDS, or the radiation disease from nuclear waste that persists for hundreds of years.

*Doomed Families.* Husbands and wives will be separated from each other (Deut. 28.30) and children from their parents (v.32). Today war and famine cause many broken families. In many different countries, all over the world, broken marriages and single-parent families become more and more frequent. Thousands of children wander the streets of cities like Bangkok, Manila or Rio de Janeiro. Parents may desire a better life for themselves so strongly that they allow or even encourage their daughters to become prostitutes in order to bring in more income for them.

*Doomed individuals.* People will suffer deep distress of mind and heart, whether from disasters at home or in exile. They will be frustrated and confused in all they do, and become sick in mind as well as body.

*A doomed nation.* The once victorious people will meet humiliating defeat (28.25) after a siege so severe that people will eat the flesh of their dead sons and daughters (28.53–57). They will be 'oppressed and crushed' (28.33) and serve the occupying power 'in hunger and thirst, in nakedness and lack of everything' (28.48

NRSV). The once numerous population will be reduced to a mere remnant (28.62). The once strong and unified people will be scattered in weakness 'among all peoples from one end of the earth to the other' (28.64; see 4.27). They will be so poor that they cannot even find slave owners to buy them (28.68).

## REFLECTIONS ON DEUTERONOMY 28

1. The vision of blessedness and peace always lay ahead for Israel, but was never completely realized. The nightmare of ruin and doom was like a storm cloud on the horizon, as prophets and teachers warned. Israel lived between the vision and the nightmare for most of the nation's history. The people were never obedient enough to deserve the restored Eden, though later historians regarded Solomon's reign as a golden age (1 Kings 4.25). Similarly, the nightmare was always ahead (e.g. Jer. 5.15–17), but never became full reality until the Exile in Babylon (e.g. Lam. 1.3). Yet even in the darkest days of the Exile, the words of Deuteronomy showed the way to a return to the vision (Deut. 4.29–31; 30.1–5).

This vision of a restored Eden reveals God's loving will for all human societies. Similarly, the nightmare of disaster is a dark shadow threatening the doom which hangs over all humanity when people rebel against the created moral and natural order (e.g. Isa. 24.4–13). Human societies also live between the vision and the nightmare, between success and disaster, life and death, blessing and curse. The new heaven and new earth beckon each generation, despite the cruel realities of the present and dread of the future.

2. Throughout this chapter we find the words 'if . . . then' (28.1–2, 13–14, 15, 58–59), and 'because . . . therefore' (28.45, 47–48). They tell us that humans can choose to live toward the vision. We are not victims of inscrutable fate. A resolute effort to live by the law of love (Deut. 6.5) in all aspects of our lives will give us new possibilities to make the blessed society a reality.

*Cities* in this vision can become centres of life instead of death. They can be filled with peace instead of violence, friendliness instead of terror, shelter and support for all instead of grinding poverty and homelessness, and justice for those in need. There can be good education for all, and the opportunity of meaningful employment for young and old. Public services and industries can improve standards of living for humans and protect the environment of all, including plants, animals, water and air. This vision may become reality in unlikely places. Calcutta in India, with a population of eleven million, has been called the dirtiest city in the world. Yet 225 poor families in south Calcutta have turned a toxic industrial wasteland into an abundant aquafarm where they catch 2,500 kilograms of fish a day in water clean enough to drink.

A resolute effort to live by the law of love will give new possibilities. Ruined cities and fields can become centres of life instead of death. In a desert area of India patients queue for medicine from dispensaries specially set up for underprivileged people. A renewed Covenant is a challenge to relieve suffering in all parts of society.

*Fields* can become sources of vibrant rural life with abundant crops and flocks, the opposite of the fields doomed to infertility and degradation by human sin (Gen. 3.17–18). In this vision, people can work their own fields for the good of the whole society. Agricultural businesses can plan for the good of the people, and preserve the bounty of nature by use of wise agricultural methods. Vibrant villages can enhance the life of the people. Different ethnic or economic groups can live in harmony and peace. Again in east Calcutta, hundreds of poor families have converted a sprawling garbage dump into rich farmland, where they grow spinach, cauliflower, corn and egg-plant.

Recently 10,000 war refugees in Central America demonstrated the power of this vision when they returned from camps in Honduras to their ruined fields in El Salvador. They pooled the $50 which the United Nations had given to each family to create their own bank. They have planted fields, built a clinic, school and community centre. They are trying to build a new society on their reclaimed land.

*Economic life* blessed by God can mean abundance for all, care for the poor and defenceless, generous help for those in need (Deut. 15.7–11). Food production can enable all to live in plenty without deprivation or starvation. Science and technology can find cures to many diseases, and help to preserve natural resources for the benefit of all (see pp. 71–72).

*Nations* blessed by God can be strong in the cause of righteousness and justice, able to help neighbouring nations or peoples in need (28.12).

In short, it is possible that justice will indeed 'roll down like waters and righteousness like an everflowing stream' (Amos 5.24).

3. We cannot expect to discover the causes of all suffering. If we read this chapter by itself, we might conclude that people who meet disaster are themselves 'evil', or that social breakdown is the direct result of the sinfulness of those who suffer from it. The parallel thought is that people who prosper are always 'good' in God's sight. We should remember Jesus's reply to those who thought that blindness was the result of sin by the blind person or his parents: 'Neither this man nor his parents sinned; he was born blind so that God's works might be revealed in him' (John 9.3 NRSV). Suffering in any part of society is a challenge to all members to work toward health and abundant life.

4. Deuteronomy 28 does not tell us that good or evil actions bring *immediate* results of blessing or disaster. There was an interval of more than 600 years between the time of Moses, when both vision and nightmare lay ahead, and the time of the Narrator, when the nightmare was nearly a full reality.

The wicked will not always suffer disaster immediately after they do their wicked acts. Even though they oppress the poor (Ps. 10.2,9), and the state of society and nature grows worse because of their evil deeds, wicked people themselves often grow rich and prosper (see Ps. 73.3–9). The sins of the powerful will cause the powerless to suffer. The righteous will not always prosper (Eccles. 7.15), but may suffer from the injustice of others (Ps. 34.19). A long process is at work, with human choices possible at every stage. During this waiting period, disaster provides us with an opportunity to practise the love of God, repent of disobedience and open our hands and hearts to the victims of injustice or disaster.

## NOTES

**28.21. Pestilence:** This term may be an intentional reference to the pestilence which struck the Egyptian animals and people (Exod. 9.3,15), here applied to disobedient Israelites. 'Pestilence' often occurs in a phrase along with famine and war (e.g. Jer. 14.12; Ezek. 7.15; Rev. 6.8).

**28.53. You shall eat the offspring of your own body, the flesh of your sons and daughters:** See also Lev. 26.29. This terrible warning about starvation during times of war actually came true during the sieges of Samaria (2 Kings 6.29) and of Jerusalem (Lam. 2.20).

**28.63. The LORD will take delight in bringing ruin on you and destroying you:** The meaning is not that God enjoys bringing ruin on people, but that ruin and destruction are not random events that happen by chance. They happen according to God's loving purpose for His people and all of humankind. Another Hebrew word which is sometimes translated as 'delight in' may also in other contexts refer to God's purpose or God's will (Isa. 1.11; 46.10; 53.10).

## STUDY SUGGESTIONS

### REVIEW OF CONTENT

1. What do the phrases 'the work of your hands', 'your basket', and 'your kneading bowl' tell us about the life of a blessed people?
2. What effect will the prosperity or ruin of Israel have on other nations?
3. In what ways are the disasters described in 28.15–65 more severe than the hardships the Israelites experienced in the wilderness?

BIBLE STUDY

4. The Narrator lived at the same time as Jeremiah. Read the following passages from the Book of Jeremiah and say what similarities or differences you notice between them and Deut. 28.15–65. (a) Jer. 6.6–7;9.21 on 'doomed cities' (b) Jer. 8.13 and 9.10 on 'doomed fields' (c) Jer. 4.23–26 on 'Eden ruined'
5. Which of the diseases mentioned in 28.22 are found in your country? In what ways, if any, are they related to wrong actions by individuals or society?
6. Describe in your own words the 'afflictions' and 'sicknesses' mentioned in Deut. 28 (a) v.20, (b) v. 28, (c) v. 34, and (d) v. 65. What are some of the ways in which people can be helped to overcome such problems?

CONTEXTUAL APPLICATION

7. Many people living in industrial areas today, are afflicted by caused by pollution from factories which discharge poisonous gases or chemicals into the air or water. According to the teaching of Deut. 28, these diseases are the result of human sin.
(a) Whose sin and what sort of sin do you think chiefly cause this sort of suffering?
(b) In your country what, if anything, are (i) the government, (ii) the Churches, (iii) individuals doing to prevent this sort of pollution? What more could they do?
8. Chs. 27 and 28 describe the benefits of God's blessing in terms of material prosperity for everyone. But today many people think of the benefits of God's blessings only in terms of financial profits.
(a) What are the chief differences between creating material prosperity and creating profits?
(b) How much 'material prosperity' is enough?
9. In some countries today land is becoming less productive because of overpopulation and overgrazing of land by cattle, sheep and goats; rains fail because of the destruction of forests, and deserts are spreading. Does this mean we need to reinterpret such verses as Deut. 28.4? If not, what does it mean?
10. Many people consider AIDS as a modern 'pestilence' sent by God as a punishment on sinful humans.
(a) What is your opinion?
(b) What should be the attitude of Christians towards people suffering from AIDS?

# 29.1–28
# The Ever-New Covenant (1)

## OUTLINE

29.1: The Renewed Covenant.
29.2–9: More Reflections on the Wilderness Period.
29.10–15: The Re-formed Community.
29.16–28: Covenant Warnings.

## INTERPRETATION

All we have read so far in Deuteronomy has been preparation for the Covenant at Moab and for later renewals in the Promised Land. In the early chapters, the Narrator presented Moses as recalling lessons from the wilderness (1.6—3.29), and the encounter with God at Sinai/Horeb (4.1–40); and then interpreting the Primary Covenant at Sinai/Horeb for the 'wilderness generation' in Moab (4.44—11.32).

### THE RENEWED COVENANT

As we saw in Deut. 12.1, Moses began preparation for the Covenant in Moab by presenting an additional set of 'statutes and ordinances' applying the Primary Covenant to public, family and social life (21.1—25.19). He then gave the people liturgical forms to use in worship (26.1–15; 27.1–6.11–26), and outlined the mutual obligations to be undertaken in each renewal of the Covenant relationship (26.16–19). Next he set before them the hope of a restored Eden for an obedient people, and warned them of the terrible disasters which would result from disobedience (28.1–68). Finally, with the Levitical priests, he proclaimed the ever-renewed mystery of divine grace: 'This day you have become the people of the LORD your God' (27.9–10). So the stage was set for the Covenant at Moab.

Now the Narrator writes of 'the covenant which the LORD commanded Moses to make with the people of Israel in the land of Moab, besides the covenant which he had made with them at Horeb' (29.1). As we have seen, the Covenant at Moab was a renewal of the Primary Covenant with additional teaching, challenging the people to *become* by their personal and collective life what God in His grace had *chosen them to be*: 'the people of the LORD your God'.

## CHANGING CIRCUMSTANCES

The places and situations of covenant renewal will change. With each renewal there is need for new understanding of what constitutes covenantal worship and a just and righteous society. The basic nature of the covenant relationship between God and His people does not change, but it is always in a living relationship with the situation where renewal takes place. When Joshua renewed the Primary Covenant at Shechem, he 'made statutes and ordinances' suitable for the new situation (Josh. 24.24–25). When King Josiah 'made a covenant before the LORD' in Jerusalem, the 'book of the covenant' was his guide (2 Kings 23.2–3; see pp. 2–3). This was probably most of Deuteronomy, which was a new interpretation of the Mosaic teaching for the new occasion.

Jesus's words 'You have heard that it was said to the men of old . . . but I say to you . . .'. (Matt. 5.21–22) were a new interpretation of Covenant commands, pointing to God's ongoing intention rather than the 'letter' of the law.

## MORE REFLECTIONS ON THE WILDERNESS PERIOD

Once again, like a theme in a work of art (see Special Note E), Moses is shown as reflecting on the experiences of the people in the wilderness, with two new reflections on the occasion of renewing the Covenant.

### FIRST REFLECTION: KNOWLEDGE OF GOD

Moses told the people that God's underlying purpose in liberating them from slavery and leading them through the wilderness was not merely to give them the land He had promised, but 'that you may know that I am the LORD your God' (29.2–3,5–6). In other passages Moses appeals to the people to 'know that' their God is the true God (4.35,39; 7.9), or that God acts in certain ways (7.9; 8.5; 9.3). In this reflection, Moses tells the people of God's purpose that there should be a direct relationship of 'knowing' between Himself as 'I' and the people as 'you'. According to God's plan, the wilderness generation would come to know Him by *experiencing* (i.e. 'seeing,' see 29.2–3) His acts of power and care. Similarly, God's intention for each new generation who enter the Covenant is that they will themselves come to know Him through their experience of His acts of power and grace in their time.

Knowledge of God is more important than religious ritual, as Hosea said (Hos. 6.6; see Matt. 9.13). It is the basis of love for God and neighbour, and is essential for 'partners in God's new creation' among the nations.

## SECOND REFLECTION: AN UNRESPONSIVE PEOPLE

Moses expressed his deep disappointment with the whole wilderness experience in the words: 'To this day the LORD has not given you a mind to understand, or eyes to see, or ears to hear' (Deut. 29.4). We would expect that the trials, disappointments, defeats, and deliverances from numerous troubles in the forty years of wilderness wanderings would have taught the people what God expected of them. This had not happened. In a previous outburst Moses had said 'From the day you came out of the land of Egypt until you came to this place, you have been rebellious against the LORD' (9.7). Here Moses says that God Himself was responsible for not opening their hearts, eyes or ears!

Was Moses really blaming God for the people's dullness? No! He was expressing his discouragement at the people's lack of response to God's discipline which was part of His love for His people. God is always ready to give good gifts to His people. However, if the people are stubborn and fail to respond with love and obedience, God will not force them to accept His gifts. When God chose the people of Israel He took the risk of giving them freedom to frustrate His purpose to 'do you good in the end' (Deut. 8.16)!

When we read the words 'to this day' in context, they seem to suggest that unless there was some change, the people would continue to go stumbling blindly toward the nightmare of ruin already described in 28.15–68. Such pessimism would certainly apply to the people of Judah and their leaders in the time of the Narrator, when the disaster was very near, as the words 'as at this day' (29.28) suggest. The renewal of the Covenant was intended to be an opportunity for each generation to make that change.

### THE RE-FORMED COMMUNITY, 29.10–15

Covenant renewal will create a new community. The community at Sinai/Horeb was the newly formed people of Israel. The community at Moab was the re-formed people of Israel. The Covenant at Shechem brought together peoples and tribes living in Canaan and groups of Canaanites such as Rahab's family. The re-formed community at Moab had three characteristics.

### A MORE INCLUSIVE COMMUNITY

*First of all,* membership of the community was expanded to include people belonging to an underclass: the wood-cutters and water carriers (29.11), not previously mentioned in 12.7,12 or 16.14. In later years this group of people may have been the descendants of the Gibeonites of Joshua's time (see Josh. 9.23,27), but in the period of the monarchy they were probably slaves in the Jerusalem Temple.

The Narrator may have inserted this group of 'non-persons' in this chapter to call the attention of the leaders of Judah to the need for greater inclusiveness. We find a clue to this in Jeremiah's criticism of the upper class who released their slaves according to a promise, and then broke the promise by taking them back as slaves again (Jer. 34.8–16). A renewed Covenant should include non-persons, women, children, those who are homeless, poor, physically or mentally handicapped, prisoners, and all sorts of oppressed people today.

God is making the same call through His people in many parts of the present-day world. Groups of students and staff in the Shikoku Christian College in Japan are working for equal rights for two minority groups: the Buraku people, and Korean residents of Japan. The Christian community in India consists mostly of people from the 'scheduled castes' (formerly called 'untouchable') who in many cases are still excluded from the mainstream of society.

## A COMMUNITY IN THE PROCESS OF TRANSFORMATION

*Secondly*, Covenant renewal was an opportunity for those who had by God's grace become 'the people of the LORD your God' (Deut. 27.9) to '*enter* the sworn covenant of the LORD your God' once again (29.12). The Hebrew word translated 'enter' means to cross over from their former lives of rebellion and idolatry under the influence of false gods, into the renewed community (see note on 29.12). Crossing from the realm of death to the realm of life is a complicated process which involves a change of the 'heart . . . soul . . . and might' (6.5).

When the people 'cross over,' God is ready to 'establish,' strengthen or restore His people in their resolve to fulfil their role in His plan (29.13, see note; see also 28.9). With this sort of strengthening or restoration, blind eyes would see, deaf ears would hear, and dull minds would again understand.

## A COMMUNITY OF MANY GENERATIONS

*Third*. Finally, the Covenant community which began at Sinai/Horeb and included the generation at Moab, 'who are all of us here alive this day' (5.3), extends into the future to include 'those who are not here with us today' (29.15 NRSV). These are the 'children's children' (4.9) 'to a thousand generations' (7.9), 'a people yet unborn' (Ps. 22.31). These generations of 'a time to come' (Deut. 6.20; see 29.22) will need their own 'today' of covenant renewal, so that they too may 'cross over' into the covenant community, be transformed and receive God's strengthening help.

## COVENANT WARNINGS, 29.16–28

The double risk of Covenant-making, both for God and for the Israelites, is a recurrent theme in Deuteronomy. When God 'attempted to go and take a nation for himself' (4.34), He had to deal with the basic problem of the Covenant relationship: the rebellious nature of the human heart. God took this risk because of His love for His people (7.7–8), and for the sake of His plan for the nations. The risk for Israel in 'crossing over' into the Covenant relationship was that their rebellious behaviour would bring God's anger and punishment (4.25–28; 28.15–68). The theme of risk is expressed again here by means of three pictures.

POISONOUS FRUIT

The *first* picture shows a beautiful field of grain ready for harvest. But the harvester sees 'a root sprouting poisonous and bitter growth' (Deut. 29.18 NRSV) that could spoil the entire crop. This root is the worship of false gods. Amos pointed to the practical dangers of this poisonous fruit: 'You have turned justice into poison, and the fruit of righteousness into wormwood' (Amos 6.12; see Deut. 32.32–33). The risk is that the poison will spread to God's people (7.4). The poison spreads from an individual, whether man or woman, to a family, and from there to an entire tribe and nation (29.18,19; see note). The author of Hebrews saw this same sort of 'root of bitterness' as a danger to the Christian community (Heb. 12.15). Poisonous fruit such as racial prejudice, violent aggression, ethnic pride, and greed still sprout and grow in Christian communities.

Even regular reading and hearing of the Covenant Teaching does not always remove this poison. It begins with self-deception. Although the entire assembly hears the reading of the Covenant Teaching, some of the listening people will congratulate themselves, thinking in their hearts 'we are safe even though we go our own stubborn ways' (Deut. 29.19 NRSV). Thus the poison spreads, and if it is not checked, will destroy the community.

A SICK LAND

In the *second* picture, a once fertile garden land has been ruined by 'sicknesses' (29.22). The signs of sickness are sulphur and salt, 'and a burnt-out waste, unsown, and growing nothing, where no grass can sprout' (29.23). This follows from the first picture. The poisons from the bad plants have polluted the land so that it cannot fulfil God's good purpose in creation to 'put forth vegetation, plants . . . fruit trees' (Gen. 1.11). Today we think of the pollution caused by garbage and toxic industrial waste products that poison water, land and air.

TWO GROUPS OF DOUBTERS

The *third* picture shows two groups of people reflecting on the ruins of what had been a 'good land' (Deut. 8.7). One group expresses doubt about God's goodness and power. These people are 'the generation to come, your children who rise up after you' (29.22). They are exiles in a distant land (29.28), victims of the sins of their parents and grandparents. Yet the Covenant was meant for them (29.15; see 4.31). They ask 'in time to come' about the meaning of the laws of life given by God in the Covenant (6.20). In their exile they ask 'Why has the LORD done thus to this land'? (29.24). They wonder whether they will be able to inherit the ruined land again?

The other group show doubts about Yahweh's power to save His own people, and by implication, the people of other nations. This group are 'the foreigner who comes from a far land', and indeed, 'all the nations' (29.22,24). Once again, the reactions of the nations to what happens to God's people are emphasized. As we have seen, God's ultimate goal in calling His people was the well-being of all the nations (see note on 4.6). They are the ones who should have said 'Surely this great nation' (Israel) 'is a wise and understanding people' (4.6), but now question God's power. Moses used this argument in his intercession with God for Israel on Mount Sinai/ Horeb. If the other nations sensed that God's people might not reach the Promised Land, they would say that it was 'because the LORD was not able to bring them into the land . . . because he hated them' (9.28). The answer given by both the exiles and the nations ('They will conclude . . .'. (Deut. 29.25 NRSV) is that the ruin of the good land was a sign of *God's faithfulness to the Covenant* which His people had abandoned.

The questions of doubt (29.24) fit in well with the actual situation of the exiles, speaking 'as at this day' (29.28). They echo the doubts expressed by the Israelites exiled in Babylon:

> My way is hid from the LORD,
>   and my right is disregarded by my God (Isa. 40.27).

The people then answer their own doubts by confessing that the disasters had come because both their ancestors ('they') and the exiles themselves had sinned:

> Was it not the LORD against whom we have sinned,
>   in whose way they would not walk,
>   and whose law they would not obey? (Isa. 42.24)

## NOTES

**29.1. The words of the covenant:** Covenant (as we saw in Special Note D), is a major theme in the Book of Deuteronomy which

'Doom' is God's judgement on people who do not live according to His Covenant—doomed cities, doomed fields, doomed families. Today war and famine and a disregard of God's commandments cause many broken families. Orphaned and abandoned children, 'the generation to come', roam the streets of many cities, like this little group in Guatemala.

comes to a climax in chs. 29—30. The word 'covenant' appears eight times in ch. 29 and five times in ch. 31.

**29.4. Eyes to see, or ears to hear:** Isaiah had to face the same kind of blindness and deafness of the people who will 'hear and hear, but . . . not understand; see and see, but . . not perceive' (Isa. 6.9; quoted by Jesus, Matt. 13.14–15). In the days of the Narrator, Jeremiah spoke of a 'foolish and senseless people, who have eyes, but see not, who have ears, but hear not' (Jer. 5.21). During the Exile in Babylon, Deutero-Isaiah, speaking for God said: 'Who is blind but my servant, or deaf as my messenger? . . . He sees many things, but does not observe them; his ears are open, but he does not hear' (Isa. 42.19–20). Eyes that see and ears that hear are signs of the messianic age (see Isa. 29.18; 35.5; Matt. 11.5).

**29.12. Enter:** The literal meaning of the Hebrew word translated 'enter' is to cross a geographical boundary like a river (21.3–14). It may also describe the act of transgressing the moral boundary of the Covenant Teaching (26.13). In 29.12 it means the act of crossing over into a new realm, the realm of life.

**29.13. Establish:** The Hebrew word translated 'establish' can also mean 'raise up' (18.15) or 'restore' (Isa. 49.6).

**29.19. Moist and dry:** This agricultural image may be a way of referring to the entire garden, both the well-watered and the dry parts. Here it probably means the whole nation, including both the prosperous and the poor.

## STUDY SUGGESTIONS

### REVIEW OF CONTENT

1. Where did Yahweh make 'the Primary Covenant' with Israel? What was the location of Covenant renewal described in Deuteronomy? In what other locations did the Israelites renew their Covenant with Yahweh?

2. What was God's purpose in leading His people through the hardships of the wilderness?

3. According to Deuteronomy 29.4 God had not yet given His people the insight and understanding they needed. What was the reason for this?

4. (a) What new group or groups of people was the renewed Covenant community to include?
   (b) What group of people did the Covenant community include in addition to the 'present' generation?

5. What three 'pictures' in ch. 29 describe possible dangers to the covenant people?

## BIBLE STUDY

6. Read 2 Kings chs. 22—23. What three differences were there between the Israelites' situation at the time of the covenant renewal in Jerusalem and their situation in Moab?
7. In what way does 2 Cor. 4.6 give an answer to the 'not yet' of Deut. 29.4?
8. How does 1 Cor. 1.26–29 help us to understand the reference in Deut. 29.11 to the 'underclass' in Israelite society?
9. Compare Matt. 13.24–30 with Deut. 29.18–22. In what ways does Jesus's teaching differ from that of Moses?

## CONTEXTUAL APPLICATION

10. What do you think could be done to make the 'Covenant community' you belong to more inclusive?
11. What are some of the ways in which Christians behave as members of society, that can have a good or harmful effect on the well-being of (a) their fellow citizens, (b) people of other nations?


# 29.29—30.20
# The Ever-New Covenant (2)


## OUTLINE

29.29: Covenant Encouragement: Clear Enough to Live By.
30.1–10: Covenant Encouragement: God's Promises.
30.11–14: Covenant Encouragement: Close Enough to Taste.
30.15–20: Choose Life!


## INTERPRETATION

### COVENANT ENCOURAGEMENT: CLEAR ENOUGH TO LIVE BY

Risks of failure also imply the possibility of success. God's people must know that His thoughts and decisions are His own, beyond human control. They are the 'secret things,' which humans, even God's treasured people, cannot know. However, in His mercy God has 'revealed' enough of the mystery of His will to give His people a guide to the way of life and peace and community to which they may return. God will reveal new aspects of His truth from generation to generation in proportion to their faithfulness. We learn from the New Testament that 'grace and truth came through Jesus Christ' (John 1.17), and that 'when the Spirit of truth comes, He will guide you into all the truth' (John 16.13). Doubts may remain about the 'secret things,' but there should be no doubt about the 'revealed things' which are available to, and sufficient for all.

## COVENANT ENCOURAGEMENT: GOD'S PROMISES

Covenant renewal is possible when the people in their distress return to God. This 'return', already mentioned in ch. 4, is given great emphasis in Deut. 30.1–10 by the Hebrew word *shub*, which appears four times with the Israelites as the subject. First they 'call . . . to mind' (literally *bring back* to their attention) the covenant promises and warnings. Then they *'return* to the LORD your God' (v.2), and *once again* obey God's voice and keep His command-ments (v.8). The process is repeated regularly when the people *'turn* to the LORD your God with all your heart and with all your soul' (v.10). This is similar to the thoughts of the prodigal son in Jesus's parable, when he 'came to himself' and 'arose and came to his father' (Luke 15.17,20).

We may call this turning, or *re*turning to God 'conversion'. It involves being ready for insight (opened eyes) and understanding (opened ears) in a process which will transform all aspects of our lives as individuals, families ('you and your children', Deut. 30.2) and societies.

In response to the people's return, God will turn to them in motherly compassion (30.3; see note). The Hebrew word *shub* describes His action to *'restore* your fortunes,' to 'gather you *again'* and 'fetch you' (30.3–4), and *'again* take delight in prospering you' (30.9; see 28.63).

God promises a new gathering of His scattered people. This is a frequent theme of writers in the period immediately before and during the Exile, as well as in New Testament times (Jer. 31.10; Isa. 43.5; 54.7; Ezek. 20.34; John 11.52). The intentional use of the same Hebrew word in Deuteronomy 30.4 and 4.34 (see note on 30.4), suggests a new act of liberation like the first, when God formed Israel as 'a people of His own possession' (4.20).

God also promises to 'circumcise' or 'open up' the heart of His people and their children, so that they will be able to love Him fully (30.6; see note). Moses had commanded the people to 'cut away . . . the thickening about your hearts' (10.16 NJPS; see note). But God in His grace promises to do what the people cannot do for themselves: to change and overcome their stubbornness of heart, just as surgeons today can change and give renewed life to people whose physical hearts are spoilt by disease.

Other writers have expressed a similar view of human need for God's help in making a new heart. Ezekiel said that God would remove the 'heart of stone' and replace it with a new 'heart of flesh' (Ezek. 36.26). Jeremiah said that God would write His Covenant Teaching on the hearts of His people (Jer. 31.33). Paul spoke of 'a spiritual circumcision' (Col. 2.11 NRSV). Hearts hardened or closed by fear, guilt, grief, prejudice, pride, greed or luxury will cause people to refuse to act in ways that are vital and life-giving. God is ready to 'open up' our hardened hearts if we are willing.

*That you may live.* The emphasis of this entire section is on the words 'that you may live' (Deut. 30.6). This major theme in Deuteronomy comes to a powerful climax in ch. 30 where it appears three times. God's purpose in taking a people to himself, in giving them Covenant Teaching, and in gathering them again from the ends of the earth is *that they, and through them all nations, may have life in all its fullness* (see John 10.10).

## COVENANT ENCOURAGEMENT: CLOSE ENOUGH TO TASTE

The scholar Raymond E. Brown has called Deuteronomy 30.11–20 'one of the great sermons of all time'. The introduction to this 'sermon,' is a word of encouragement to a discouraged, frightened people about to go into exile: this commandment to love God wholly (6.5) is 'not too hard' (30.11) or idealistic, or mysterious. Not only is it the most important of 'the things that are revealed' (29.29), but God himself will make the yoke easy by opening up the hearts of people for love (30.6). In this way the command will be 'in your heart' to practise it and 'in your mouth' to taste, teach and preach it for others to hear and put into practice (30.12–14).

## CHOOSE LIFE!, 30.15–20

The key to the meaning of this passage is in the words 'life' and 'live' which appear seven times. The theme comes from 30.6, 'that you may live'. God's will is life, but individuals and groups must choose 'life and good', and reject 'death and evil' by a lifelong commitment to love God fully, and by daily decisions to obey God's voice and keep His commandments. Moses's final words summarize the central appeal of the Book of Deuteronomy:

'Therefore choose life that you and your descendants may live, loving the LORD your God, obeying his voice, and cleaving to him; for that means life to you and length of days' (30.19–20).

## NOTES

**30.3. Compassion:** The word means 'mother love' for a child, as we see from the example of the mother whose heart 'yearned for her son' (1 Kings 3.26; see Isa. 49.15). This sort of divine mother love is also referred to in Hosea 11.8 and Isaiah 54.7,8,10. In Deuteronomy 13.17 and 32.36 it refers to God's motherly compassion for His sinful people.

**30.4. Fetch:** The same Hebrew word describes God's action to '*take* a nation for himself from the midst of another nation' (4.34), and to 'fetch' them again from among the nations (30.4).

**30.6. That you may live:** For previous instances of this phrase see 4.1; 5.33; 8.1; 16.20. In each case the statement is related to keeping commands and dwelling on the land.

**30.11–14.** Paul used this passage to explain that Jesus Christ is very close to believers in the proclamation of the gospel. He concludes by saying 'the word is near you, on your lips and in your heart (that is, the word of faith which we preach)' (Rom. 10.6–8).

## STUDY SUGGESTIONS

### REVIEW OF CONTENT

1. What are the 'secret things' and the 'revealed things', and how will God's people recognize the latter?
2. What is the meaning of 'conversion' in 30.1–10?
3. What two promises does God make for people who return to Him?
4. (a) For what reasons is God's command to love him 'easy' to fulfil?
   (b) In what circumstances do people chiefly find it difficult to fulfil?

### BIBLE STUDY

5. Read Isaiah 35.5 and Matthew 11.4–5. In what way are each of these passages a fulfilment of God's promise in Deuteronomy 30.6?
6. (a) What was God's purpose in taking a people to Himself?
   (b) What do we learn from John 8.12 about the fulfilment of that purpose?

### CONTEXTUAL APPLICATION

7. Select some short Bible readings and compose two or three prayers for use in a service of Covenant renewal, using passages from Deut. 26—30, and adapting them so as to relate to the experience of the congregation you belong to.
8. There are always risks of failure and chances of success in renewing our Covenant with God. Discuss the following attitudes to those risks: (a) Forget the risks and go for success.

(b) Remember the risks and try to avoid them. (c) Don't take any risks; if we can't be sure of success, back off.

9. What do you think the words 'that you may live' (Deut. 30.6) would mean for the following people?

(a) Villagers in an area where rains have failed for the third year in succession.

(b) A person with incurable cancer.

(c) A family who have lost their land through an illegal act by government officials.

(d) A teen-aged young woman from a minority group who has been trapped in the prostitution business.

(e) Rich people who are supporting the regime of an oppressive dictator.

(f) A prisoner serving a twenty-year sentence for drug trafficking.

# PART 4: 31.1—34.12

# LIFE AFTER MOSES

---

## INTRODUCTION

Four problems dominate the last four chapters of Deuteronomy. Each is related to the fact that the people of Israel had to enter the Promised Land without their great leader.

1. The first problem was *how to maintain continuity after Moses*. Moses's death made change inevitable, but a new leader would be needed to continue reminding the people of God's promises and warnings, and to help them to follow the guidance he had already given them. Chapter 31 deals with this problem.

2. The second problem was *how to maintain the people's true identity after Moses*. We have already met this theme in Deut. chs. 4 and 7 (see pp. 16–17, 61–62). One way of maintaining an identity would be to adopt the values of popular religion as a way of being 'modern', or 'popular', while pretending to be loyal to Yahweh. Another way would be to use political power to assert a new self-proclaimed identity. This was the path chosen by the powerful world emperor of Babylon, who boasted 'I am, and there is no one besides me' (Isa. 47.8,10).

But God's people would only find their true identity in their relationship to God whose name is 'I Am'. Chapter 32 deals with this problem of identity.

3. The third problem was related to the future. The burden of sinfulness, their own and others', could bring such suffering and darkness that the people could easily lose hope. Their problem was how to follow Moses's *vision of hope in time of darkness*. Chapter 33 is Moses's legacy of hope.

4. The fourth problem was *how to remember Moses*. How could the people preserve the memory of their great leader in a way that would show the honour due to him, but not make him some sort of superman or god-like hero, nor use his memory to prevent necessary change in the future. This is the subject of ch. 34.

The people were also experiencing these four problems in the time of the Narrator, five hundred years after the death of Moses, as we can see from references in literature of the time. In the work of a historical writer whose views were similar to those of the Narrator, we can detect a longing for *continuity* with the 'law' of

Moses (2 Kings 18.11–12; 21.8). The prophet Jeremiah complained that his people did not know 'the ordinance of the LORD' (Jer. 8.7), and called for a continuity with the past by referring to some of the Ten Commandments in his Temple sermon (7.9–10). He told them to 'stand by the roads, and look, and ask for the ancient paths' (6.16), and to 'hear the words of this covenant' (11.2).

In the midst of the ruins of warfare, Jeremiah asked the question of *identity*: 'Is Israel a slave? Is he a homeborn servant? Why then has he become a prey?' (Jer. 2.14). He saw the Israelites seeking a false sense of identity. He compared the people of his time to a woman who said 'It is hopeless, for I have loved strangers, and after them I will go', and then said 'I am innocent' (Jer. 2.25,35).

At the same time Jeremiah held up to the Israelites, who had been scattered in exile, the *vision of hope* that 'in those days the house of Judah shall join the house of Israel, and together they shall come . . . to the land that I gave to your fathers for a heritage' (Jer. 3.18). He told them that Yahweh would make a 'new covenant with the house of Israel and the house of Judah' (Jer. 31.31).

## PROBLEMS FOR GOD'S PEOPLE TODAY

Similar problems confront Christian leaders in the modern world. The problem of *continuity* takes the form of a search for roots of faith in an age of secular attitudes, greed for money, and nationalistic power-seeking.

The problem of *identity* is relevant to younger generations of Christians in rapidly changing cultures and societies with conflicting values. They might ask 'are we Christians who are Thais (or Bengalis or Brazilians or Zambians or any other national or ethnic group), or Thais or Bengalis or Brazilians or Zambians who happen to be Christians? Where does our true loyalty lie?'

The problem of *vision* involves questions about the future of the Christian faith in a world dominated by unfriendly powers, and about the future of our planet in a time of nuclear weapons, environmental pollution and pandemic disease.

The problem of *right remembering* arises in relationship to strong leaders of past years, who laid foundations for the present, but who were associated with colonial or oppressive regimes which are no longer acceptable as providing guidance for the future.

# 31.1–30
# Continuity After Moses

## OUTLINE

31.1–6: Moses Prepares the People for his Death.
31.7–23: Joshua as Moses's Successor.
31.24–30: The Book of the Covenant Teaching.

## INTERPRETATION

Chapter 31 deals with three themes which have appeared earlier in Deuteronomy, and gathers them together in a summary way.

### MOSES PREPARES THE PEOPLE FOR HIS DEATH

Although the whole of Deuteronomy so far has been a preparation for Moses's death (see 1.37; 3,27; 4,21–22), in this chapter it is a major theme. Here, for the first time, God speaks the words of solemn finality to Moses: 'You must die' (v. 14), and 'You are about to sleep with your fathers' (v. 16). Moses's words 'after my death' (vv. 27,29) refer to that death as inevitable, and seem to threaten that chaos might follow it. Continuity after Moses was an urgent matter of life or death for the generations following him.

All leaders, even the greatest and most influential, are mortal, and must eventually cease from their labours, either by retirement or death. When a wise pastor begins his ministry in a congregation, he immediately takes steps to prepare the people for the time when he will leave them. He does this by: (a) continuous education in Christian faith and practice at all levels, (b) developing a vital worship tradition which can be adapted to changing circumstances, (c) choosing and training potential leaders, and (d) helping his people to put God's love into action through service projects. When the time comes, the congregation will be ready for change of leadership while maintaining continuity of mission.

### JOSHUA AS MOSES'S SUCCESSOR

The appointment of a successor to Moses is a second theme that runs throughout Deuteronomy (1.38; 3.21–22; 3.28; 32.44; 34.9). Entry into the Promised Land was the final step in the process that began with liberation from slavery in Egypt and continued at Mount Sinai/Horeb and on through the wilderness period. A new leader was necessary to complete the task Moses had begun. With great foresight as inspired by God, Moses had prepared Joshua for

A new leader was needed to complete the task Moses had begun. In this century many newly-independent nations have had to educate and train new leaders for various sorts of work—starting from adult literacy classes, as above in Tanzania, through to universities. And training new leaders has been an important task of the Churches in Bible Schools and Theological Seminaries, as below in the Philippines.

this work by encouraging and strengthening him in the presence of the people (1.38; 3.28). Here in ch. 31 we find the outlines of a commissioning service for Joshua in five steps which may serve as a pattern for preparing new leaders today.

1. *Moses prepared the people* to understand and accept Joshua's leadership (31.3–6). There were two reasons for them to be strong and courageous: (1) God would go over with them into the new land, and (2) they would experience God's powerful presence through the leadership of Joshua. 'Joshua will go over at your head' (31.3). The people needed assurance that the new leader would continue the work of Moses.

2. *Moses prepared Joshua* (31.7–8). He told Joshua that God's presence would give him power for his task of enabling the people to inherit the land. More importantly, Moses charged Joshua to go *with* the people all the way as they entered the land (31.7; see note). A good leader must stay close to his people. He should not think of himself as superior to them, or separate himself from their fears and concerns.

3. *Moses brought Joshua into the tent of meeting* so that he could come into direct contact with Yahweh (31.14). Moses wanted Joshua to meet God as he himself had done (Exod. 24.15–18). Leaders must know and understand the spiritual side of their task.

4. *Yahweh invited Joshua to share the burden of 'this people'* (Deut. 31.16–18). Yahweh's speech about the stubborn and rebellious character of 'this people' (31.16) seems like an interruption in the commissioning service. Yahweh shares with Moses and Joshua his knowledge of 'the purposes which they are already forming' (31.21; see note). The Hebrew word translated as 'purposes' implies a comparison between God's people and humanity's 'evil imagination' before and after the flood (Gen. 6.5; 8.21). In fact this speech is not an interruption: it emphasizes the importance of Joshua's leadership in continuity with that of Moses, in spite of the evil in the hearts of God's people. Leaders must be prepared to maintain their goals in spite of disappointments and difficulties.

5. *Yahweh commissioned Joshua* for the challenging and difficult task ahead (Deut. 31.23). Joshua's basic authority for his great task came not from Moses but from Yahweh Himself.

The training of new leaders is one of the most important tasks of the Churches in all parts of the world today. The Christian community in China was tested by persecution during the years of the cultural revolution (1965–75), and has grown rapidly in more recent times. Now seminaries are working hard to develop new leaders who will take the place of the older generation, and give pastoral leadership to new generations of Christians.

## THE BOOK OF THE COVENANT TEACHING, 31.24–30

At the beginning of Deuteronomy, the Narrator had shown Moses explaining the Covenant Teaching ('this law') to the wilderness generation of Israelites gathered in Moab (Deut. 1.5). Now, at the end, Moses gives them the Covenant Teaching in portable written form to take with them into the future. It contains the sum of the 'things that are revealed . . . to us and to our children for ever, that we may do all the words of this law' (Covenant Teaching (29.29). It will always be 'very near to you . . . in your mouth and in your heart, so that you can do it' (30.14). Future generations who read and hear the Covenant Teaching will hear the voice of Moses speaking again to them.

Two things stand out in this description of the written Covenant Teaching.

1. It would serve to *control the greed and pride of the powerful*. The appointed time for the recitation of the Covenant Teaching was 'the year of release' (31.10; see 15.2). On that occasion, creditors would forgive their debtors, slave-owners would free their slaves, and the people as a whole would make a new attempt to solve the problem of poverty.

2. Justice and spirituality, though separate, are both a part of Covenant Teaching. The *public authorities* (*elders*; see 27.1) would be in charge of *administration of justice*. The *religious leaders* (*priests*, 31.9,25; see 27.9) would be in charge of *interpreting the Covenant Teaching* and leading in worship.


## NOTES

**31.6. He will not fail you or forsake you:** The author of Hebrews used these words to encourage Christians to remember people in prison and oppressed, to hold marriage in honour, and to keep their lives 'free from the love of money' (Heb. 13.3–5).

**31.7. Put them in possession of it** (the land): The literal meaning of the Hebrew word translated 'put them in possession' is 'cause them to inherit'. This includes helping them to win victory over the rulers of the land, and also giving them the Covenant Teaching as a guide so that they can live long in the land (see pp. 8–10 and Joshua 1.7–8).

**31.21. I know the purposes which they are already forming:** The Hebrew word translated 'purposes' in this verse is translated as 'imagination' in Gen. 6.5 and 8.21. NRSV makes the connection clear by use of the word 'incline' in both places. 'I know what they are *inclined* to do' (Deut. 31.21). 'Every *inclination* of the thoughts of their hearts . . . .'. (Gen. 6.5; 8.21). This expression thus links

Israel to the universal problem of human wickedness (see pp. 77–78).

**31.26. This book of the law.** If 'the words of this law' on the stones on Mount Ebal (27.8; see Josh. 8.32) were the Ten Commandments, 'this book of the law' could refer to the Book of Deuteronomy itself, or some parts of it.

## STUDY SUGGESTIONS

### REVIEW OF CONTENT

1. What *four* problems dominate the last four chapters of Deuteronomy?
2. What *three* themes related to continuity appear in ch. 31?
3. What were the *five* steps in Joshua's commissioning service?
4. What was the occasion for the reading of the 'book of the law'? What does this tell us about the purpose and use of that book?

### BIBLE STUDY

5. Moses was preparing his people for the fact that he would not be with them when they entered the Promised Land. In what ways is Deut. 31 like and unlike the farewell speeches of Joshua and Jesus (Josh. 23—24; John 17).
6. Read Amos 6.4–7. Do you think that the people described there had heard the 'book of the law' read regularly? If so, why did it have no effect on them?

### CONTEXTUAL APPLICATION

7. Choose two of the four problems (see question 1) that were important for the 'Moab generation', and say in what ways they are important for people of your generation today.
8. Compose a commissioning service for newly elected officers of a Church group to which you belong (youth, women, older people). Include as many of the five steps of Joshua's commissioning service as you can. What else would you include?
9. The four steps taken by the wise pastor to prepare his people for the future were Christian education, vital worship, leadership development, and active service (see p. 180). Which do you think are most important, or least important: (a) for the congregations concerned, (b) for pastors when they first begin pastoral work?

# 32.1–43
# Identity After Moses

## INTRODUCTION

Chapter 32 is in the form of a song which, in poetic form, reminds the Israelites of their identity and helps them to resist the temptation of the false gods of the land. Already in ch. 31 Yahweh had told Moses to 'write this song, and teach it to the people of Israel' so that it would 'confront them as a witness (for it will live unforgotten in the mouths of their descendants)' (31.19,21). The Narrator has placed this second song at the end of Moses's long life as part of his legacy, along with the written Covenant Teaching.

The Old Testament records three 'songs' of Moses. The first (Exod. 15.1–18) celebrates Yahweh's victory over the forces of oppression at the crossing of the sea, and looks forward to the settlement of His people in the Promised Land. The second is Moses's song in Deut. 32. For the third song, see Deut. 33.

Because of its poetic form, this song does not present ideas in an orderly way, but rather as four themes, each relating to the people's identity after the death of Moses. The Narrator presents Moses's words to the people following the conclusion of the song (32.44–47)

## OUTLINE

First Theme: You are part of God's Wider Plan.
Second Theme: You are God's Special People.
Third Theme: You are a Perverse Generation.
Fourth Theme: You can be a New Generation.

## INTERPRETATION

### FIRST THEME: YOU ARE PART OF GOD'S WIDER PLAN

The beginning and ending of this song place God's people in a universal context of all creation and the whole family of nations on the earth. Yahweh is not the God of a city state like Marduk, the god of the city of Babylon. Yahweh is not a tribal god of Israel like Chemosh the god of the Moabites, concerned only in the fortunes of one people. Yahweh is Lord of heaven and earth (Deut. 10.14; see 4.39), and Lord of *all* nations, who is also God of Israel (see pp. 24–25).

The poem begins with Moses's call to heaven and earth (meaning all of creation) to listen carefully to his words of warning and promise to the people. The poem closes with an appeal to all nations to praise Yahweh's people as the beginning of a new earth (32.43; see note). Israel's first identity is rooted in Yahweh's deep concern for the right ordering of all that He has created and is continuing to create: sky and land, mountains and rivers, forests and seas, plants and animals, together with human beings in their nations and groupings.

The effect of this summons to heavens and earth at the beginning of the song is to suggest that when Yahweh's people choose between life and good, and death and evil, their decision will affirm or threaten the integrity of the whole environment and the *shalom* of all nations. Doing 'evil in the sight of the LORD' (31.29) has consequences for all of nature ('heaven and earth' v.28) and for the nations God has made. On the other hand, living according to the Covenant Teaching will refresh both nature and the nations like 'gentle rain upon the tender grass' (32.2).

Christians who realize that they are part of God's wider plan will gladly join hands with people of other faith traditions to work for righteousness and justice in society and in the natural environment, and for the peace and integrity of creation. There is no separate Hindu, Buddhist, Christian or Muslim solution to universal problems like the ozone hole, global warming, or pollution of many sorts that threaten life on our planet. In Thailand Christians and Buddhists together fight tourist-funded prostitution. Christians and Buddhists from nine Asian countries met in Seoul, Korea, not long ago to protest against use of the Pacific as a dumping ground for nuclear waste.

### SECOND THEME: YOU ARE GOD'S SPECIAL PEOPLE

God has chosen 'a people for His own possession, out of all the peoples that are on the face of the earth' (7.6; see note). On their part, God's people are to follow the pattern which He has set for them. To use the words of Paul, they must be 'imitators of God, as beloved children' (Eph. 5.1).

The present King of Thailand employs a staff of agriculturalists on his spacious palace grounds to improve methods of producing crops like rice, potatoes, strawberries and coffee which can be imitated by people throughout the entire nation. In the same way, God has chosen a particular people to conduct demonstration projects for the benefit of all nations. The people who recite this song will learn about God's nature and what they must do to be like Him.

First, God is like a *Rock* to Israel (32.4,15,18). He is absolutely dependable, and 'will not fail . . . or forsake' His people (31.6,8; see 4.31). The Rock of their salvation will protect them from enemy attacks (32.15; see Ps. 62.2). God's work of creation and new creation is 'perfect', that is, wholly good and true, and 'without iniquity' (Deut. 32.4; see note).

Other pictures also help us to understand the special relationship between God and His people. God is like a *mother* who carried the Israelites like a child in the womb and 'gave you birth' (32.18), showing motherly compassion on them (32.36). God is like a *father* who brought His people up and made them strong (v. 6), or the leader of a *rescue team* who found and saved someone dying in a 'howling waste', and then protected, cared for, and kept that person 'as the apple of his eye' (32.10; see note). Again, God is like a *mother eagle* teaching its young to fly by pushing them out of the nest one by one, then swooping down to allow the inexperienced young bird to rest on her outstretched wings (32.11; see note and Exod. 19.4).

These pictures help God's people to remember who they are and what they should do. Because their Rock's 'ways are justice' (Deut. 32.4), they must follow ways of 'justice, and only justice' (16.20). They must protect innocent people from injustice (19.4–10) and strive to be 'faithful' like Him (32.4 NRSV; see v.20). Because God's 'work is perfect' they must be 'blameless' (18.13; see note on Deut. 32.4 and Matt. 5.48).

The people will give fatherly discipline and motherly care to their children to make them strong (8.5). They will love the stranger in their midst (10.19), be generous to the poor (15.7–14), and give new life to the weak and vulnerable in the year of release (15.12–18). Today we may think of many brave people who help others in times of trouble, like ambulance teams or lifeboat crews, or like the Reverend Kiyoshi Tanimoto, pastor of a congregation in Hiroshima, Japan, who showed this sort of imitation of God by his compassion for the victims of the nuclear bomb blast of 1945. Without thought of personal danger, he rescued people from the raging fires and offered cups of water to people crying out for medicine.

## THIRD THEME: YOU ARE A PERVERSE GENERATION

Alongside the knowledge that the Israelites are specially chosen by Yahweh, is the realization that they have turned away from their Rock, father, mother, guardian, and teacher! The expressions accumulate like links in a chain: 'dealt corruptly . . . no longer his children . . . perverse and crooked (v.5), grew fat, bloated and gorged, . . . abandoned God who made him, and scoffed at the Rock of his salvation' (v.15 NRSV), 'with abominable practices they provoked him to anger', (v.16), 'sacrificed to demons which were no gods' (v.17), 'forgot the God who gave you birth' (v. 18).

They are 'void of counsel', with 'no understanding', unable to see where their ways are leading (v.28). They are lured by the poisonous grapes of the Canaanite culture that brings death (vv. 32–33) — a serious warning to the people who 'have eaten and are full and grown fat' (31.20).

This description of Israel fits the situation in the time of the Narrator, as we can see from the words of Jeremiah, who compared the people to 'well-fed lusty stallions, each neighing for his neighbour's wife', or to a 'horse plunging headlong into battle' (Jer. 5.8; 8.6). They were a 'senseless people who have eyes, but see not . . . ears, but hear not' (5.21), a people 'uncircumcised in heart' (9.26). They had 'become great and rich . . . fat and sleek,' and 'know no bounds in deeds of wickedness' (5.27–28). The second and third themes, when taken together, show that God's people are both chosen and sinful, living in a 'fallen world' just like other humans!

A Christian doctor who is director of a home for AIDS patients in a large city wrote: 'We at Joseph House are very much immersed in the fallenness of the world. We see, of course, our own fallenness too. Relapses into drugs or alcohol, relapses into unloving or suspicious behaviour, relapses into taking more care of ourselves than we do of one another, relapses into fearing for our future rather than trusting that we will be taken care of.'

### FOURTH THEME: YOU CAN BE A NEW GENERATION

This song of Moses ends with a picture of a chorus of nations praising the new generation of God's people who can be a sign of God's new earth. The good news is that, despite their failure and rebellion, with the resulting darkness and disaster, God will restore *shalom* by defeating the powers of death (32.35, 40–42, 43; see note on 32.35,41): He will vindicate and, once again, show compassion on His defeated, hungry, helpless people (32.36).

God's saving action for His people is in keeping with His wider plan to bless the nations. He is concerned lest the 'adversaries . . . misunderstand' His restorative judgement on His people (32.27 NRSV). When the nations see that the God of Israel has power to restore life to the dying, heal the wounded, and 'cleanse the land for his people' (32.43 NRSV), they will join the chorus of praise for the 'wise and understanding people' (4.6) who taught them about the divine source of wisdom and understanding. Then the nations will be able to

> See now that I, even I, am he,
> and there is no god beside me;
> I kill and I make alive;

I wound and I heal;
and there is none that can deliver
out of my hand (32.39).

## NOTES

**31.30. The words of this song:.** The contents of 32.1–43 suggest that
in its present form the song is addressed to readers of much later
times, perhaps the generation of Manasseh or Jehoiakim, or even
the time of the Exile (see pp. 2–3). For example, the predictions
that 'they will forsake' God (31.16), and 'will surely act corruptly'
(31.29) had come true: 'he forsook God who made him' (32.15),
and 'they have dealt corruptly' (v. 5). 'The generation to come'
(29.22) was now 'a perverse and crooked generation' (32.5, see v.
20). The possibility that Israel would 'provoke' God's anger (4.25)
was now a fact (32.16,19,21). The nation had suffered defeat at the
hands of an aggressive power (32.30). Although the final
destruction of the nation was still in the future, the whole of human
society and the natural environment had become profoundly
disturbed (32.22–25).

**32.1. Give ear, O heavens . . . let the earth hear:** The Book of Isaiah
begins with a similar appeal to the entire creation to listen carefully
as Yahweh makes His charge against His people (Isa. 1.2). The
consequences of Covenant violation appear further on in the Book
of Isaiah: 'The earth mourns and withers . . . the heavens languish
together with the earth. The earth lies polluted under its inhabitants; for they have transgressed the laws, violated the statutes,
broken the everlasting covenant' (Isa. 24.4–5; see 50.3).

Jeremiah also described creation's reaction to human violation of
the Covenant of creation. He said that the heavens would be
'appalled . . . shocked . . . utterly desolate' because God's people
have forsaken the Lord of all creation for gods of death (Jer. 2.12–
13). When human actions make 'the fruitful land . . . a desert', the
earth will 'mourn' and the heavens grow dark (4.26,28; see Hos.
4.3). Yet, the redemption of God's people is the beginning of a new
creation, causing the heavens and earth to sing for joy (Isa. 44.23;
49.13).

**32.4. Perfect:** The same Hebrew word *tamim* appears in Deut.
18.13 translated as 'blameless'. See pp. 105–06 and 112–13 for a
discussion of the meaning of this Hebrew word *tamim*.

**32.10. The howling waste:** The Hebrew word is *tohu*. This recalls
the original chaos when 'the earth was a formless void (*tohu
wabohu*) before creation (Gen. 1.2 NRSV), and also the return to a
chaotic state in the time of Jeremiah, when he saw that the earth
was 'waste and void' (*tohu wabohu* Jer. 4.23). Deutero-Isaiah told

'They are a perverse and crooked generation, foolish and senseless' (32.5–6).
Moses's forecast that the Israelites' greed and corruption would bring disaster was
confirmed when later prophets wrote: 'the earth mourns and withers' and 'the
fruitful land was a desert'. People today face the same choice between the 'doom' of
rapidly spreading desert in many countries, or the blessing of abundant life in a
'restored Eden'—exemplified below in the 'Promised Land' of Israel itself—if they
'keep all the commandment'.

the exiles in Babylon that God's will for the world was not that it should be in a state of 'chaos' (*tohu*), but that it should be a place and space for meaningful habitation (Isa. 45.18). When God rescued Israel from the 'howling waste' (*tohu*), He was beginning to create a new earth.

**32.11. Flutters over its young:** The Hebrew word translated 'young' is in plural form. Martin Buber has written that these young eaglets must refer to the peoples to whom God gave an inheritance (32.8).

**32.35,41. Vengeance:** The true meaning of the Hebrew word *naqam*, translated as 'vengeance', is to right a wrong or restore a condition of peace by taking action against those who have done the wrong, or violated the peace. In this case, both Israel and her enemies had destroyed God's *shalom*. As Paul emphasized in Romans 12.19 (see Heb. 10.30), 'vengeance' belongs to God, not to humans (Lev. 19.18).

**32.43. Praise his people, O you nations:** This translation follows the Hebrew and is used by RSV and NJPS. The Greek and Qumran versions have 'heavens' instead of 'nations' and add a second line to the Masoretic text. The NRSV has adopted this to read 'Praise, O heavens, his people, worship him, all you gods!' Paul quotes the first line in Rom. 15.10 but changes the interpretation to read 'Rejoice O Gentiles *with* his people'.

## STUDY SUGGESTIONS

### REVIEW OF CONTENT

1. Where can we find the three songs attributed to Moses?
2. What are the *four* themes of ch. 32 which show the identity of God's people?

### BIBLE STUDY

3. Psalm 146.7–9 describes some of God's actions. *Give three* examples of actions by Christians which reflect those actions of God.
4. Compare Isaiah 44.23 with Hosea 4.1–3. Why do the heavens and earth 'mourn' or 'rejoice' in each case? In Deuteronomy 32.1 are they mourning or rejoicing?

### CONTEXTUAL APPLICATION

5. 'When Yahweh's people choose between life and death . . . their decision will affirm or threaten the integrity of the whole environment and the *shalom* of nations' (p. 186). Do you agree? Give reasons for your answer.
6. Give examples of Christians working with people of other faiths

to preserve the natural environment, or to improve the conditions of life for their fellow citizens. How are these examples of interfaith co-operation related to the identity of Christians?

7. Why was God willing to take the risk of calling His own 'special people', when He knew that they would become 'a perverse generation'?

8. (a) In what ways, if any, do you think that people in your country today are 'following God's pattern' more closely than people of past generations?

(b) In what ways, if any, are they 'following God's pattern' *less* closely?

# 33.1–29
# Moses's Vision of a New Israel

## INTRODUCTION

Deuteronomy concludes not with law but with a vision of a reunited Israel in a restored Garden of Eden (see pp. 53, 152–53, 160–62). Moses's vision brings Deuteronomy to a climax with the completion of the task he set out to do according to 1.5, 'to explain this law' (Covenant Teaching), thus 'making living water accessible to those who would not be able to find it by themselves' (see note on 1.5). Moses's last word to the people gathered at the boundary of the Promised Land was not a set of commands but a vision of hope, reaching beyond their history of past revolt and defeat, and beyond the disaster that was yet to come to them (see 31.29).

In the time of the Narrator, 'all Israel' (1.1; 31.1,7) was mostly scattered in exile among the nations (30.1). Of the twelve tribes mentioned in 33.6–25, only Judah remained, living in a greatly reduced part of the original land of Israel, and they too would soon be 'uprooted . . . from their land' (29.28). The Narrator must have had these scattered people in mind when he placed this song of hope at the end of Deuteronomy.

## OUTLINE

33.1–5: Foundations for Renewal.
33.6–25: A Diverse but Reunited People.
33.26–29: A People Saved by the Lord.

## INTERPRETATION

### FOUNDATIONS FOR RENEWAL

In 33.1–5, Moses reminds the people of three foundations necessary for a renewed, reunited Israel.

1. The first is a firm *faith in divine deliverance* as in times past. Yahweh, who 'came from Sinai' at the head of the armies of heaven ('the ten thousands of holy ones', 33.2), is still their powerful Lord, as described in the Song of Moses (32.36; see 7.17–24).

2. The second foundation is the constitution or *set of laws based on righteousness and justice*. This took the form of *a written manual of direction and instruction* ('a law') as 'a possession for the assembly of Jacob' (33.4; see 31.9, 24–25)), to serve as a guide for their life together in times of prosperity and disaster.

3. The third foundation is a *structure of government* to administer righteousness and justice in public life. This took the form of a righteous *king* (a descendant of David), governing with a council of *elders* representing 'the united tribes of Israel' (33.5 NRSV; see note). As we have seen, this government would function according to Yahweh's instruction, because the king would be guided by the Covenant Teaching (17.14–20). The structure of representative government here suggested is not necessarily tied to a monarchical form of government.

### A DIVERSE BUT REUNITED PEOPLE, 33.6–25

We find here a picture of a restored people, enriched by diversity, and bound together by their covenant loyalty to God. We can best understand the purpose of this section of Deuteronomy by comparing it with other visions of a future Israel blessed by God. *Ezekiel* pictured a restored land with all twelve tribes gathered around a new Jerusalem with twelve gates, one for each tribe (Ezek. 48.1–7, 23–26, 30–34). From the Temple in the centre of Jerusalem flows a life-giving river producing food for the hungry and medicinal leaves for healing wounds (Ezek. 47.12).

Similarly, the new Jerusalem pictured in *Revelation* has twelve gates named for the twelve tribes (Rev. 21.12). The gates are always open (Rev. 21.25) so that all nations and their leaders may enter and learn from the light of God's presence (Rev. 21.24). The tree of life which grows by the river of life in that restored Eden will produce fruit for food and leaves for the healing of the nations (Rev. 22.1–2).

### SPECIAL BLESSINGS

These pictures of future blessing give us a clue to the meaning of this passage in Deuteronomy 33. The Narrator pictures Moses as giving to the scattered people, who have survived the 'nightmare' of disaster pictured in Deut. 28.15–63 and 31.16–18, a vision of a renewed and reunited people of God in the midst of the nations.

Each tribe included in this vision would receive a particular blessing, related to its own situation and abilities, as its unique contribution to the whole. For Reuben, it is escape from death, for Judah, victory over adversaries (33.6,7). Benjamin's blessing is security (33.12), while Joseph (which includes Manasseh and Ephraim) receives 'the choicest gifts of heaven above . . . the abundance of the everlasting hills . . . the best gifts of the earth and its fullness' (33.13–16). For Zebulun and Issachar there is 'the affluence of the seas and the hidden treasures of the sand' (33.19). Gad receives 'the best of the land' (33.21), Dan the strength of a lion (33.22), Naphtali the land by the lake of Galilee (33.23). Asher is blessed with the good-will of fellow tribes, and abundant crops of olive oil 33.24).

SPECIAL TASKS

In two cases, blessing means the assignment of special tasks. Levi, the priestly tribe, does not receive land or abundant crops, but will have the task and privilege of interpreting the will of God (v.8, see note), instructing the people in the Covenant Teaching and representing the people before God in worship (v.10).

Zebulun and Issachar will 'call peoples to their mountain' (v.19). This may refer to periodic feasts to which neighbouring peoples would be invited, and at which the hosts would tell of Yahweh's saving power and the Covenant Teaching. In the words of a psalmist, they would 'say among the nations, "the LORD reigns!" ' (Ps. 96.10). On their part, the visitors would say 'Surely this great nation is a wise and understanding people' (Deut. 4.6).

In this vision, the people of God will be bound together in a federal unity of diverse tribes, in which each will bring its particular contribution to the whole. At the same time, Israel is once again taking its place among the peoples of the earth. Yahweh who delivered Israel and gave them His Covenant Teaching is also 'lover of the peoples' (33.3 RSV and NRSV margins; see note). We find a similar insight in the writings of one of the prophets of Israel during the exilic period: according to Isaiah ch.49, the task of 'the servant of the LORD' is to 'raise up the tribes of Jacob', that is, to restore the federal unity which was Moses's vision in Deuteronomy 33. This restored people will then be 'a light to the nations' and invite them to become a part of the federal unity of the Covenant People (Isa. 49.6,8).

## A PEOPLE SAVED BY THE LORD

This final section summarizes the major themes of the entire poem. A people 'saved by the LORD' (v.29) will receive three sorts of *blessing*.

1. God who is 'the shield of your help, and the sword of your triumph' (v. 29) will give them *victory* over the powers of oppression and death (their 'enemies', v. 27b).

2. God, whose 'heavens drop down dew' (v.28) will give them *material blessings* for the support of life ('grain and wine' (v.28) in a restored Eden.

3. The third and most important blessing is God Himself! What makes this people special ('who is like you'? v.29) is the assurance that:

> The eternal God is your dwelling place,
> and underneath are the everlasting arms. (v.27a)

Of the two gifts of God to His people—the Covenant Teaching, and His nearness to them (4.7–8)—the second is the most important. The Commandment above all others is that God's people should love Him wholly (6.5), and thus remain close to Him, who is 'our dwelling place in all generations' (Ps. 90.1).

When the Israelites built a 'sanctuary' or a 'house' in response to God's command, God promised to 'dwell in their midst' (Exod. 25.8). In fact, God chose to 'make his name dwell' in the sanctuary (Deut. 12.11); when people went there to worship, they would feel close to Him (see Ps.73.17, 23–26, 28). The sanctuary was the symbol of God's presence with His people. The Psalms are filled with a yearning to dwell in the house of God (Ps. 27.4), to see God's power and glory (63.2), to take refuge under God's wings (91.1), and to find protection in God's holy Temple (26.8)

This affirmation of faith tells all scattered and homeless people in every generation and place that no matter how far away they may be from the central sanctuary, no matter what suffering and temptations may come to them in the future, they can live close to God as their true home or 'habitation' (Ps. 91.9). A theological student once said that Christians 'must learn to throw themselves into God's everlasting arms'. God will not only rescue His people from slavery and oppression (Deut. 26.8), but will give them victory over the enemy. His arms are arms of love and compassion, always ready to revive the dying (Deut. 32.10) and carry the weak (Isa. 40.11).

We find the same theme in the New Testament. Jesus invites Andrew to His home (John 1.39), and finally reveals that He Himself is the new sanctuary (2.21). He invites His followers to 'make your home in me as I make mine in you', and then adds

'Those who remain in me, with me in them, bear fruit in plenty' (John 15.4–5, translation by Henri Nouwen). Their prayers will be effective (v.7), since 'God is love, and those who abide in love abide in God, and God abides in them' (1 John 4.16 NRSV).

## NOTES

**33.1. This is the blessing with which Moses . . . blessed the children of Israel before his death:** These are the Narrator's words introducing the poem which follows. The Narrator probably used a poem from a time long after Moses's death, and placed it at the end of Deuteronomy for his own purposes. Scholars are not agreed about the date when this poem was composed. Some believe it was a hymn of national thanksgiving used in worship after the division of the Kingdom of Israel which took place following the death of Solomon. They suggest that the original intention of the poem was to urge the separated northern tribes to reunite with Judah as before, and thus be blessed. The Narrator has placed it at the end of Deuteronomy to hold out to the scattered people a vision of hope for reunion.

**33.3. He loved his people:** The Hebrew of this line has 'peoples' in the plural (see marginal notes in RSV and NRSV). But that does not fit in with the rest of the poem, which focuses on Israel. Most translators, therefore, both ancient and modern, assume the plural to be an error, and change it to the singular 'his people'. However, the plural form may be correct after all. Yahweh's regard for the nations is also expressed elsewhere in Deuteronomy.

**33.4. When Moses commanded us a law:** Reference to Moses in the third person suggests that Moses was not the author of this poem.

**33.5. There arose a king in Jeshurun** (NRSV): The Hebrew does not indicate who the king was. RSV interprets the king as Yahweh. The gathering of the heads of all the tribes of Israel in this verse suggests a reference to the coronation of David when 'all the tribes of Israel . . . all the elders of Israel . . . made a covenant . . . before the LORD' with David, and anointed him king over Israel (2 Sam. 5.1, 3).

**33.8. Thummim . . . and . . . Urim:** These were small objects with symbols written on them indicating a positive or negative reply from God. The priests kept them in the pocket of their aprons ('*ephod*'), and used them to cast lots. Hosea may have been referring to this way of consulting God when he blamed the people for inquiring of a wooden idol (Hos. 4.12).

**33.19. Call peoples to their mountain:** Some scholars believe that this is a reference to Mount Tabor which lay on the border between Zebulun and Issachar. It was also at the crossing of the east-west road between the Valley of Jezreel and the Sea of Galilee, and the north-south road from Damascus to Megiddo. There may have been an important shrine on Tabor, where festivals were held.

**33.27. And he thrust out the enemy:** The Hebrew form may refer to either past or future action. NIV translates with the future tense: 'He will drive out your enemy'. JB uses the participle form to describe typical or continuous action of Yahweh: 'driving the enemy before you'.

**33.28. So Israel dwelt in safety:** The Hebrew verb translated 'dwelt' can mean present or future. NRSV has 'Israel lives in safety'; NIV, 'Israel will live in safety'.

## STUDY SUGGESTIONS

REVIEW OF CONTENT

1.  (a)  What people did the Narrator have in mind when he placed ch. 33 at the end of Deuteronomy?
    (b)  In what way had the situation of the Israelites in Moab been different from the situation of their descendants in the time of the Narrator?
2.  What were the *three* 'foundations' necessary for a renewed Israel?
3.  What two other passages in the Bible help us to understand 33.6–25?
4.  What 'blessings' would God give to the tribes of Reuben, Gad and Naphtali in a re-united Israel?
5.  What were the special tasks given to Levi, Zebulun and Issachar?
6.  (a)  What three blessings accompany salvation by God?
    (b)  What is God's most important gift to His people?

BIBLE STUDY

7.  In what ways is the picture of a renewed Israel in Deuteronomy 33.6–25 (a) similar to, and (b) different from, the picture in Ezekiel 48.1–7, 23–26?
8.  Read Psalm 73.23–28 and John 15.4–5. In what ways do these passages help you to understand the words 'The eternal God is your dwelling place' (Deut. 33.27)?

CONTEXTUAL APPLICATION

9.  How far do the three 'foundations' described in Deut. 33.1–5 apply to your own country? What other foundations, if any, does it have or need?
10.  Read Deuteronomy 33.6–25 as a picture of 'federal unity in

diversity'. In what ways can this picture be a model for international relationships, or for a multi-cultural and multi-racial society today?

11. (a) What might be the meaning of 'the everlasting arms' for a person whose house has burned down, and who has lost everything?

(b) In what ways, if any, have you yourself experienced 'the everlasting arms'?

# 32.48–52 and 34.1–12
# Remembering Moses

## INTRODUCTION

When the Narrator described Moses's death five hundred years after the event, he also told his own and later generations how they (and we) should remember Israel's greatest leader.

According to Deut. 34.5, God Himself buried Moses in an unmarked grave outside the Promised Land. The Narrator was telling his readers to remember Moses not by making a pilgrimage and putting flowers on his grave, but by *living* as Moses had taught them. He gave his readers three brief portraits of that heroic figure to help them remember him rightly.

## OUTLINE

32.48–52, 34.1–4: The Man who Saw the Promised Land from Afar.
34.5–9: The Servant of the Lord.
34.10–12: Israel's Greatest Prophet.

## INTERPRETATION

### THE MAN WHO SAW THE PROMISED LAND FROM AFAR

The *first* portrait is of Moses as an old man, who, though 'no longer able to go out and come in'(31.2), had ascended alone through mist and wind to a craggy mountain-top in sight of the Promised Land. In his heart were Yahweh's last words to him: 'I have let you see it' (i.e. the land) 'with your eyes, but you shall not go over there' (34.4 and see 32.52). As we look at this portrait, we can feel Moses's deep disappointment, and recall another portrait of him pleading with God for His stubborn and rebellious people on Mount Sinai/Horeb (Deut. 9). We may also remember Moses's willingness to bear the burden of their guilt in the wilderness so that they might enter the land (3.25–26, see p. 15; 4.21).

Israel's greatest leader, with clear eyesight and undiminished natural strength (34.7), bowed in humble obedience to 'the LORD's command' (34.5 NRSV; see note). His work was complete.

## A MAN OF VISION

The Narrator's words 'The LORD showed him all the land' (v.1) imply that what Moses saw when he gazed at the Promised Land was God's own dream of a 'wise and understanding people' (Deut. 4.6) in a restored garden land (28.1–14; 33.6–25). In the words of the New Testament, Moses, like Abraham, 'looked forward to the city that has foundations, whose architect and builder is God' (Heb. 11.10 NRSV). The portrait of Moses gazing at the land points to a continuation and ultimate fulfilment of the work he had begun. The Narrator was telling his readers that the right way to remember this great leader would be to join the prophets and faithful people in every generation, in the struggle for the fulfilment of the vision.

This picture of Moses on Mount Nebo was what inspired the Black American civil rights leader and martyr, Martin Luther King Jr. In the midst of a struggle for racial equality which in the end cost him his life, he told his people that he too had 'been to the mountain', and 'seen the Promised Land'. And from his own 'Mount Nebo', came his famous words 'I have a dream that one day this nation will rise up and live out the true meaning of its creed . . . that all men are created equal'.

## THE SERVANT OF THE LORD

The *second* portrait shows Moses as Yahweh's faithful servant being laid to rest (v.5). 'Servant' is here a title of distinction and honour for those who have given special service to Yahweh, like Abraham (Gen. 26.24), Joshua (Josh. 24.29), and David (2 Sam. 3.18). The particular title 'servant of the LORD' is applied to Moses eighteen times, more than to any other individual in the Old Testament (see note on 34.5). Moses was the first model for the title 'servant of the LORD'.

We must also note the symbolic importance of the *location* of Moses's unmarked grave between Beth-peor (Deut. 34.6) and Jericho (v.1). This was the very place where Moses reminded the people of the Primary Covenant between God and Israel (4.46). At Beth-peor a group of Israelites had corrupted themselves by worshipping the Canaanite Baal, with disastrous results (see note on 4.3). Jericho, on the other hand, was the gateway to the Promised Land with its promise of new life. The Covenant Teaching given to the people as a 'possession' (33.4) would guard against corruption from the false gods of Canaan, and guide them in the new society they were to set up.

Leaders in later generations could say with Joshua, 'Take good care to observe the commandment and the law which Moses the servant of the LORD commanded you, to love the LORD your God, and to walk in his ways, and to keep his commandments, and to cleave to him, and to serve him with all your heart and with all your soul' (Josh. 22.5).

The portrait of Moses as a model 'servant of the LORD' points forward to the suffering Servant of the Lord described in the second part of Isaiah. God's 'servant' would carry the Covenant Teaching ('law') given by Moses to the waiting peoples in distant lands (Isa. 42.4). By him the Covenant Teaching would 'go forth' from God to guide the peoples (Isa. 51.4). As Moses interceded for his people and bore their guilt, so the nations would say of that servant that 'he was wounded for our transgressions, . . . bruised for our iniquities . . . poured out his soul to death . . . bore the sin of many, and made intercession for the transgressors' (Isa. 53.5, 12).

The line from Moses as servant of the Lord extends beyond the suffering servant to Jesus. He gave His disciples a re-interpretation of the Covenant commands, and, like Moses who laid his hands on Joshua, commissioned His disciples to teach all nations 'to observe all that I have commanded you' (Matt. 28.19–20; see John 20.21; Acts 1.8). John wrote that Jesus 'is the expiation of our sins, and not for ours only but also for the sins of the whole world' (1 John 2.2).

## ISRAEL'S GREATEST PROPHET

In the *third* portrait of Moses we see him as a prophet. Prophets, like lawgivers, were used by God to make His will known to the people. Receiving their messages from God, their task was to communicate His words of instruction for present and future generations (Deut. 18.18). Although Yahweh had promised to 'raise up' for the people a prophet like Moses (18.18; see note on 18.15), the Narrator tells his readers that 'there has not arisen a prophet since in Israel like Moses' (34.10). He pictured Moses as Israel's first and greatest prophet.

### A PROPHET FILLED WITH POWER

In earlier chapters of Deuteronomy the phrase 'All the mighty power and all the great and terrible deeds' has referred to what *God* did in the wilderness (3.24; 11.2; see note). *God* performed 'signs

Readers of Deuteronomy 'should remember Moses as a man of vision, a servant of the Lord, and a prophet, pointing forward to Jesus who told His disciples to make God's will known 'in all the world'. People like Fritz Schumacher, warning against pollution of the land, and the Christian evangelist explaining God's word to villagers in East Africa, may help us to 'remember Moses' today.

and wonders' in Egypt (4.34; 6.22) by His 'mighty hand' (3.24; 7.19; 26.8). Here in ch. 34 the Narrator tells his readers that *Moses* himself 'performed' them (34.11–12 NRSV). Israel's greatest prophet was God's mighty hand at work!

## A PROPHET CLOSE TO GOD

Moses's words carried much authority because he was very close to God. Although God once spoke to the people of Israel 'face to face' (5.4), they could not endure this intimacy (v. 5). They had to depend on Moses (v.27). According to tradition, God used to speak to Moses 'mouth to mouth' (Num. 12.8) 'as a man speaks to his friend' (Exod. 33.11). In this final memorial to Moses, the Narrator comments that God 'knew' Moses 'face to face', suggesting a steady, ongoing intimate relationship, a sort of mystical communion. We may use the words of Jeremiah to describe Moses as one who had 'stood in the council of the LORD to perceive and to hear his word . . .' (and had) 'proclaimed' God's words to His people in order to turn them 'from their evil way' (Jer. 23.18,22). This is what gave Moses's words such great authority.

## NEW TESTAMENT ECHOES

In the New Testament we can find many echoes of the Narrator's words about Moses as prophet. Jesus was seen as 'the prophet who is to come into the world' (John 6.14; see 11.40), fulfilling the word of Deuteronomy 18.15,18. Like Moses, Jesus was 'a prophet mighty in deed and word before God and all the people' (Luke 24.19; see Acts 7.22). As God had worked through the hands of Moses, people were amazed at the 'deeds of power . . . being done by his' (Jesus's) 'hands'! (Mark 6.2 NRSV). As described by John the Evangelist, Jesus knew that 'the Father had given all things into his hands' (John 13.3), and saw His work as a continuation of the Father's work (John 5.17).

Just as 'signs and wonders' had testified to Moses's authority, they also attested to the authority of Jesus (Acts 2.22). Signs and wonders gave authority to the Apostles (2.43), when performed 'through the name' of Jesus (4.30; see 2 Cor. 12.12). Paul spoke of the 'signs and wonders' (Rom. 15.19) which 'Christ has accomplished through me' (Rom. 15.18, NRSV). Throughout the history of the Church there have been people whom God has used to perform 'wonders', healing the sick, whether in body or in mind, through the laying on of hands and with prayer, as well as by using scientific means of healing.

The Narrator's comment that God knew Moses 'face to face' (Deut. 34.10) expresses an important idea. God knows each one of us, even when we don't acknowledge Him (see Ps. 139.2.4). Yet He is always testing His people to 'know' what is in their hearts (Deut. 8.2), that is, to find out whether there is any response to Him. To say that God 'knew Moses face to face' describes an intimate two-way relationship and trust between Moses and God.

Jesus's communion with God was even more intimate than that of Moses. In the Gospel of John we read Jesus's words that 'the Father knows me and I know the Father' (John 10.15), and 'What I say, therefore, I say as the Father has bidden me' (12.50).

According to Paul, although Christians are able to see 'the light of the knowledge of the glory of God in the face of Christ' (2 Cor. 4.6), only in the life after death will they be able, like Moses, to see and know God 'face to face', and 'understand fully, even as I have been fully understood' (1 Cor. 13.12).

The death of Moses was both an end and a beginning. It marked the end of his life and the completion of his work. Yet his influence continued. Chapter 34 is an epilogue to Deuteronomy and to the entire Pentateuch, and at the same time a prologue to the subsequent history of Israel. Moses's name appears 120 times in the Old Testament outside the Pentateuch, and 79 times in the New Testament. Moses appeared in conversation with the transfigured Jesus (Matt. 17.3). The three great monotheistic religions of the world, Judaism, Christianity and Islam all acknowledge their debt to the influence of Moses. Moses is indeed a figure of world-wide importance.

## NOTES

**34.1. To Mount Nebo, to the top of Pisgah:** Nebo and Pisgah may have been different names for the same mountain, or perhaps one was a particular peak in a range of the other. Nebo appears alone in Deut. 32.49 and Pisgah alone in 3.27.

**34.5. The servant of the LORD:** Moses is called by this title 17 times in Deuteronomy, 14 times in Joshua, and also in 2 Kings 18.12, and 2 Chronicles 1.3 and 24.6. Elsewhere the title 'servant of the LORD' is used for Joshua (Josh. 24.29; Judges 2.8), for David (in the superscriptions of Psalms 18 and 36), and for God's servant (in Isa. 42.19).

**34.5. According to the word of the LORD:** The Hebrew word translated 'word' means 'mouth'. Rabbinic commentators have suggested that this meant that God 'kissed' Moses as He died.

**34.11. The signs and the wonders:** This phrase occurs seven times in Deuteronomy. False prophets may even do 'a sign or a wonder' in order to tempt the people to follow other gods (13.2).

**34.12. All the mighty power:** A literal translation of the Hebrew behind the English phrase is 'all the mighty hand'; that is, Moses's powerful hand. In six instances this refers to God's power in rescuing His people from slavery in Egypt (Deut. 4.34; 5.15; 6.21; 7.8; 9.26; 26.8). Twice the phrase 'his mighty hand' refers to God's deeds of judgement and salvation in the wilderness (3.24; 11.2).

## STUDY SUGGESTIONS

### REVIEW OF CONTENT

1. What were Yahweh's last words to Moses?
2. What did Moses 'see' from Mount Nebo?
3. What famous Christian of today was inspired by the picture of Moses on Mount Nebo?
4. What was the symbolic meaning of the place where Moses was buried?
5. In what *two* ways was the 'suffering servant' described in Isaiah 42 like Moses?
6. In what *two* ways was Moses a great prophet?
7. In what way was Moses's death both an end and a beginning?

### BIBLE STUDY

8. Read Isaiah 42.4 and 51.4. In what way is the picture of the servant of God in these verses (a) similar to, or (b) different from that of Moses as a teacher of 'law' (Covenant Teaching)?
9. Compare Deuteronomy 34.9 with Matthew 28.19–20. What are the similarities and differences between Moses's commissioning of Joshua and Jesus's commissioning of the disciples?

### CONTEXTUAL APPLICATION

10. Choose a 'prophetic' person from recent history, and compare his or her life and death to that of Moses as described in Deut. 34.
11. (a) What do you understand by the phrase 'deeds of power'?
    (b) If Christians today are 'close to God' does that mean that they are able to do deeds of power?
12. (a) Find out if any Churches or individual Christians in your country are healing people of their sicknesses by the use of prayer, laying on of hands, or other similar means.
    (b) What differences are there, if any, between that sort of healing and being healed by modern medicine?
13. In what way is Moses a model for the life of individual Christians today? In what way is he a model for your own life?

# Key to Study Suggestions

**Introduction and 1.1–5**

1. (a) See p. 2, para. 3.   (b) See p. 2, last para.   (c) See p. 3, paras 2 and 3.
2. See p. 4, para. 1.
3. See p. 4, last para.; p. 5, Note on 1.1, para. 1; and Special Note A, paras 1 and 2.

**1.6–46**

1. See p. 8, last 2 paras.
2. (a) See p. 9, last 3 paras.   (b) See p. 10, lines 1–7.   (c) See p. 10, section headed 'Qualities of Good Leaders'.   (d) See p. 10, section headed 'Qualifications of Good Leaders'.
3. See p. 11, lines 2–5.
4. See p. 11, section headed 'Rebellious Action and Inaction': (a) first 5 lines;   (b) lines 6–end.   (c) See p. 11, section headed 'The Consequences of Rebellion', first 5 lines.   (d) See p. 11, last 2 lines and p. 12, lines 1–10.

**2.1—3.39**

1. See p. 13, last 6 lines and p. 14, lines 1 and 2.
2. See p. 14, sections headed 'Victories are not Ends but Beginnings' and 'Further Reflections on Victory'.
3. See p. 15, para. 2.
4. See p. 15, para. 3.

**4.1–14**

1. (a) See p. 17, lines 10–2 from foot of page.   (b) See p. 17, last line and p. 18, lines 1–6.   (c) See p. 18, section headed 'Unique Blessings from God's Grace'.
2. See p. 18, section headed 'Lest you forget', last 6 lines.
3. See p. 18, last 5 lines and p. 20, lines 1 and 2.
4. See p. 20: (a) section headed 'Remembering the Fire', para. 2; (b) section headed 'Remembering the Mystery'.
5. See p. 20, section headed 'Remembering the Voice'.

**4.15–23**

1. See p. 23, para. 1.
2. See p. 23, section headed 'The Risk'.
3. See p. 25, paras 2, 3 and 4.
4. See p. 25, last para. and p. 26, lines 1 and 2.
5. See p. 28, last 6 lines, and p. 29, lines 1–14 and 22–25.

**4.44—5.15**

1. See p. 32, paras 1–3.
2. See p. 33, section headed 'An Educational Process'.

3. See p. 33, last 4 lines and p. 35, lines 1–7.
4. See p. 34, paras 3–7.
5. See p. 34, last 9 lines and p. 35, lines 1–11.
6. See p. 35, para. 4.

### 5.16–33

1. See p. 39, para. 3.
2. See p. 40, para. 2, lines 3–7.
3. See p. 40, para. 6.
4. See p. 41, para. 1.
5. See p. 41, paras 2 and 3.
6. See p. 42, para. 3.
7. See p. 43, para. 5.
8. See p. 44, Special Note C:  (a) numbered para. 1;  (b) numbered para. 2;  (c) numbered para. 3.

### 6.1–25

1. See p. 46, last para. and p. 47, lines 1–3.
2. See p. 49, numbered paras 1, 2, and 3.
3. See p. 49, last 3 lines and p. 50, numbered paras 1 to 6.
4. See p. 51, numbered paras 1 to 6, and p. 52, lines 1–4 and numbered paras 1 and 2.
5. See p. 53, last 2 paras and p. 54, lines 1–10.
6. See p. 55, para. 3.

### 7.1–26

1. See p. 59, last 3 paras and p. 60, first 2 paras.
2. (a) See p. 60, paras 3 and 4.  (b) See p. 60, last 2 lines and p. 61, lines 1–3.
3. (a) See p. 65, Notes on 7.2 and 7.26, and Special Note D, paras 1 to 3.  (b) See p. 61, para. 2.  (c) See p. 61, paras 4 and 5 and p. 61, paras 1 and 2.
4. (a) See p. 59, para. 1 and p. 62, last 2 paras.  (b) See p. 63, paras 1 to 3, para. 6, lines 1 and 2, and p. 64, paras 2 and 4.
5. See p. 64, sub-paras (a) and (d).

### 8.1–20

1. See p. 67, last 3 lines and p. 68, lines 1–3.
2. See p. 68, paras 3–5.
3. See p. 68, last 3 paras and p. 70, paras 1–3.
4. See p. 71, para. 2.
5. See p. 71, paras 3 and 4 and p. 72, paras 1 and 2.
6. See p. 72, last para.

### 9.1—11.32

1. See p. 77, para. 3.
2. See p. 77, last para. and p. 78, paras 1 and 2.

**3.** See p. 78, last 4 lines and p. 80, paras 1–4.

**4.** See p. 81, paras 2, 3 and 4.

**5.** (a) and (b) See p. 81, last 7 lines and p. 82, lines 1–8.

**6.** See p. 82, numbered paras 2 to 4.

**7.** See p. 83, para. 2.

**8.** See p. 84, section headed 'Knowing God'.

**9.** See pp. 84 and 85, whole of section headed 'How shall we respond to God?'.

**12.1—16.22(1)**

**1.** See p. 91, last para.

**2.** See p. 91, last para. and p. 92, paras 1, 2, and 3, lines 1–4.

**3.** See p. 92, para. 3, lines 4–10.

**4.** See p. 92, last para. and p. 93, lines 1–3.

**5.** See p. 93: (a) paras 2 and 3; (b) para. 4.

**6.** See p. 93, last 12 lines.

**7.** (a) See p. 94, last 3 lines and p. 95 paras 1 and 2. (b) See p. 94, paras 3 and 4.

**8.** See p. 94: (a) para. 5; and (b) para. 6.

**12.1—16.22(2)**

**1.** See p. 100, paras 1–4.

**2.** See p. 100, last 4 lines and p. 101, lines 1–8.

**3.** See p. 101, para. 2 and p. 102, para. 3.

**4.** See p. 101, paras 2 and 3, and p. 102, paras 3 and 5.

**16.18—21.9(1)**

**1.** See p. 105, final para. and p. 106 lines 1 and 2, and pp. 112–113, Note on 18.13.

**2.** (a) See p. 106, para. 3. (b) See p. 106, paras 4, 5, and 6, p. 107, para. 1, and p. 108, para. 3.

**3.** See p. 106, para. 5, lines 3–6.

**4.** See p. 107, first para. lines 6–10, and numbered paras 1–4.

**5.** (a) See p. 108, para. 3. (b) See p. 108, last para. (numbered 1), and p. 109, lines 1 and 2 and numbered para. 2.

**6.** See pp. 110 and 112, Note on 18.12 and numbered paras 1–7.

**7.** See Note on 18.15.

**16.18—21.9(2)**

**1.** See p. 114, last para. and p. 115, numbered paras 2 and 3.

**2.** See p. 115, last 2 lines and p. 116, lines 1–3.

**3.** (a) See p. 117, numbered paras 1, 2 and 3. (b) See p. 117, last 2 lines, and p. 118, lines 1–12.

**16.18—21.9(3)**

**1.** See p. 120, paras 2 and 3 and p. 112, lines 1–8.

**2.** See p. 122, numbered paras 1, 2 and 3, and p. 124, numbered para. 4.

# KEY TO STUDY SUGGESTIONS

**21.10—25.19(1)**

**1.** See p. 127, para. 2.

**2.** (a) See p. 127, last para.   (b) See p. 128, lines 1 and 2 and numbered paras 1–4.

**3.** (a) See p. 129, para. 4.   (b) See p. 129, last 3 lines, and p. 131, paras 1–3.

**4.** See p. 132, paras 2 and 3.

**5.** See p. 132, para. 7.

**6.** See p. 135, Notes on 23.17–18.


**21.10—25.19(2)**

**1.** See p. 137, paras 2 and 3 and p. 138, paras 1–5.

**2.** See p. 138, last para. and p. 140, lines 1–3 and para. 2.

**3.** See p. 140, paras 3 and 4.

**4.** See p. 140, last para. and p. 141, lines 1–5 and para. 2.

**5.** See p. 141, para. 2, lines 2–7.


**26.1–19**

**1.** See p. 144, para. 1, lines 4–13.

**2.** See p. 144, last 2 paras, and p. 145, lines 1–3 and para. 2.

**3.** (a) See p. 145, numbered para. 1, lines 3–5 and p. 147, numbered para. 2, lines 1 and 2, and numbered para. 3, lines 1–3.   (b) See p. 145, last 10 lines, and p. 147, lines 1 and 2; p. 147, numbered para. 2, lines 2–4 and numbered para. 3, lines 3–4.

**4.** See p. 147, last 9 lines and p. 148, lines 1–11.

**5.** (a) See p. 149, para. 3, lines 3–10.   (b) See p. 148, last 4 lines and p. 149, lines 1 and 2; p. 149, para. 2 and p. 149 para. 3, lines 1–3.

**6.** See p. 149, last 2 paras. and p. 150, lines 1 and 2.


**27.1–26**

**1.** See p. 152, para. 2, lines 1–7.

**2.** (a) See p. 152, para. 3.   (b) See p. 153, paras 2 and 3.

**3.** See p. 153, last 7 lines.

**4.** See p. 155, paras 2 and 3.


**28.1–68**

**1.** See p. 157, last 3 lines and p. 158, paras 1 and 2.

**2.** See p. 158, paras 3 and 5.

**3.** See p. 158, para. 4 and last 5 lines, p. 159, and p. 160, lines 1–5.


**29.1–28**

**1.** See p. 165, paras 1 and 3, and p. 166, paras 1 and 2.

**2.** See p. 166, paras 3 and 4.

**3.** See p. 167, paras 1–3.

**4.** (a) See p. 167, paras 4 and 5, and p. 168, last para.   (b) See p. 168, last para.

**5.** See p. 169, para. 1, last 2 lines and paras 2 and 4, and p. 170, paras 1 and 2.

**29.29—30.20**
1. See p. 173, last 8 lines and p. 174, lines 1–6.
2. See p. 174, paras 2 and 3.
3. See p. 174, paras 4–6.
4. (a) See p. 175, para. 3, last 5 lines.   (b) See p. 174, last 6 lines and p. 175, para. 1, lines 6–8, and para. 3, lines 3–5.

**31.1–30**
1. See p. 178, numbered paras 1–4.
2. See p. 180, para. 2, lines 1–3 and para. 3, lines 1 and 2, and p. 182, lines 2–4.
3. See p. 182, numbered paras 1–5.
4. See p. 183, para. 1 and numbered paras 1 and 2.

**32.1–43**
1. See p. 185, Interpretation, sub-heading and para. 1; p. 186, sub-heading and para. 4; p. 187, sub-heading and last para.; p. 188, sub-heading and para. 4.
2. See p. 185, Introduction.

**33.1–29**
1. See p. 192, Introduction:   (a) para. 2;   (b) para. 1.
2. See p. 193, numbered paras 1–3.
3. See p. 193, paras 5 and 6.
4. See p. 194, para. 2.
5. See p. 194, paras 3 and 4.
6. (a) See p. 195, numbered paras 1 and 2.   (b) See p. 195, lines 15–17.

**32.48–52 and 34.1–12**
1. See p. 198, last para.
2. See p. 199, para. 3.
3. See p. 199, para. 4.
4. See p. 199, last para. and p. 200, lines 1–5.
5. See p. 200, paras 3 and 4.
6. See p. 200, last para. and p. 202, paras 1 and 2.
7. See p. 203, para. 4.

# Index

As explained in Special Note E (p.75), much of the history and teaching in Deuteronomy is repeated again and again, and the same subjects appear in many different chapters. This index covers all the main themes in detail, but only the more important references are given for some subsidiary subjects. The names of God, Moses, and the People of Israel are not included as they appear on nearly every page.

210